Abstract Data Types in Modula-2

Abstract Data Types in Modula-2

Rachel Harrison

*Department of Electronics and Computer Science,
University of Southampton, UK*

JOHN WILEY & SONS

Chichester · New York · Brisbane · Toronto · Singapore

Other Wiley Editorial Offices

John Wiley & Sons, Inc., 605 Third Avenue,
New York, NY 10158-0012, USA

Jacaranda Wiley Ltd, G.P.O. Box 859, Brisbane,
Queensland 4001, Australia

John Wiley & Sons (Canada) Ltd, 22 Worcester Road,
Rexdale, Ontario M9W 1LI, Canada

John Wiley & Sons (SEA) Pte Ltd, 37 Jalan Pemimpin 05-04
Block B, Union Industrial Building, Singapore 2057

Library of Congress Cataloging-in-Publication Data:
Harrison, Rachael.
    Abstract data types in Modula-2   /   Rachel Harrison.
        p.   cm.
    Bibliography: p.
    Includes index.
    ISBN 0 471 92230 7
    1.   Modula-2 (Computer program language)   2.   Abstract data types
(Computer science)   I.   Title.
QA76.73.M63H35   1989   89-14773
005.13'3—dc20   CIP

British Library Cataloguing in Publication Data:
Harrison, Rachel.
    Abstract data types in Modula-2.
    1.   Computer systems.   Programming languages   :
    Modula-2 language
    I.   Title
    005.13'3

ISBN 0 471 92230 7

Printed and bound in Great Britain by Courier International, Tiptree, Essex

Contents

Preface

During the 1960s the concern over the amount of inadequate software which was being produced led to the emergence of software engineering as a bona fide academic discipline. Computer scientists began to turn their attention to the solution of the 'software crisis'. With the recognition of the value of structured programming came the language Pascal, which embodied the principles of structured programming, and which has consequently been widely adopted as a teaching language in higher education.

By the mid 1970s it had been realised that data encapsulation (the use of modules to collect together related procedures) and data abstraction (the use of data types with well-defined manipulation procedures) also played a vital part in the production of correct software. This increasing realisation of the importance of the 'divide and conquer' or 'separation of concerns' maxim is reflected in the design of imperative languages such as Modula-2 and Ada. Modula-2 provides two sorts of modules which enables specification to be separated from implementation, and opaque types which can be used to hide the implementation of a data type from the user.

This book is concerned with the theory and practice of data abstraction, and the importance of specification. Modula-2 was chosen as the implementation language because of the facilities that it provides for data hiding and its descent from Pascal, which should enable anyone with a reading knowledge of Pascal to understand the code without too much difficulty. A functional programming style is adopted, because of the clarity of expression and lack of side-effects which this encourages. The text demonstrates how easily a specification written in a functional style can be implemented in Modula-2.

The book is aimed at undergraduates and postgraduates who have completed an introductory programming course. It is assumed that the reader has some knowledge of Pascal or Modula-2: an appendix has been provided which highlights some of the differences between the two languages. The text was prepared for the first year, second semester, course on Algorithms and Data Structures which is given at Imperial College, London.

Acknowledgements

I would like to thank all those in the Functional Programming Section of Imperial College for providing a stimulating environment in which to work. I am indebted to Susan Eisenbach who gave me the chance to give the course from which this book evolved. In particular, I would like to thank Peter Harrison of Imperial and Peter Henderson of Southampton University, both of whom read early versions of the manuscript and provided many helpful suggestions, and a lot of valuable encouragement.

CHAPTER 1

Introduction

This chapter introduces the concepts of *data abstraction* and *abstract data types*. It explains the choice of Modula-2 as the programming language in which the examples in this book are set and also our reasons for using a *functional style* when programming.

WHAT IS ABSTRACTION ?

The *Concise Oxford Dictionary* gives the definition of the verb 'to abstract' as 'to deduct, remove, consider apart from the concrete'. Niklaus Wirth (1986) described the process of abstraction by saying: 'Certain properties and characteristics of the real objects are ignored because they are peripheral and irrelevant to the particular problem'. Abstraction is at the very heart of all problem solving. It can be described as ignoring all unnecessary details and thus simplifying the task under consideration. For example, if you were asked how you travel to work, the reply might be 'by bus' rather than a full description of the walk to the bus stop, the interminable wait for the correct-number bus, how many buses went past because they were already full, the route the bus took, and what colour hat the woman sitting next to you was wearing.

Abstraction is used to decompose a complex problem into smaller, more manageable subproblems. It has long been realized that the human mind has difficulty in coping with large, complex software systems. In the 1960s the term 'software crisis' was coined to describe the rapidly escalating costs of software as systems became increasingly complex. The structured programming revolution attempted to bring some methodology into the world of programming by suggesting elimination of uncontrolled jumps ('goto' statements) and use of only three control structures: sequence, selection and iteration. Following on from this, in 1971 Wirth used the phrase 'stepwise refinement' to mean successive decomposition of a task into several separate, less complicated subtasks. Abstraction furthers the aim of simplification by providing a mechanism for separating the attributes of an object or event that are relevant in a particular context from those that are not.

Abstraction is thus a logical consequence of the 'divide and conquer' approach to problem solving, and so is particularly suited to computer languages such as Pascal and Modula-2 which were designed to embody the principles of structured programming. As an example of abstraction consider the use of procedures in Modula-2 and other high-level languages to encapsulate and name a single task (this is called *procedural* abstraction). The standard utility modules of Modula-2 (Wirth 1988) such as those used for input and output are another example.

As an illustration of this approach consider a simplified hierarchy of the abstractions which constitute a program (figure 1.1). Each level is constructed only of entities from the levels below.

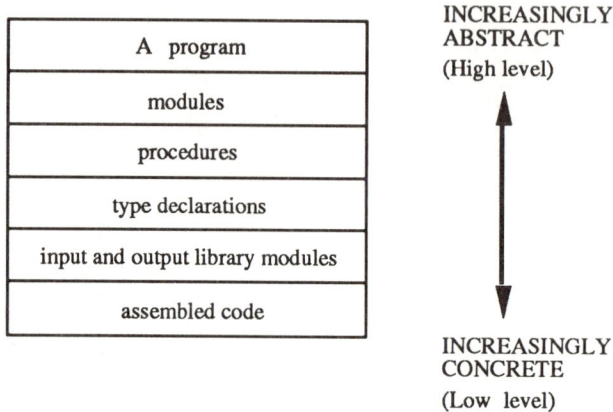

A program
modules
procedures
type declarations
input and output library modules
assembled code

INCREASINGLY
ABSTRACT
(High level)

↑

↓

INCREASINGLY
CONCRETE
(Low level)

Figure 1.1 A hierarchy of abstraction

EXAMPLE

As an example of an abstract concept, consider our idea of dates (this example was first given by Christopher Strachey). We usually consider dates to be of the form Day, Month, Year. There are only a limited number of operations which we would wish to perform on dates (for example, finding the number of days between two dates, checking a year to see if it is a leap year). Operations such as multiplication of two dates would be nonsensical.

A computer could store dates in the form Year, Month, Day. For example, January 2nd, 1971 would be 71 01 02. This could be stored in binary coded decimal format.

Another representation which is quite frequently used to store dates on computers is the Julian form, proposed by Joseph Scalizer in 1582. A Julian date is represented as the number of elapsed days since a known start date. On a computer the date may be stored as four binary coded decimal digits. For example, if the start date were January 1st, 1970, then January 2nd, 1971 would be represented by the number 0366, or 0000 0011 0110 0110 in binary coded decimal notation.

Figure 1.2 shows the relationship between the abstract concept of a birthday and the different possible representations of it.

Note that the underlying representation of dates is immaterial. In fact the representation may change without affecting our use of dates. It is much easier for us to manipulate dates in the *abstract* form Day, Month, Year. A date is thus an *abstract data type*.

One of the advantages of abstraction is that we can think of the data type in ways that are easy to understand, without having to consider the details of the implementation.

In order to progress further we must define some terms. A *data structure* or *structured data type* is an organized collection of data elements. Data structures are created by using predefined *constructors* such as arrays, records, sets and pointers together with other predefined types such as REAL, CHAR, CARDINAL, INTEGER and BOOLEAN. User-defined data types can

EXAMPLE   3

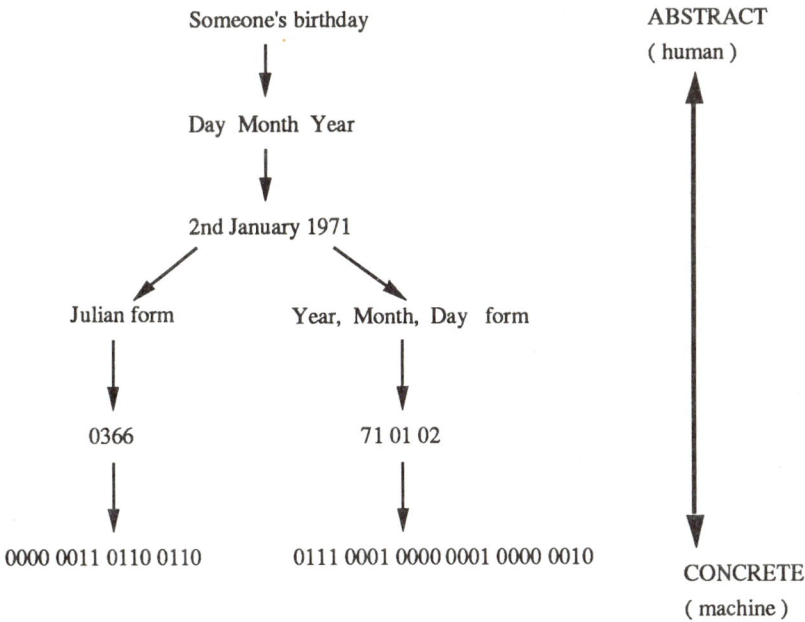

Someone's birthday

Day Month Year

2nd January 1971

Julian form   Year, Month, Day form

0366   71 01 02

0000 0011 0110 0110   0111 0001 0000 0001 0000 0010

ABSTRACT
(human)

CONCRETE
(machine)

Figure 1.2

also be used to create data structures. For example, one way to store a list of employees' names and salaries would be to use an array of Modula-2 records with one field for the name (defined as a string, say) and one for the salary (defined as a subrange type).

In 1977 J. V. Guttag used the term *abstract data type* to refer to 'a class of objects defined by a representation-independent specification'. The separation of concept from implementation is the characteristic of abstract data types that makes them so important. This idea is also called *data hiding* or *data abstraction*. The implementation of the type is hidden from the user of the program. We are more concerned with **what** we can do with the data type than in **how** it is implemented. This leads us to the following definition:

An *abstract data type* consists of a data type together with a set of operations, called *access procedures*, which define how the type may be manipulated.

Therefore data structures are at a lower level of abstraction than abstract data types. The main difference between the two is the formal specification of the access procedures which should be provided by the implementor of an abstract data type. As an example of access procedure for a data structure, consider the indexing of an array A by an integer i: in Modula-2 $A[i]$ returns the item at position i in the array. Similarly, the selection of a field C in a record B, denoted by $B.C$, is also an access procedure. In fact data structures provide the supporting framework which is used to implement abstract data types. Using the hierarchical approach again, figure 1.3 illustrates how abstract data types (for example, the abstract data type *list*, which will be defined in the next chapter) are related to predefined language data types (such as CHAR and CARDINAL in Modula-2) and machine-level representation of data.

	EXAMPLES
ABSTRACT DATA TYPES	List
PREDEFINED STRUCTURED DATA TYPES	ARRAY OF CHAR
PREDEFINED SIMPLE DATA TYPES	CHAR, CARDINAL
MACHINE LANGUAGE TYPES	10110111

INCREASINGLY
ABSTRACT

INCREASINGLY
CONCRETE

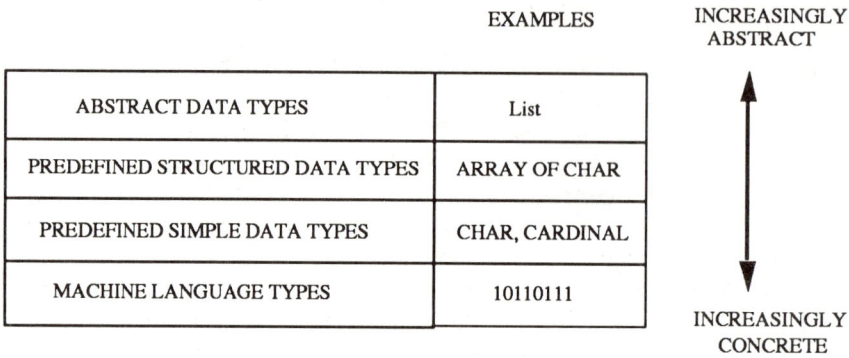

Figure 1.3 The hierarchy of data types

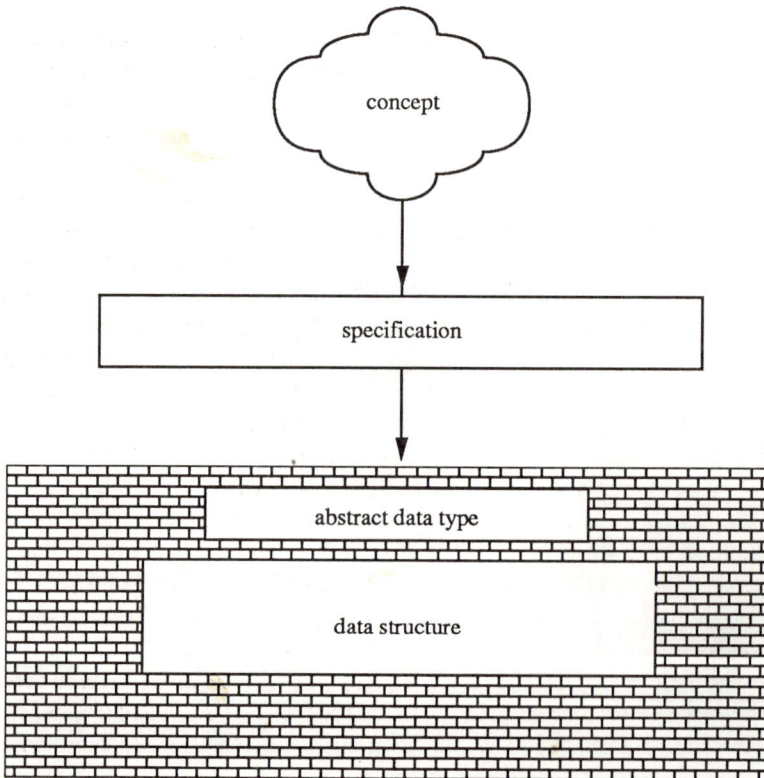

concept

specification

abstract data type

data structure

Figure 1.4

DATA ABSTRACTION

Data abstraction, the use of abstract data types, can be described as a method of expressing the interaction between a program and its data structures. This controlled access can be thought of as building a black box or wall around a program's data structures (figure 1.4).

The interaction of a program with its data structures is defined by the operations that describe the abstract data type. These are the *access procedures* which are used to manipulate the abstract data type and they are the only way to interact with it. Of course, a program's result must be independent of the way its abstract data types are implemented.

The term data abstraction had become recognized as a programming methodology by the beginning of the 1980s, and was hailed as the next leap forward in the evolution of software engineering. The influence of the data-abstraction revolution can be seen in the design of many recently developed programming languages such as Modula-2 and Ada.

WHY MODULA-2?

Modula-2 was designed by Wirth (Wirth 1982) and is based on Pascal, the block-structured language for which Wirth was also responsible ten years previously. Pascal does provide some facilities for abstraction: it gives us the ability to hide an implementation within procedures and to create our own data types.

However, one significant shortcoming of Pascal is that it does not provide us with the facility of separate compilation for procedures and functions, and so deprives us of any means of hiding the implementation of an abstract data type. In the design of Modula-2 there was an attempt to rectify this and encourage the use of abstract data types by having *modules* which can be compiled separately.

There are two sorts of modules: *definition* and *implementation*. This is one of the most significant differences between the two languages. The access procedures of an abstract data type are contained in a definition module in the form of procedure headings. The user of an abstract data type need only be concerned with the definition module, which provides the interface to the implementation module. We also have the ability to declare a type in a definition module as *opaque*, and so hide the implementation from the user. The actual implementation of the type (declarations of data structures and code to implement the access procedures) is given in the implementation module, access to which can be limited.

Ada[1] is similar to Modula-2 in many ways but it was developed by the US Department of Defense for military applications and is a much larger language. The first version of Ada was proposed in 1979. The ability to separate the specification of a data type from its implementation is provided by means of 'packages' which correspond to the modules of Modula-2. (See the Ada Manual produced by the US Department of Defense in 1983 for further details.)

Since specification can be separated from implementation in Modula-2 it was the natural choice as the programming language for this text. This decision has several fortuitous consequences. Both Pascal and Modula-2 are frequently used as teaching languages because of their simplicity and the clarity of code which can be produced using them. Those who already know Pascal should have no difficulty in understanding Modula-2 code, as the syntactic differences

---

1   Ada is a registered trademark of the U.S. Government.

are fairly minor. Also there are numerous implementations of Modula-2, including many for microcomputers.

The influence of data abstraction on the design of programming languages is continuing with much research now going on into the design of 'object-oriented' programming languages such as Smalltalk-80[1] (Goldberg and Robson 1983) and C++ (Stroupstrup 1985). An *object* is considered to be some private data and a set of operations that can access the data. Many of the various functional languages which exist such as Miranda[2] (Turner, 1985), Hope (Burstall *et al* 1980) and ML (Harper *et al* 1986) also provide data-abstraction facilities. For example, MacQueen (1985) describes the design of a set of constructs to support modular programming in Standard ML. Functional programming will be discussed in more detail later in this chapter.

ADVANTAGES OF ABSTRACT DATA TYPES

'Abstract data types can play a significant role in the development of software that is reliable, efficient and flexible' (Guttag 1977). An abstract data type can be thought of as a 'black box' in that we can use the abstract data type without worrying about how it actually works. Consider the following analogy: a television is a black box—we understand how to use it, there are controls which we can adjust to change the channel, volume, etc., but we do not actually need (or, probably, want) to know what is inside the television and why it works the way it does. The switch to change the channel is analogous to a parameter to a procedure, and the picture is the result of the procedure.

In this way the use of abstract data types allows us to concentrate on the desired properties of the data type and *what* it should do for us, rather than on *how* it should do it. It is generally accepted that the human brain can only cope effectively with a small number of tasks at any one time, and so anything which reduces complexity is to be welcomed.

The separation of the definition of an abstract data type from its implementation means that there can be several equivalent implementations, giving the programmer the opportunity to change the implementation without having any effect on the rest of the system. This is particularly easy in Modula-2 because of the separation of the definition of an abstract data type (in a definition module) from its implementation (in a corresponding implementation module).

The definition of an abstract data type provides us with a specification which can be used in a formal verification of a program's correctness. Over the past twenty years or so computer scientists have become increasingly concerned with the need to produce software which has not only been tested on some limited set of input data but which has been actually *proved* to be correct in all cases. Consider how important this is in the production of an air-traffic control system, for example, or a system to control a nuclear reactor. This interest in verification has led to much research on specification techniques, since there must be a correct and formal specification against which an implementation can be verified. This interest in formalism is part of the endeavour to transform software engineering from an art to a science.

A specification is a description of a system which is to be produced to solve some problem. We may consider two levels of specification: the user/designer and the designer/programmer interfaces. Various techniques have been developed to produce specifications which users will be able to understand, most of which involve the use of graphics to some extent, and are well documented: for example, data flow diagrams are used in SSADM (Downs *et al* 1988). We are

1   Smalltalk-80 is a registered trademark of the Xerox Corporation.
2   Miranda is a trademark of Research Software Ltd.

more concerned with the designer/programmer's specification. The specification at this level must be unambiguous so that the implementors (the programmers) can understand and work with it, always producing the same solution, even if by different methods. The use of a natural language such as English is therefore not sufficiently precise: a more *formal* specification is needed.

We have already stated that the specification of an abstract data type is maintained in a definition module. In fact this is only part of the story, because we must not only state formally the names and parameters of the access procedures (their *syntax*) but also give a set of rules which define the relationships between them and the way they can be manipulated (their *semantics*).

We will define the syntax of the access procedures by a list of procedure headings in Modula-2 (this will exist in a definition module). The semantics of the access procedures will be defined by a list of rules or *axioms* which will define the meanings of the operations. This form of specification is called *algebraic* (Guttag 1977, 1978) and will be used throughout the text (an example will be given in the next chapter). The term algebraic is used because the syntax of the access procedures together with their semantics can be regarded as defining an algebra. The term *axiomatic* specification is also used. The technique falls within the broader classification of '*definitional*' or '*implicit*' specification because we are stating the behaviour of the procedures implicitly by definition, without any concrete representation such as data structures and code. Jones (1986) calls this method 'property oriented specifications of data types'. See Liskov and Zillies (1975) for a discussion of specification techniques for abstract data types. The algebraic specification of an abstract data type gives us a list of axioms which we can use to verify all the implementations of the data type. The construction of such a specification prior to any implementation is extremely useful not only in formal program verification but also in clarifying the details of the implementation. Ensuring that the implementation satisfies its specification enables us to guarantee its behaviour.

PROGRAMMING STYLE

One of the aims of this text is to encourage a *functional* style of programming. This is quite different to that which is often used to write code in conventional languages. Such languages (for example, Pascal, Cobol, Ada and Modula-2) are called *imperative* because of the way that programmers use the computer by commanding it to execute statements in a certain order. Programmers are taught to consider the action of their program on a set of memory cells. The result of an assignment statement such as

$$x := 5$$

is to put the value 5 in a memory cell which will be called x. The reason for this style of programming is the underlying von Neumann architecture, which has remained unchanged for the past forty years. We are promoting a functional style of programming in the belief that it facilitates the production of correct programs: instead of issuing commands to the machine to tell it *how* to calculate a result we simply write down *what* we want to calculate. Programming style should not be dictated by the design of the hardware.

Much research has been done on the design of functional languages, some of which were mentioned earlier. However, these languages have not yet reached the maturity necessary for widespread commercial use. This text shows that that a conventional, imperative language, Modula-2, can be used to program in a functional style. The ramifications of this statement will be explained in more detail in the next section.

Note: We will use the term *function* to refer to a procedure which returns a value by means of a RETURN statement, i.e. the equivalent of a Pascal function.

PROGRAMMING IN A FUNCTIONAL STYLE

Two of the characteristics of a functional style are: (1) the avoidance of *side-effects* and (2) the preference for recursion over iteration. The reasoning that gave rise to these characteristics, and some of the shortcomings of the traditional, *procedural* programming style, is expounded below.

Side-effects

The interchangeability of two expressions which have the same meaning is called *referential transparency*. An example of a language which is referentially transparent and with which we are all familiar is mathematics. For example, if we were told that the value of x is 3, and then asked to evaluate the expression:

$$5 - x$$

we would all be able to give the answer 2 without too much trouble. Since x and '3' denoted the same value they could be interchanged. Referentially transparent functions can be reasoned about more easily because they can be expressed as normal mathematical functions. However, functions written in imperative languages are often not referentially transparent: the value of a variable is said to be *history sensitive*, because it depends on what has happened previously in the program. Therefore if we had a variable called x, say, which occurred several times in a program, and we happened to know that at one point in the program the value of x was 3, then we could not rewrite the program substituting the value 3 wherever we saw the variable x. This is one of the stumbling blocks of imperative languages. To ensure that functional languages are referentially transparent the concept of the assignment statement has been rejected.

If a function has more than one effect during the course of its execution then it is said to have a *side-effect*. An example of a side-effect is any change to a non-local variable. Writing functions with side-effects is now considered bad programming style, as such code tends to be very difficult to reason about, and so is more likely to have unforeseen consequences. For example, given a function **sqrt** to calculate the square root of a number we assume that

$$\text{sqrt}(x) + \text{sqrt}(x) = 2*\text{sqrt}(x)$$

If the function **sqrt** changed the value of its argument or of a global variable used to compute its result then this relation would no longer hold. Many functions written in imperative languages are not referentially transparent because of the use of side-effects and because there is no restriction on the use of the assignment (:=) statement.

Using a functional style means that all procedures should in fact be functions which only perform a single task and return a single result, and so do not have any side-effects. Consequently each function should take only *value* parameters, that is, parameters which are passed by value: their value can be used in the function but they cannot be altered. *Variable* parameters, which are identified by the reserved word VAR in the procedure heading, are passed by *reference*. This means that the address of the variable is passed to the procedure, so that any alterations to the variable actually cause the variable to change its value. By using only value parameters a function can be made to behave like a black box, and this leads to programs which are transparent and so are easier to understand and maintain.

The use of black boxes to decompose problems into simpler units is a technique which is well known in engineering. For example, we take for granted the fact that switching on the headlights of a car will not cause it to brake. Each unit is self-contained.

However, generations of programmers have carried on producing code, unaware of this 'separation of concerns' maxim. Assigning a value to a global variable within a procedure is a side-effect, exactly like arranging a car's braking system to depend on whether its lights are on or off.

It has long been realized that interaction between modules should be kept to a minimum. The technical term for the extent of interaction between modules is *coupling*. (This term was coined by Stevens *et al* 1974.) The use of a functional style of programming discourages such interaction between modules and so leads to clearer, less obscure code.

To summarize: the use of global variables and variable parameters should be avoided in order to minimize the possibility of side-effects.

Recursion and Iteration

In computer science a function is *recursive* if in the course of its execution a call is made to the function. A similar, but more restricted concept than recursion is *iteration*, which can be defined as the repeated execution of a block of code where the repetition is controlled by a FOR, WHILE, REPEAT or LOOP command.

Recursion is often the most natural way of expressing a solution to a problem. One good example of this is the Fibonacci function, the definition of which for positive integers is given below:

> *if* $n \le 2$ *then* Fib $(n) = 1$
> *else* Fib $(n) =$ Fib $(n-1) +$ Fib $(n-2)$

So the sequence of Fibonacci numbers is: 1, 1, 2, 3, 5, 8, 13, 21, 34, ...

The definition naturally leads us to a recursive version of the function:

```
PROCEDURE Fib ( n : CARDINAL ) : CARDINAL ;
(* Precondition: n > 0
   Postcondition: returns the nth Fibonacci number *)


BEGIN
    IF n <= 2 THEN
        RETURN 1
    ELSE
        RETURN ( Fib ( n - 1 ) + Fib ( n - 2 ) )
    END (* if *)
END Fib ;
```

(*Note*: Each procedure in this text will be accompanied by a short comment explaining its function. We will follow the example of Dijkstra and give *pre-* and *postconditions* for each procedure, which state the conditions which hold before and after a procedure's execution respectively. Usually the precondition merely states the type of the procedure's parameters, and so will be omitted for brevity.

It is left as an exercise for the reader to develop an equivalent iterative algorithm.)

As we are using a functional style of programming we will use the definition of a function when we are designing code instead of trying to derive complicated iterative algorithms. For example, consider writing a function to sum the integers between the bounds 'lower' and 'upper':

$$\text{lower} + (\text{lower} + 1) + (\text{lower} + 2) + \ldots + \text{upper}$$

or

$$\sum_{\text{lower}}^{\text{upper}} i = \text{lower} + \sum_{\text{lower}+1}^{\text{upper}} i$$

We can easily produce a specification for this function, which we have called sum:

$$\text{sum (lower, upper)} <= \textit{if } \text{lower} = \text{upper } \textit{then } \text{lower}$$
$$\textit{else } \text{lower} + \text{sum (lower} + 1, \text{upper)}$$

where the symbol '<=' is read 'is defined as'. This is very similar to the way the function would be written in a functional language such as Hope, and it is very simple to produce a recursive function in Modula-2 which mirrors this definition:

```
PROCEDURE sum (lower, upper : INTEGER ) : INTEGER ;
(* Postcondition: returns the sum of the integers
between lower and upper *)

BEGIN
    IF lower = upper THEN
        RETURN lower
    ELSE
        RETURN (lower + sum (lower + 1, upper ))
    END
END sum ;
```

The aim of using a functional style is to help the reader develop a more 'foolproof' method of programming. The full power of recursion will become apparent in later chapters.

Functional programming has been criticized in the past as being extremely inefficient, both in terms of execution speed and memory usage. However, we would argue that such considerations are irrelevant here for two reasons. First, this book is primarily about abstract data types and their use: efficiency is an entirely separate concern. Second, hardware is being developed at such a rate that we will soon not need to be concerned about our machine's limitations. The cost of hardware has decreased considerably over the past 20 years: today's personal computers are cheaper and more powerful than many of the mainframes that were used in industry a couple of years ago.

Another point to consider is the research which is currently in progress into machine architecture. As mentioned earlier, most computers which are in use today are based on the conventional von Neumann architecture, with a single processor connected by a bus to an amount of memory. This design has not changed since it was first conceived about 40 years ago. However, if programs are written in referentially transparent functional languages then different parts of a program can be evaluated in parallel, with processors working simultaneously. We need no longer tell the machine *how* it must evaluate a sequence of expressions to arrive at the answer to a problem, but instead we simply tell it *what* the problem is, and let it do the rest. The functional style used throughout the text typifies this approach, using a conventional language.

IMPLEMENTATION OF ABSTRACT DATA TYPES

Although implementation is not the main concern of this book we will consider some of the possible implementation techniques for abstract data types. These can be classified as either *static* or *dynamic*. By *static* we mean that the memory requirements for the data structure have been determined at compile time. *Dynamic* implies that memory may be allocated as required at run time and consequently data structures which are created dynamically are extremely versatile.

To facilitate the creation of *dynamic data structures* Modula-2 provides a **pointer** type. Such pointer (or dynamic) variables are a powerful and common feature of 'Algol-like' languages such as Pascal and Modula-2. The choice between static and dynamic implementations depends on many factors, including the amount of memory available and data to be stored, the required efficiency of operations which access the data structure and the capabilities of the language. Generally, arrays are used for static implementations and structures containing pointer variables for dynamic. Arrays are a common feature of nearly all modern languages and the reader is assumed to be familiar with them. Static data structures (such as arrays) cannot change their size or shape once they have been declared. This may constrain the solutions of some problems. A full understanding of the use of pointers is necessary when discussing possible implementations of abstract data types. Consequently, Appendix 1 of this book is devoted to a discussion on the use of pointers in Modula-2 and defines some of the notation used.

ORGANIZATION OF THE TEXT

The philosophy of this book is as follows. In each chapter we will start by considering why we may need a particular abstract data type, what properties we would like it to have, the necessary access procedures and the axioms which govern their behaviour. Later, after establishing the abstract concept of the data type by means of its algebraic specification, we will discuss possible implementations.

This book is about abstract data types and how to use them, in a functional style, to solve problems. Functional programming is not merely an alternative to procedural programming, it will play an increasingly important role in the future as languages which have been designed specifically to facilitate a functional style of programming come into use.

We are not overly concerned with their implementation—although implementations will be suggested, we invite the reader to consider alternatives. Any implementation will suffice, as long as the access procedures still satisfy their specification.

SUMMARY

A *data structure* is an organized collection of data.

An *abstract data type* consists of a data type together with a set of operations, called *access procedures*, which define how the type may be manipulated.

Data structures are used in the implementation of abstract data types.

Data abstraction is the use of abstract data types to control the interaction between a program and its data structures.

Modula-2 allows us to separate the definition of the access procedures for an abstract data type from its implementation.

The advantages of abstract data types are:

(1) The separation of specification from implementation helps to reduce the complexity of the task in hand.
(2) Implementation independence is assisted.
(3) The formal specification of abstract data types can be used in verifying the correctness of the implementation.

An *algebraic specification* consists of two parts: the *syntax* of the access procedures and their *semantics*, which is given by a set of *axioms* defining the relationship between them.

In the *functional style* of programming, procedures take only value parameters and return only a single result. Instead of developing complicated iterative algorithms, procedures are developed using recursion to prescribe what task they are to perform.

The use of a functional style facilitates the production of correct programs: instead of issuing commands to the machine to tell it *how* to calculate a result we simply write down *what* we want to calculate. Programming style should not be dictated by the design of the hardware.

The interchangeability of two expressions which have the same meaning is called *referential transparency*.

CHAPTER 2

The Abstract Data Type List

INTRODUCTION

In Chapter 1 we stated that an abstract data type consists of a data type together with a set of operations (called access procedures) that are used to manipulate the type. The first abstract data type we will consider is the *list*. After giving the algebraic specification of a list we show how the access procedures can be used to develop higher-level functions which operate on lists. The second half of the chapter is devoted to a discussion of the implementation of the access procedures.

DEFINITION

The abstract data type *list* is a linear sequence of an arbitrary number of items of the same type together with a number of access procedures.

The list is one of the most fundamental abstract data types. Lists abound both in the 'real world' and in computing applications. For example, consider a sequence of people standing at a checkout in a supermarket or of books arranged alphabetically on a shelf. A Modula-2 type text file consists of a list of characters. The operations which are allowed on a file include creating a file, adding characters, removing characters, checking for an empty file, etc.

REPRESENTATION AND NOTATION

There are several ways that we can represent lists. We will follow common practice and denote a list by parentheses, with the elements of the list separated by commas. For example:

A list of numbers: (1, 9, 3, 2, 7, 8, 0)
A list of characters: ('C', 'A', 'T', 'S')
A list of names: ('Sue', 'Pam', 'Jill') etc.

By convention, the first item in a list is referred to as the *head* of the list. We will assume that this is the leftmost item if the list is represented as above. For example, the item at the head of the list of names ('Sue', 'Pam', 'Jill') is 'Sue'. Removing the head of a list leaves us with a list which is called the *tail* of the list. So the tail of the list of names ('Sue', 'Pam', 'Jill') is the list ('Pam', 'Jill').

ALGEBRAIC SPECIFICATION

In order to understand how we can manipulate the abstract data type list we must give its algebraic specification.

As explained in Chapter 1, the algebraic specification of an abstract data type consists of two parts: the syntax of the access procedures, which gives their names, parameters and result type, and their semantics, which consists of a list of axioms specifying the relationships between them.

We will assume for generality that we have declared a type InfoType, which will be used as the type of the items in the list. This declaration will be given in a definition module, and every module which uses items of type InfoType will need to import it from this module. The aim of doing this is to ensure that the abstract data type list is not implemented for only one particular type of item but can easily be adapted to any type.

Syntax of the access procedures

There are five access procedures for the abstract data type list from which all other procedures can be built. They can be split into three groups: *constructor* functions, which are so called because they are used to construct or create the data type, *predicate* functions, which are boolean valued functions used to test the data type, and *selector* functions, which select different parts of the type.

1. Constructor functions

There are two constructor functions, the first of which creates an empty list.

```
PROCEDURE Empty ( ) : List ;
```

This procedure returns an empty list, that is, one that does not contain any data items. Note that the empty parentheses after the call to Empty are optional according to Wirth (1988).

The other constructor function takes two parameters, an item and a list, and constructs a new list with the item at its head and the list parameter as its tail. This function is called Cons, which is short for 'construct'. For example, the result of Cons ('Amy', ('Sue', 'Pam', 'Jill')) is the list ('Amy', 'Sue', 'Pam', 'Jill').

```
PROCEDURE Cons (I : InfoType ; L : List ) : List;
```

This procedure inserts item I at the head of the list L.

2. Predicate functions

There is only one predicate function that we need: as it is an error to try to determine the head or tail of an empty list we require a predicate function to determine whether a list is empty.

```
PROCEDURE IsEmpty (L : List ) : BOOLEAN ;
```

This procedure checks the list to determine whether it is empty.

3. Selector functions

There are two selector functions:

```
PROCEDURE Head ( L: List ) : InfoType ;
```

This procedure returns the item at the head of the list.

```
PROCEDURE Tail ( L : List ) : List ;
```

This returns the list which results from removing the head of the list L. These access procedures constitute the definition module for the abstract data type list, which is given below.

```
DEFINITION MODULE Lists ;
(* Access procedures for the abstract data type list.*)

FROM Items IMPORT InfoType ;

TYPE List ; (* an opaque type: see implementation module
for details *)

PROCEDURE Empty ( ) : List ;
(* Postcondition: returns an empty list *)

PROCEDURE IsEmpty ( L : List ) : BOOLEAN ;
(* Postcondition: returns TRUE if L is empty,
   otherwise FALSE *)

PROCEDURE Cons ( I : InfoType ; L : List) : List ;
(* Postcondition: returns a list with I as its head
   and L as its tail *)

PROCEDURE Head ( L : List) : InfoType ;
(* Postcondition: returns the item at the head of
   list L *)

PROCEDURE Tail ( L : List ): List ;
(* Postcondition: returns the tail of list L *)

END Lists.
```

Note that the type list is declared as an *opaque type*. The availability of such types is an extremely important feature of Modula-2 as it enables us to hide the declaration of the abstract data type so that it cannot be seen in the definition module. The user only needs to see the definition module in order to be able to use the abstract data type, the actual implementation of which will be completely hidden in the implementation module. This is the correct way to use an abstract data type, as it ensures that it can only be manipulated by use of the access procedures. This facility, which makes Modula-2 eminently suitable as a data-abstraction language, is not provided by earlier languages such as Pascal.

Semantics of the access procedures

Note that there are only two possible forms of list: either a list is empty or it is of the form `Cons (h,t)` where `h` is an item and `t` is a list (which may, of course, be empty). The access procedures for the abstract data type list must satisfy the following axioms:

1. IsEmpty (Empty ( )) = TRUE
2. IsEmpty (Cons (h, t)) = FALSE
3. Head (Cons (h, t)) = h
4. Tail (Cons (h, t)) = t
5. Head (Empty ( )) = error
6. Tail (Empty ( )) = error

A result which is an error (as in axioms (5) and (6)) should result in the termination of the program's execution.

Consistency and completeness

We must ensure that the axioms are both *consistent* and *sufficiently complete*. The definitions of these terms, which are given below, are due to Guttag (1977, 1978), who was responsible for much of the theoretical foundations of data abstraction.

Definition

If any two axioms are contradictory then the specification is said to be *inconsistent*.

Consistency is relatively straightforward to determine by inspection, as the axioms are formulated according to our intuitive understanding of the abstract data type which is under discussion.

To prove that the axioms are sufficiently complete we must show that every access procedure has a predictable outcome when given a list which is either empty or of the form `Cons (h, t)`. More formally:

Definition

If the behaviour of the abstract data type is undefined in any situation then the axioms are said to be not *sufficiently complete*.

If the axioms are not sufficiently complete then it may be impossible to determine the behaviour of some program which uses the abstract data type.

`Empty` and `Cons` are constructor functions. The behaviour of these procedures is fully described by the syntactic part of the specification. That of `IsEmpty` is given by axioms (1) and (2); `Head` by axioms (3) and (5); and `Tail` is given by axioms (4) and (6).

What, if any, of the procedures was passed an error as an argument? A procedure is said to be *strict* if it returns an error as a result in such a case. We will assume that the access procedures are all strict. So we expect, for example:

IsEmpty (error) = error

Hence our definition of a list is both consistent and sufficiently complete.

The type list is one of the most widely used and researched of all abstract data types, and the access procedures which we have given here can be considered to be the canonical set. More generally, the criteria we use when specifying an abstract data type is to provide access procedures which will enable it to be constructed, tested and parts of it selected.

APPLICATIONS OF THE ACCESS PROCEDURES

We will assume the existence of the five access procedures. Remember that these procedures are the only way that we can manipulate the abstract data type list. Using them we will show how we can construct more complex procedures, such as joining (or *appending*) two lists, searching the list for a particular item, finding the length of the list, sorting a list and so on. These higher-level procedures will be independent of the way the access procedures are implemented. We can think of these five procedures as 'building bricks' which we can use to help us to form more complex operations (figure 2.1).

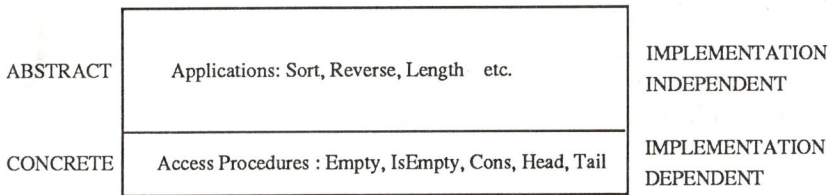

Figure 2.1

Later, we will consider possible implementations of the access procedures for the abstract data type list. However, we do not need to know how the procedures are implemented in order to be able to use them. One of the advantages of data abstraction is that we can change the implementation of the abstract data type simply by altering the way in which the access procedures are implemented. Provided that they still satisfy their specifications after the change, no other procedures should need to be altered. Also, if the higher-level procedures are to be ported to a different machine running a different compiler all that needs to be done is to implement the access procedures again.

Another advantage, which will become apparent as we progress through the chapter, is that the implementation of the higher-level procedures is greatly simplified. We do not need to be concerned with the implementation (the data structures and code), since this has been taken care of by the access procedures; we have followed the '*divide and conquer*' or '*separation of concerns*' maxim.

HIGHER-LEVEL PROCEDURES

We can now demonstrate how to build higher-level procedures using only the 'building bricks' provided for us by the procedures. We will assume that the access procedures have already been implemented and that they satisfy their specifications (i.e. they have been shown to function correctly).

EXERCISES

1. Write a procedure which takes a list as a parameter and returns its length.

Solution

We will derive the procedure by considering each of the possible forms that a list could take in turn. There are two cases, corresponding to the two constructor functions; either the list is empty or it has one or more items. The first case is trivial:

```
IF IsEmpty (L) THEN
    RETURN 0
```

If the list is not empty, its length is one greater than the length of its tail. To find the length of the tail of the list we can use recursion. So we have:

```
ELSE
    RETURN (1 + Length (Tail (L)) )
```

The derivation of the procedure is now very simple:

```
PROCEDURE Length ( L: List) : CARDINAL ;
(* Postcondition: returns the length of the list L *)

BEGIN
    IF IsEmpty (L) THEN
        RETURN 0
    ELSE
        RETURN (1 + Length (Tail (L)) )
    END (* if *)
END Length ;
```

To see how this works, we will execute the call[1]

Length ('A', 'C', 'M')

by a process which is called *rewriting* or *reduction*. We *rewrite* or *reduce* the expression to its simplest form. We will use parentheses ( ) to represent the empty list and an arrow ($\rightarrow$) to indicate each step of the rewriting.

Length ('A', 'C', 'M')	
$\rightarrow 1 +$ Length (Tail ('A', 'C', 'M'))	(by definition of the procedure Length)
$\rightarrow 1 +$ Length ('C','M')	(by axiom 4)
$\rightarrow 1 + 1 +$ Length (Tail ('C', 'M'))	(by definition of the procedure Length)
$\rightarrow 1 + 1 +$ Length ('M')	(by axiom 4)
$\rightarrow 1 + 1 + 1 +$ Length ( )	(by definition of the procedure Length and axiom 4)
$\rightarrow 1 + 1 + 1 + 0$	(by definition of the procedure Length)
$\rightarrow 3$	

---

1   When a function is known to take a list as parameter we omit one pair of parameters during rewriting, for clarity.

2. Write a procedure which takes two lists as parameters and returns a list which consists of the two lists appended together. For example, if we append the two lists of characters ('C','A','R') and ('R','O','T') we produce the list ('C','A','R','R','O','T').

Solution

Again there are two cases to deal with: either one list is empty or it has one or more items. The easiest case to deal with occurs when the first list is empty. Then the result of Append is simply the second list (which could, of course, be empty):

```
IF IsEmpty (L1) THEN
    RETURN L2 ;
```

Now suppose that the first list has one item in it. For example,

```
Append ( ('R'), ('R','O','T'))
```

All that needs to be done is to somehow add the item 'R' to the beginning of the second list. We know that we can use Cons to add an item to a list in this way. To obtain the item which is in the list all we need do is to take the head of the list. So we have

```
RETURN Cons ( Head ( L1) , L2 )
```

Now suppose that one list has more than one item in it (say two). For example,

```
Append ( ('A', 'R'), ('R','O','T'))
```

Again, we can follow the same procedure. The difference is that this time we have to Cons the head of the first list onto the list which we obtained in our previous example, i.e. the result of appending the rest of the list onto the second list. To obtain the rest of the list all we have to do is to use the access procedure Tail:

```
RETURN Cons ( Head ( L1) , Append ( Tail (L1) , L2 )
```

The result is the same if L1 has more than two items. Putting the two cases together we obtain:

```
PROCEDURE Append (l1,l2 : List ) : List ;
(* Postcondition: returns the result of appending
    list l2 to list l1 *)

BEGIN
    IF IsEmpty (l1) THEN
        RETURN l2
    ELSE
        RETURN Cons (Head (l1), Append(Tail(l1),l2))
    END (* if *)
END Append ;
```

For example, the rewriting of

Append(('C','A','R') , ('R','O','T'))

proceeds as follows:

Append(('C','A','R') , ('R','O','T'))
→ Cons (Head ('C','A','R') , Append (Tail ('C','A','R') , ('R','O','T')))
→ Cons ('C', Append (('A','R') , ('R','O','T')))
→ Cons ('C', Cons (Head ('A','R'), Append (Tail ('A','R') , ('R','O','T'))))
→ Cons ('C', Cons ('A', Append (('R') , ('R','O','T'))))
→ Cons ('C', Cons ('A', Cons (Head ('R') , Append (Tail ('R'), ('R','O','T')))))
→ Cons ('C', Cons ('A', Cons ('R' , Append (( ), ('R','O','T')))))
→ Cons ('C', Cons ('A', Cons ('R', ('R','O','T'))))
→ Cons ('C', Cons ('A', ('R','R','O','T')))
→ Cons ('C', ('A','R','R','O','T'))
→ ('C','A','R','R','O','T')

3. Write a procedure which takes a list as a parameter and returns the list with its items reversed. For example,

Reverse ('T','A','R') should give ('R','A','T').

Solution

Again there are two distinct cases: either the list is empty or it has one or more items. The former case is trivial:

```
IF IsEmpty (L) THEN
    RETURN L
```

In the latter case we need to take the item from the front of the list and place it at the end of the list, and do this for each item in the tail of the list (using recursion). For example, consider the call to

Reverse ('T', 'A')

First take the head of the list: this gives us the item 'T'. This must be converted to a list by using Cons:

```
Cons ( 'T', Empty ( ) )
```

so that it can be added (by using Append) to the end of the rest of the list. In this example the rest of the list only contains the single item 'A'.

```
RETURN Append ( ('A') , ('T') )
```

If there were more than two items in the list then the rest of it would also have to be reversed. So the code would be:

```
RETURN Append ( Reverse (Tail (L)), Cons (Head (L), Empty ( )) )
```

Putting the two cases together gives the procedure below:

```
PROCEDURE Reverse ( L: List ) : List ;
(* Postcondition: return the reverse of the list L *)

BEGIN
    IF IsEmpty (L) THEN
        RETURN L
    ELSE
        RETURN Append (Reverse (Tail (L)),Cons (Head (L),Empty
                                                          ( )))
    END (* if *)
END Reverse ;
```

4. Write a procedure (PrintList) which takes a list as a parameter and prints its contents to the screen.

Solution

Again we can use case analysis on the two possible forms a list can take. Obviously, if the list is empty then there is nothing to do, so we should check first to determine whether the list is empty or not. Otherwise we take the first item in the list (using Head) and write it out:

```
IF NOT IsEmpty (L) THEN
    WriteItem ( Head (L));
```

The procedure WriteItem must be implemented when the type of the items in the list is known. We then print the rest of the list (which is obtained using Tail):

```
PrintList (Tail (L))
```

So the procedure to print a list is:

```
PROCEDURE PrintList (L: List) ;
(* Postcondition: print the elements of the list L *)

BEGIN
    IF NOT IsEmpty (L) THEN
        WriteItem ( Head (L));
        PrintList (Tail (L))
    END (* if *)
END PrintList;
```

To reduce the number of modules which have to be edited if the item type is changed, all procedures which depend on the type of item (for example, procedures to read and write items, compare them for equality and inequality, etc.) should be kept together in a separate module.

A slightly more sophisticated version, the body of which is given below, separates the individual items by commas:

```
BEGIN
    IF NOT IsEmpty (L) THEN
        WriteItem ( Head (L));
        IF NOT IsEmpty ( Tail ( L)) THEN
            Write (" , " )
        END ; (* IF *)
        PrintList (Tail (L))
    END ; (* if *)
END PrintList;
```

5. Write a procedure which takes a list as a parameter and returns a list in which the items are sorted.

Solution

The items in the lists given above are not in any particular order. Occasionally we need to sort the items in a list in some way, for example, alphabetically (a list of names) or numerically.

The method we will use is to take the head of the list and insert it into the tail of it in such a way as to maintain the order of items in the list. First we must develop an insert procedure (InsertInOrder) which inserts a single item I into an ordered list L.

If the list is empty, then we simply form a list containing the item:

```
IF IsEmpty(L) THEN
    RETURN Cons ( I, Empty ( ) )
```

Otherwise, we compare the item we are trying to insert with the item at the head of the list. For generality, we should implement a procedure (IsLess) which takes two parameters of type InfoType and compares them for ordering. If the item is less than the head of the list then we can insert it at the head:

```
ELSIF IsLess ( I, Head (L)) THEN
    RETURN Cons (I, L)
```

Otherwise we must insert the item in the tail of the list by calling the insert function recursively:

```
ELSE
    RETURN Cons ( Head (L), InsertInOrder(I, Tail (L)))
```

The entire function is given below.

```
PROCEDURE InsertInOrder (I: InfoType ; L : List) : List ;
(* Postcondition: insert item I in the list L in order *)

BEGIN
    IF IsEmpty(L) THEN
        RETURN Cons ( I, Empty ( ) )
```

```
ELSIF IsLess (I , Head (L)) THEN
        RETURN Cons (I, L)
    ELSE
        RETURN Cons ( Head (L), InsertInOrder(I, Tail (L)))
    END (* if *)
  END InsertInOrder ;
```

Using this insert procedure we can now write a procedure to sort a list. First, we must sort the tail of the list to ensure that there is an ordered list in which to insert items.

```
  PROCEDURE Sort (L : List) : List ;
  (* Postcondition: returns a list containing the
      elements of list L sorted in order *)
  BEGIN
    IF IsEmpty(L) THEN
        RETURN L
    ELSE
        RETURN  InsertInOrder  (Head (L),  Sort  (Tail (L)) )
    END (* if *)
  END Sort ;
```

For example, to sort the list ('C','M','A') we first have to sort the list ('M','A'). We can do this in exactly the same way by taking the head and inserting it in the right place in the tail. Since 'A' < 'M' this should give us the list ('A', 'M'). Thus we have:

> Sort ('C','M','A')
> → InsertInOrder ('C', Sort ('M','A'))
> → InsertInOrder ('C', InsertInOrder('M', Sort ('A')))
> → InsertInOrder ('C', InsertInOrder('M', InsertInOrder ('A',( ))))
> → InsertInOrder ('C', InsertInOrder('M', ('A')))
> → InsertInOrder ('C', ('A','M'))
> → ('A', 'C', 'M')

Of course, this is not the only way to sort a list, nor is it the most efficient, but what it lacks in efficiency it makes up for in simplicity and elegance.

Exercise 2.1

Write the procedures below:

1.  ```
    PROCEDURE Last (L: List) : InfoType ;
    (*Postcondition: returns the last (i.e.
      rightmost) item of the list L *)
    ```

2.  ```
    PROCEDURE IsIn ( I : InfoType; L : List) : BOOLEAN ;
    (*Postcondition: return TRUE if item I is in
      list L, otherwise FALSE *)
    ```

Note: For generality, use a procedure 'IsEqual' to check for equality of two items. This would have to be implemented when the type of the items in the list is known.

3. PROCEDURE Duplicate (L : List) : List ;
    (*Postcondition: returns a list in which each item is
       duplicated. For example, Duplicate ('A', 'C', 'M')
       should return ('A','A','C','C','M','M') *)

4. PROCEDURE AllOut (I : InfoType; L : List) : List ;
    (*Postcondition: returns a list in which all occurrences
       of the item I have been removed. *)

5. PROCEDURE FirstOut (I : InfoType; L : List) : List ;
    (*Postcondition:returns a list in which the first
       occurrence of the item has been removed. *)

6. PROCEDURE Take (n : CARDINAL ; L : List) : List;
    (*Postcondition: returns a list which consists
       of the first n items of the list L. *)

7. PROCEDURE Drop (n : CARDINAL ; L : List) : List;
    (*Postcondition:returns a list without the first n items
       of the list. *)

8. PROCEDURE PrettyPrintlist (L : List);
    (*Postcondition: prints the contents of the list to the
       screen in such a way that the list is enclosed by
       brackets and consecutive items are separated by
       commas.*)

9. PROCEDURE Replace (new, old: InfoType; L: List) : List ;
    (*Postcondition: returns a list in which the first
       occurrence of old has been replaced by new *)

10. PROCEDURE ReplaceAll (new, old: InfoType; L: List)
    : List ;
    (*Postcondition: returns a list in which all occurrences
       of old have been replaced by new *)

11. PROCEDURE InBefore (new, old: InfoType; L: List) : List ;
    (*Postcondition: returns a list in which new has been
       inserted before every occurrence of old *)

12. PROCEDURE InAround (new, old: InfoType; L: List) : List ;
    (*Postcondition: returns a list in which new has been
       inserted before and after every occurrence of old *)

HIGHER-ORDER FUNCTIONS

Suppose now that the items in the list are of type CARDINAL (i.e. integers ≥ 0), and we wish to write a procedure Double which takes a list and returns a list in which the value of each of the items has been doubled. For example,

Double (1, 3, 14, 25) = (2, 6, 28, 50).

As usual, there are two cases. If the list is empty there is nothing to do:

```
IF IsEmpty (L) THEN
    RETURN L
```

Otherwise we must double the item at the head of the list and then Cons this onto the tail of the list, each item of which must also be doubled:

```
ELSE
    RETURN Cons ( 2 * ( Head ( L )), Double ( Tail ( L )))
```

and this gives us the procedure below:

```
PROCEDURE Double (l : List ) : List ;

BEGIN
    IF IsEmpty (l) THEN
        RETURN l
    ELSE
        RETURN Cons (2 * Head(l), Double (Tail(l)))
    END (* if *)
END Double ;
```

However, writing the procedure in this way has one disadvantage: if we wish to apply some other function to every item in a list (for example, triple or square) or return the factorial of each, we would have to write another procedure. A more general procedure, which could take a function as a parameter together with a list and return the list in which the function had been applied to each item in it, would be much more useful. Fortunately, Modula-2 allows us to pass a procedure as a parameter to a procedure (this is an extension of a similar facility provided by Pascal). The way this is done is described below.

Modula-2 allows us to declare a *procedure type*. For example:

```
TYPE MONADIC = PROCEDURE ( CARDINAL ) : CARDINAL ;
```

This declares a type which is a procedure that takes a cardinal number as a parameter and returns a value of type CARDINAL. This is a *monadic* function, that is, it has only one parameter. Now we can declare variables of this type (which are called *procedure variables*) in the same way as usual, and also pass variables of this type to procedures as parameters. A function which takes a procedure as a parameter or returns one as its result is called a *higher-order function*. Unfortunately, one of the restrictions of Modula-2 is that procedures cannot be returned as results. However, functional programming languages do not suffer this restriction and higher-order functions are a very powerful feature of such languages. We will now write the procedure which was described above:

```
PROCEDURE Map ( Funct: MONADIC; L : List) : List ;
```

If the list is empty, there is nothing to do.

```
IF IsEmpty (L) THEN
    RETURN L
```

Otherwise, we must take the head of the list, apply the function `Funct` to it, and also do this to each item in the tail of the list by calling `Map` recursively. To add the result onto the tail of the list we use `Cons`, which gives us:

```
ELSE
    RETURN ( Cons ( Funct ( Head ( L )),
                    Map ( Funct, Tail ( L ))))
```

The full procedure is given below:

```
PROCEDURE Map ( Funct: MONADIC; L : List) : List ;
(* Precondition: takes a monadic function Funct and a list L
   Postcondition: returns a list in which the function
   Funct has been applied to each item of the list L in
   turn *)

BEGIN
    IF IsEmpty (L) THEN
        RETURN L
    ELSE
        RETURN ( Cons ( Funct ( Head ( L )),
                        Map ( Funct, Tail ( L ))))
    END ;
END Map ;
```

Suppose we are given the monadic function below, `Times2`:

```
PROCEDURE Times2 ( n : CARDINAL ) : CARDINAL ;
(* Postcondition: returns twice its argument *)

BEGIN
    RETURN 2 * n ;
END Times2 ;
```

We can now double every item in a list by passing this function and the list to `Map`. For example, the execution for the list of even numbers (2, 4, 6) is rewritten below:

```
Map ( Times2, 2, 4, 6 )
→ Cons ( Times2 ( Head ( 2, 4, 6 )), Map (Times2, Tail ( 2, 4, 6 )))
→ Cons ( Times2 ( 2 ), Map ( Times2, ( 4, 6 )))
→ Cons ( 4, Cons ( Times2 ( Head ( 4, 6 )), Map ( Times2, Tail ( 4, 6 ) )))
→ Cons ( 4, Cons ( Times2 ( 4 ), Map ( Times2, ( 6 ) )))
→ Cons ( 4, Cons ( 8, Cons ( Times2 ( Head ( 6 )), Map ( Times2, ( Tail ( 6 ))))
→ Cons ( 4, Cons ( 8, Cons ( Times2 ( 6 ), Map ( Times2, ( ) ))))
→ Cons ( 4, Cons ( 8, Cons ( Times2 ( 6 ), ( ) )))))
→ Cons ( 4, Cons ( 8, Cons ( 12, ( ) )))
→ Cons ( 4, Cons ( 8, ( 12 ) ))
→ Cons ( 4, ( 8, 12 ))
→ ( 4, 8, 12 )
```

As a second example, suppose we have a function Square which returns the square of the number which is passed to it. The rewriting of a call to Map using this function and the list of numbers (2, 4, 6) is shown below:

Map (Square, (2, 4, 6))
→ Cons (Square (Head (2, 4, 6)), Map (Square, Tail (2, 4, 6)))
→ Cons (Square (2), Map (Square, (4, 6)))
→ Cons (4, Cons (Square (Head (4, 6)), Map (Square, Tail (4, 6))))
→ Cons (4, Cons (Square (4), Map (Square, (6))))
→ Cons (4, Cons (16, Cons (Square (Head (6)), Map (Square, (Tail (6))))
→ Cons (4, Cons (16, Cons (Square (6), Map (Square, ( )))))
→ Cons (4, Cons (16, Cons (Square (6), ( )))))
→ Cons (4, Cons (16, Cons (36, ( ))))
→ Cons (4, Cons (16, (36)))
→ Cons (4, (16, 36))
→ (4, 16, 36)

Note:
(1) We have assumed for these examples that the items in the list are cardinal numbers, i.e. that we have TYPE InfoType = CARDINAL;
(2) There is a restriction on the use of procedure types in Modula-2: predefined intrinsic functions cannot be passed as parameters. However, this can be circumvented by implementing a procedure which then calls the predefined function.

Now suppose that we wish to sum all the items in a list. The procedure is simple to write; take the head of the list and add it to the sum of the items in the tail. Again, the only problem with this solution is that it is too specific. We really need a higher-order function, so that we could also (for example) easily obtain the product of the items or the length of the list. This operation can be expressed by a higher-order function, which has come to be known as Reduce, since the items of the list are reduced by the function to a single result.

To implement this function, we will need to declare a new procedure type, which takes two parameters (and so is a *dyadic* function)

```
TYPE DYADIC = PROCEDURE ( CARDINAL, CARDINAL ) : CARDINAL ;
```

The function Reduce takes a dyadic function, F, a list, L, and a base case, b and returns a result which is of the same type as the base case. We can derive the function by considering the two cases of an empty and non-empty list. If the list is empty, we return the base case:

```
IF IsEmpty (L) THEN
    RETURN b
```

Otherwise we apply the function to the head of the list and the result we obtain by calling Reduce recursively with the tail of the list:

```
F ( Head ( L ), Reduce ( F, Tail ( L ), b ))
```

The entire procedure is given below.

```
PROCEDURE Reduce ( F: DYADIC; L : List ; b : CARDINAL) :
                                        CARDINAL ;
(* Precondition: takes a dyadic function F, a list L and
   a base case b
   Postcondition: reduces L to a single value by applying
   F to 2 values at a time *)

BEGIN
   IF IsEmpty (L) THEN
      RETURN b
   ELSE
      RETURN F ( Head( L ), Reduce ( F, Tail ( L ), b ))
   END ;
END Reduce;
```

Alternatively, we can write a *tail-recursive* version of the procedure Reduce (tail recursion will be discussed in Chapter 4) which takes a dyadic function, F, a list, L, and an *accumulating parameter*, acc, which will accumulate the result which is to be returned. If the list is empty, we return the accumulating parameter:

```
IF IsEmpty (L) THEN
   RETURN acc
```

Otherwise we apply the function to the head of the list and the accumulating parameter to obtain a new value for acc:

```
F ( acc, Head ( L ))
```

and then repeat this for each item in the tail of this list by calling Reduce recursively until the list is empty.

```
Reduce ( F, Tail ( L ), F ( acc, Head ( L )))
```

The procedure is given below.

```
PROCEDURE Reduce ( F: DYADIC; L : List ; acc : CARINAL) :
                                        CARDINAL ;

(* Precondition: takes a dyadic function F, a list L and an
   accumulating parameter acc
   Postcondition: returns acc, which accumulates the result
   of applying F to 2 values at a time *)

BEGIN
   IF IsEmpty (L) THEN
      RETURN acc
   ELSE
      RETURN Reduce ( F, Tail (  L ), F ( acc, Head ( L )))
   END ;
END Reduce;
```

Suppose we have written a function Sum which takes two parameters and returns their sum. We can use Reduce with this function and an accumulating parameter which is the identity element for Sum, i.e. zero, to sum the items in a list. For example:

Reduce (Sum, (2, 4, 6), 0)

$\rightarrow$ Reduce (Sum, Tail (2, 4, 6), Sum (0, Head (2, 4, 6)))
$\rightarrow$ Reduce (Sum, (4, 6), Sum (0, 2))
$\rightarrow$ Reduce (Sum, (4, 6), 2))
$\rightarrow$ Reduce (Sum, Tail (4, 6), Sum (2, Head (4, 6)))
$\rightarrow$ Reduce (Sum, (6), Sum (2, 4))
$\rightarrow$ Reduce (Sum, (6), 6)
$\rightarrow$ Reduce (Sum, Tail (6), Sum (6, Head (6)))
$\rightarrow$ Reduce (Sum, ( ), Sum (6, 6))
$\rightarrow$ Reduce (Sum, ( ), 12)
$\rightarrow$ 12

Note that the equivalence of these two versions of Reduce depends on the fact that F is associative and that zero is its identity element.

Consider the function below:

```
PROCEDURE Increment ( i,  j : CARDINAL ) : CARDINAL ;
(* Postcondition: returns the result of incrementing
   the second parameter *)

BEGIN
    RETURN i + 1
END Increment ;
```

If we use this function as a parameter to Reduce, with an accumulating parameter which is initially 0, the result will be obtained by adding 1 to the accumulator for each item in the list, which is actually the number of items in the list. For example:

Reduce (Increment, (2, 4, 6), 0)

$\rightarrow$ Reduce (Increment, Tail (2, 4, 6), Increment (0, Head (2, 4, 6)))
$\rightarrow$ Reduce (Increment, (4, 6), Increment (0, 2))
$\rightarrow$ Reduce (Increment, (4, 6), 1)
$\rightarrow$ Reduce (Increment, Tail (4, 6), Increment (1, Head (4, 6)))
$\rightarrow$ Reduce (Increment, (6), Increment (1, 4))
$\rightarrow$ Reduce (Increment, (6), 2)
$\rightarrow$ Reduce (Increment, Tail (6), Increment (2, Head (6)))
$\rightarrow$ Reduce (Increment, ( ), Increment (2, 6))
$\rightarrow$ Reduce (Increment, ( ), 3)
$\rightarrow$ 3

which is the length of the list.

Exercise 2.2

How can we find the length of a list using two higher-order functions? Does this method have any drawbacks ?

We have demonstrated how an abstract data type can be used by a programmer without any knowledge of the implementation: indeed, we have not yet given an implementation. However, the next part of the chapter is devoted to this subject.

IMPLEMENTATIONS OF THE ACCESS PROCEDURES

We are now going to consider possible implementations of the access procedures for the abstract data type list. The definition module containing the five access procedures was given earlier.

Diagrammatic representation

The definition of the abstract data type list stated that a list is a linear sequence of an arbitrary number of items together with the access procedures given above. Therefore, if the list is not empty there is one particular value at the front of the list, then another value following it, etc., until we get to the end of the list.

To clarify this, when discussing the implementation of the abstract data type list we will represent the structure of a list as shown in figure 2.2.

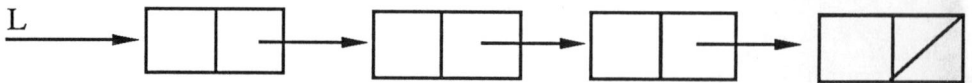

Figure 2.2

Here, L points to the item at the head of the list. Each of the boxes will contain an item and (as can be seen from the figure) an indication of the next item. The boxes will be referred to as *nodes*. Thus each node can be said to have a *data field* and a *link field*. If a node does not have a successor then a diagonal line is drawn through its link field.

For example, the list of characters ('C', 'A', 'T', 'S') can be represented by:

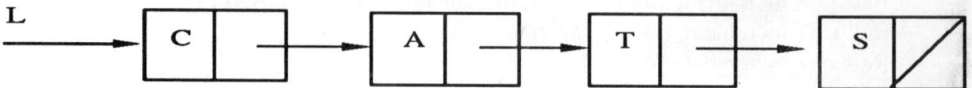

and the list of integers (7, 3, 25, 1) by:

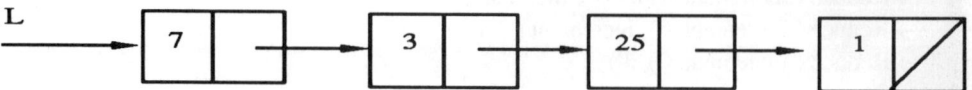

and so on.

Of course, the access procedures for an abstract data type must be independent of the type of items that the abstract data type contains: hence the use of the type InfoType, which should be defined in a separate module and imported into the definition and implementation modules containing the access procedures.

In the last chapter we used procedures `IsLess` and `IsEqual` when we wanted to test the order and equality, respectively, of two items. These must be implemented when the type of the items in the list is known. Such procedures should be kept in a single implementation module, together with any others which depend on the knowledge of the type of the items (for example, procedures for input and output of items).

The *stack* and *queue* abstract data types are very similar to the abstract data type list, the only differences being the way that insertion and deletion can be performed. These abstract data types will be discussed later.

Methods of implementation

We stated in Chapter 1 that there are two classes into which implementations may fall: static and dynamic. We will start by discussing a dynamic implementation using pointer variables, and then go on to discuss a static implementation. Readers unfamiliar with the manipulation of pointer variables should refer to Appendix 1.

Recall that the access procedures must be the only procedures which depend on the method of implementation. We must be able to replace an implementation by any other and find that our higher-level procedures (`Append`, `Reverse`, `Length`, etc.) will function without alteration.

Dynamic implementation

Implementing the list using pointers means that the list is a *dynamic* data structure. The storage for dynamic variables is allocated from the *heap* at run time. The term *linked list* is often used to describe this structure.

Each node in a linked list consists of both a data value (for example, this could be an integer) and a pointer to the next node. Therefore the nodes can be defined as records. For example:

```
TYPE
   NodePtr = POINTER TO Node ; (* Node has not been defined
                                                    yet *)

   Node = RECORD
               Info: InfoType;
               Link : NodePtr ;
           END ;
```

This sets up a record called `Node` which contains two fields. The first is devoted to data and may be any type. The second field is a pointer which points to the next node in the list. The two types `NodePtr` and `Node` are said to be *mutually recursive*. This is one of the few cases in which mutual recursion is allowed in Modula-2. We can then identify lists with pointers to nodes which are at the head of lists and declare our abstract data type list by:

```
TYPE List = NodePtr;
```

For example, if the type `InfoType` was defined as

```
TYPE InfoType = CARDINAL ;
```

it should now be possible to construct a list of the form shown in figure 2.3.

L

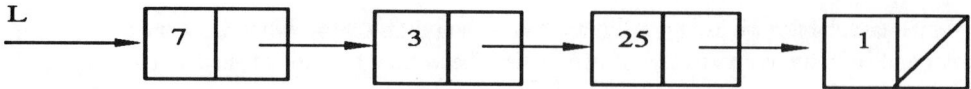

Figure 2.3

The Link field of the last Node in the list is set to NIL so that we know when we have reached the end of the list. This is shown by the diagonal line in the last pointer field.

We can now implement the access procedures. These will be written in a functional style, and so each procedure is a function which takes value parameters and returns a single value by using the RETURN statement.

1. The first access procedure we will consider is the constructor function Empty. This is very simple to implement, since we just need to return a pointer which does not point to anything, i.e. a NIL pointer.

```
PROCEDURE Empty ( ) : List ;
(* Postcondition: returns an empty list, i.e. one that does
    not contain any data items *)

BEGIN
    RETURN NIL
END Empty ;
```

2. Having done this we can easily implement the predicate function IsEmpty:

```
PROCEDURE IsEmpty ( L : List ) : BOOLEAN ;
(* Postcondition: returns TRUE if L is empty, otherwise
    FALSE *)

BEGIN
    RETURN ( L = NIL)
END IsEmpty;
```

We can verify the first axiom describing the semantics of the list by noting that the result of the function call IsEmpty (Empty ()) is TRUE.

3. The procedure Cons inserts an item at the head of a list. We will assume that the first item in the list is the leftmost one. Thus if we insert the character 'S' at the head of the list ('C', 'A', 'T') the result is ('S', 'C', 'A', 'T'). There are four steps, which can best be explained diagrammatically:

(a) Create a new node and make a new pointer (NewList) point to it.

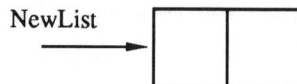

(b) Set the data field of the node to be the new item.

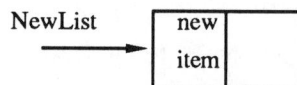

(c) Set the link field of the node to point to the head of the old list

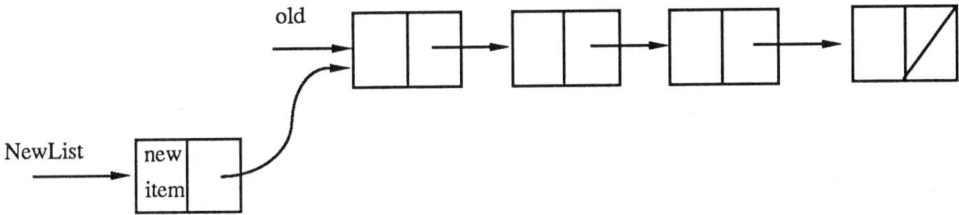

Note that the new list is constructed from the old one, but the old list is not affected by this sharing of nodes.

(d) Then return this new list.

The procedure Cons, given below in pseudocode, summarizes these operations:

PROCEDURE Cons (I : InfoType ; L : List) : List;
(* Postcondition: returns a list with I as its head and L as its tail *)

Create a new node and make a new pointer point to it.
Put the new item in the data field of the node.
Make the link field of the node point to the head of the old list.
Return the new list.

This can be translated directly into Modula-2[1]

```
PROCEDURE Cons ( I : InfoType ; L : List ) : List ;
·(* Postcondition: returns a list with I as its head and
    L as its tail *)

VAR Newlist : List ;

BEGIN
    NEW (Newlist ) ;
    Newlist^.Info := I;
    Newlist^.Link := L ;
    RETURN Newlist
END Cons ;
```

Therefore if the items in the list are characters then Cons ('A', Empty ( )) will return ('A'), i.e. a list with the character 'A' in it, as shown below.

To check the second axiom, we need to determine the result of IsEmpty (Cons (h, t)), where h is an item and t is a list. This can be done by noting (from the implementation of Cons) that the statement

---

1   Not all Modula-2 compilers provide the procedure NEW. Consequently it may be necessary to replace calls to NEW by calls to the procedure ALLOCATE. See Wirth (1988) for details.

```
Cons ( h, t ) = NIL
```

is obviously false, which verifies the axiom.

Note that the list L which is passed to Cons is not affected by the function: after executing Cons, L still contains exactly the same items as it did prior to the procedure call. Thus Cons is referentially transparent at the level of abstraction with which we are concerned.

4. The procedure Head returns the item at the head of the list. For example, the head of the list ('S', 'C', 'A', 'T') is the item 'S'.

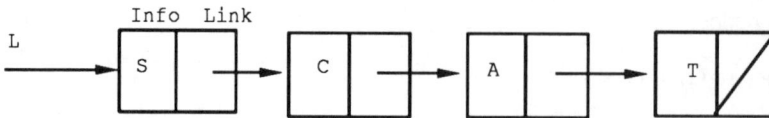

The semantics of the algebraic specification for the abstract data type list stated that the result of trying to take the head of a list which is empty should be an error, and this is ensured by the first part of the procedure:

```
PROCEDURE Head (L : List) : InfoType ;
(* Postcondition: returns the item at the head of list L *)

BEGIN
    IF IsEmpty (L) THEN
        WriteString ("Error - can't take head of empty
                                                    list " ) ;
        HALT (* tidy exit *)
    ELSE
        RETURN L^.Info
    END (* if *)
END Head ;
```

Thus the call Head (Empty ( )) results in an error message and termination of the program. The other axiom we must check is the result of the call to Head (Cons (h, t)), where h is an item and t is a list. However, by observation of the procedures Cons and Head we note that Cons assigns the item h to the Info field of the node at the head of the list, and Head returns the contents of the Info field of the list which is passed to it, i.e. h.

5. Now let us consider the selector function Tail. This is the reverse of the operation Cons in that it returns a list without the node which was at the head of the list. For example, if we remove the first item from the list ('S', 'C', 'A', 'T') we have ('C', 'A', 'T').

Note that the procedure Tail leaves the original list (which is passed in as a value parameter) unchanged. This is in keeping with our desire for a functional programming style, as any other action (such as calling DISPOSE to recover the space allocated to the head of the list) would be a side-effect of the access procedure, and, as we have already explained, side-effects are undesirable.

Consider what would happen if the head were disposed of. For example, suppose that we called the procedure PrintList which we wrote earlier. The body of PrintList is:

```
WriteItem ( Head ( L )) ;
PrintList ( Tail ( L ))
```

If `Tail` had the side-effect of disposing the head of the list, then a call to `PrintList` would result in the entire list being disposed of! Obviously this is something that we wish to avoid.

If it is essential to dispose of a list which is no longer used a procedure to do this could be implemented as an access procedure. However, care must be taken because if the list being disposed of has been assigned to another list then the memory locations used will be shared. Some people may regard the lack of an access procedure to dispose of part or all of a list as unusual. However, we would like to draw their attention not only to the reductions in the cost of memory over recent years but also to the fact that all these implementations of the access procedures only use *one* list—no memory cells in the list are ever copied, and so the amount of memory used is kept to a minimum.

To implement the function `Tail`, we have to return a pointer to the second node in the list.

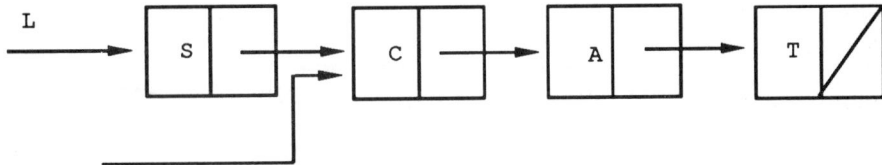

Again, the semantics for the access procedures stated that trying to find the tail of an empty list results in an error, and so this is the first thing that we check.

```
PROCEDURE Tail ( L : List ) : List ;
(* Postcondition: returns the tail of list L *)

BEGIN
    IF IsEmpty (L) THEN
        WriteString ("Error - can't take tail of empty
                                                  list ") ;
        HALT (* tidy exit *)
    ELSE
        RETURN L^.Link
    END (* if *)
END Tail;
```

Thus the call `Tail ( Empty ( ))` results in an error message and termination of the program. By observation, we see that `Tail` returns the `Link` field of the node at the head of the list, and so the result of `Tail ( Cons ( h, t ))` is the list `t`.

We have now verified all six axioms which describe the semantics of the abstract data type list. The complete implementation module for the access procedures for this list is given below.

```
IMPLEMENTATION MODULE Lists ;
(* This module contains the implementation of the abstract
    data type list *)
```

```
FROM Items IMPORT InfoType ;
FROM Storage IMPORT ALLOCATE ; (* system dependent, needed
for calls to NEW *)
FROM InOut IMPORT WriteString ; (* system dependent *)

TYPE
   NodePtr = POINTER TO Node ;

   Node = RECORD
              Info : InfoType ;
              Link : NodePtr
          END ;

   List = NodePtr;

PROCEDURE Empty ( ) : List ;
(* Postcondition: returns an empty list *)

BEGIN
   RETURN NIL
END Empty ;

PROCEDURE IsEmpty ( L : List ) : BOOLEAN ;
(* Postcondition: returns TRUE if L is empty, otherwise
   FALSE *)

BEGIN
   RETURN ( L = NIL)
END IsEmpty;

PROCEDURE Cons ( I : InfoType ; L : List) : List ;
(* Postcondition: returns a list with I as its head
   and L as its tail *)

VAR Newlist : List ;

BEGIN
   NEW (Newlist) ;
   Newlist^.Info := I ;
   Newlist^.Link := L ;
   RETURN Newlist
END Cons ;

PROCEDURE Head (L : List) : InfoType ;
(* Postcondition: returns the item at the head of the list
   L *)

BEGIN
   IF IsEmpty (L)
      THEN WriteString ("Error - can't take head of empty
                                               list ") ;
         HALT ; (* exit tidily *)
   ELSE
      RETURN (L^.Info )
   END (* if *)
END Head ;
```

```
PROCEDURE Tail ( L : List ) : List ;
(* Postcondition: returns the tail of the list L *)

BEGIN
    IF IsEmpty (L) THEN
        WriteString ("Error - can't take tail of empty
                                              list ") ;
        HALT ; (* exit tidily *)
    ELSE
        RETURN L^.Link
    END (* if *)
END Tail;

END Lists.
```

Static implementation

A very simple implementation of a list uses an array, and places the items in the array sequentially. For example, the list

('S', 'D', 'F', 'T', 'Q', 'A', 'B', 'G', 'H', 'L')

would be stored as shown in figure 2.4. The links (or 'pointers') between the items are in this case implicit, since given an array A and an index i, the item following $A[i]$ in the list is that retrieved by $A[i+1]$.

1	2	3	4	5	6	7	8	9	10
S	D	F	T	Q	A	B	G	H	L

Figure 2.4

We will now consider a variation on this, which is static in the sense that an array is used to hold the items but also dynamic in that a pointer variable is used. A list is declared as a pointer to a record which has two fields: one is an array, which is used to hold the items in the list, and the other is an integer, to record the index of the next available space. Of course, a truly static implementation should not make use of pointer variables at all. There are two reasons for declaring a list as a *pointer* to a record: first, because we have declared a list to be an opaque type in the definition module and opaque types are usually restricted to pointer types, and second, because some Modula-2 compilers do not allow structured types to be returned from functions. Therefore this implementation was forced on us by the limitations of some Modula-2 compilers and not by limitations of the language. The use of an opaque type allows us to observe the rule that the implementation of an abstract data type should be hidden from the user. The complete implementation is given below:

```
IMPLEMENTATION MODULE Lists;
(* Access procedures for lists implemented statically *)
```

```
(* N.B. The list is stored backwards, i.e. the head of the
   list has the highest index of any item in the array. *)

FROM InOut IMPORT WriteString ;
FROM Item IMPORT InfoType ;
FROM Storage IMPORT ALLOCATE ;

CONST Max = 100 ;
TYPE
   Size = [ 1..Max ] ;
   Range = [ 1..Max+1 ] ;
   List = POINTER TO Node ;
   Node = RECORD
          Buffer : ARRAY Size OF InfoType ;
          ListPtr : Range ; (* points to the
          first free slot *)
          END ;

PROCEDURE Empty ( ) : List ;
(* Postcondition: returns an empty list *)

VAR Temp : List ;

BEGIN
   NEW ( Temp) ;
   Temp^.ListPtr := 1 ;
   RETURN Temp
END Empty ;

PROCEDURE IsEmpty ( L : List ) : BOOLEAN ;
(* Postcondition: returns TRUE if L is empty, otherwise
   FALSE *)

BEGIN
   RETURN L^.ListPtr = 1;
END IsEmpty ;

PROCEDURE IsFull ( L : List ) : BOOLEAN ;

BEGIN
   RETURN (L^.ListPtr = Max+1)
END IsFull ;

PROCEDURE Cons( L : List ; NewItem : InfoType ) : List ;
(* Postcondition: returns a list with I as its head
   and L as its tail *)

VAR Temp : List ;

BEGIN
   IF IsFull ( L ) THEN
      WriteString (" The list is full !" ) ;
      HALT ; (* exit tidily *)
   ELSE
      NEW (Temp ) ;
```

```
              Temp^ := L^ ; (* make a copy of L and assign it to
              Temp *)
              Temp^.Buffer[Temp^.ListPtr] := NewItem ;
              Temp^.ListPtr := Temp^.ListPtr + 1 ;
              RETURN (Temp);
         END
     END Cons ;


     PROCEDURE Head ( L : List ) : InfoType ;
     (* Postcondition: returns the item at the head of the list
        L *)

     BEGIN
         IF IsEmpty(L) THEN
             WriteString (" attempt to use Head on an empty list
                                                  ! " ) ;
             HALT; (* exit tidily *)
         ELSE
             RETURN L^.Buffer[L^.ListPtr - 1] ;
         END ;
     END Head ;

     PROCEDURE Tail ( L : List ) : List ;
     (* Postcondition:returns the tail of the list L *)

     VAR Temp : List ;

     BEGIN
         IF IsEmpty(L) THEN
             WriteString (" attempt to use Tail on an empty list
                                                  ! " ) ;
             HALT; (* exit tidily *)
         ELSE
             NEW (Temp) ;
             Temp^ := L^ ; (* make a copy of L and assign it to
                                                      Temp *)
             Temp^.ListPtr := Temp^.ListPtr - 1;
         END ; (* if *)
         RETURN Temp
     END Tail ;

     END Lists.
```

There are two points to note about this implementation. First, it was necessary to provide a procedure to check to see whether the array is full or not. This procedure was not included in the specification because the abstract data type list does not have any limitation on its size. The implementor should try to ensure that the constant Max is as large as possible, so that this error message is never displayed.

Second, the procedures Cons and Tail both copy L and then make the necessary alterations to the copy. This is to avoid side-effecting the original list, which would otherwise be altered. This should be contrasted with the dynamic implementation, in which we had only one copy of the list but several pointers to different parts of it.

Note that it is not necessary to recompile the *definition* module for the abstract data type list, as it is unchanged. Consequently all the other procedures which were built using the access procedures (such as Append, etc.) should still function in exactly the same way. All that is necessary is to link the module containing them with the new implementation module for the access procedures.

Alternative static implementation

As with the dynamic implementation that we gave, the static implementation above does not include any procedures for garbage collection, so there is no way that we can recover a slot in the array once an item has been placed in it. Such procedures were not included as access procedures because of our wish to write code in a functional style. A program should use an abstract data type (such as a list) to hold the values which are returned as the answers to some particular problem. The need to be concerned with the recovery of space which has been allocated to the list should not arise. However, for the sake of completeness and pragmatism, we have included a static implementation which does provide garbage collection by maintaining a list of the free nodes, i.e. nodes that are available for use. With a dynamic implementation this overhead would be handled by a implementation's run-time environment.

The implementation of the access procedures uses an array of records. Each record in the array will represent a node in a list and so contains two fields. The first field is the information or data field of the items to be kept in the list. The second contains an integer which will indicate the position of the next node in the list. For this example we will limit a list to a maximum of 10 items.

```
CONST
    ListSize = 10 ;
    Nil = 0 ; (* used to denote an empty list *)
TYPE
    NodePtr = [0..ListSize];

    Node = RECORD
                Info : InfoType;
                Link : NodePtr;
           END;

    List = NodePtr;
```

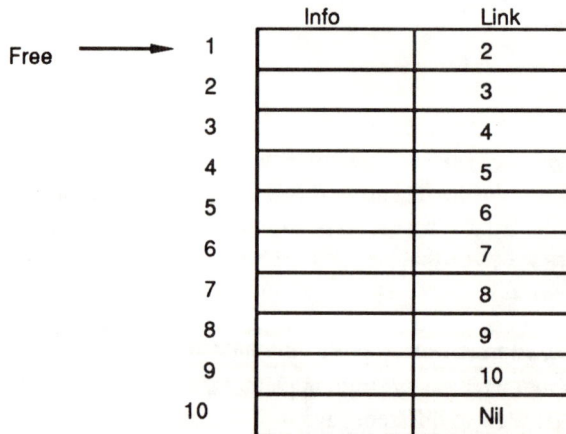

	Info	Link
Free → 1		2
2		3
3		4
4		5
5		6
6		7
7		8
8		9
9		10
10		Nil

Figure 2.5 The initial node pool (ListSize = 10)

Then we can declare a pool of nodes ready for use:

```
VAR Nodes : ARRAY [1..ListSize] OF Node;
```

As before, we will assume that `InfoType` has been defined by the user and is imported from another module. Initially all the nodes are free. This is shown by having a variable called `Free` which is used to indicate the first node in the list of free nodes.

```
VAR
    Free : List ; (* used to keep a list of free nodes *)
```

If we initially let each node point to its successor in the array then the situation can be depicted as in figure 2.5. Therefore the list pointed to by `Free` consists of ten nodes, corresponding to the slots 1 to 10 in the array.

Note that the link field of the last node in the list is given the value `Nil` to indicate that it does not point to anything. The code for the initialization of the list is given below:

```
VAR Count : CARDINAL ;

BEGIN
    FOR Count := 1 TO ListSize - 1 DO (* initialise the
                                                    list *)
        Nodes [Count].Link := Count + 1
    END ;
    Nodes[ListSize].Link := Nil ;
    Free := 1
END
```

This is also known as a *cursor-based* implementation, and is particularly useful if code is being written in a language which does not have pointer variables, such as early versions of Fortran and Algol. The complete implementation module for the access procedures is given below:

```
IMPLEMENTATION MODULE Lists ;

FROM InOut IMPORT WriteString ;

CONST
    ListSize = 10 ;
    Nil = 0 ;

TYPE
    NodePtr = [0..ListSize] ;
    Node = RECORD
                Info : InfoType ;
                Link : NodePtr
            END ;

    List = NodePtr;
```

```
VAR
    Nodes : ARRAY [ 1..ListSize] OF Node ;
    Free : List ; (* used to keep a list of free nodes *)
    Count : CARDINAL ; (* used to initialise the node pool *)

PROCEDURE Empty ( ) : List ;
(* Postcondition: returns an empty list *)

BEGIN
    RETURN Nil
END Empty ;

PROCEDURE IsEmpty ( L : List ) : BOOLEAN ;
(* Postcondition: returns TRUE if L is empty, otherwise
    FALSE *)

BEGIN
    RETURN ( L = Nil)
END IsEmpty;

PROCEDURE New ( ) : List ;
(* Postcondition: takes the node from the head of
    the Free list and return a pointer to it *)

VAR Newlist : List ;

BEGIN
    IF IsEmpty (Free) THEN
        WriteString (" No more nodes are available !")
    ELSE
        Newlist := Free ;
        Free := Nodes [Free].Link ; (* side-effect on Free *)
        RETURN Newlist
    END (* if *)
END New ;

PROCEDURE Cons ( I : CARDINAL ; L : List) : List ;
(* Postcondition: returns a list with I as its head
    and L as its tail *)

VAR Newlist : List ;

BEGIN
    Newlist := New ( ) ;
    Nodes [Newlist].Info := I ;
    Nodes [Newlist].Link := L ;
    RETURN Newlist
END Cons ;

PROCEDURE Head ( L : List) : CARDINAL ;
(* Postcondition: returns the item at the head of the list
    L *)
```

```
BEGIN
    IF IsEmpty (L) THEN
        WriteString ("error-can't take head of empty list" ) ;
        HALT
    ELSE
        RETURN ( Nodes [ L].Info )
    END
END Head ;


PROCEDURE Tail ( L : List ): List ;
(* Postcondition: returns the tail of list L *)


BEGIN
    IF IsEmpty (L) THEN
        WriteString ("error-can't take tail of empty list" ) ;
        HALT
    ELSE
        RETURN Nodes [ L ].Link ;
    END (* IF *)
END Tail;


BEGIN (* initialise the list *)
    FOR Count := 1 TO ListSize - 1 DO
        Nodes [Count].Link := Count + 1
    END ;
    Nodes[ListSize].Link := Nil ;
    Free := 1
END Lists.
```

Note that we have had to use global variables (Free, Count and Nodes). This contravenes our desire for a functional style of programming, but is necessary in order to implement the garbage-collection routines.

We also need an access procedure FreeNode which recovers a node for use. This procedure should only be used when it is known that the node at the head of a list (Old) can safely be disposed of, and that the tail of the list Old has already been assigned to some other list. Note that this procedure side-effects the global free list.

```
PROCEDURE FreeNode (Old : List ) : List ;
(* Postcondition: add the node pointed to by Old to
    the free list and return the new free list *)


BEGIN
    Nodes [Old].Link := Free ;
    Free := Old ;
    RETURN (Free )
END FreeNode ;
```

A comparison of the dynamic and static implementations is given below.

Comparison of static and dynamic implementations

Memory

With a static implementation the memory requirements for the program are defined at compile time. However, the array might be too small, which would mean that there would not be enough space for the list, or it might be far too large, resulting in a waste of memory space. Changing the size of the array will mean recompiling the program. Also, with the static implementation the constructor function Cons and the selector function Tail first copy the original list to avoid side-effecting it.

Efficiency

Since the dynamic implementation requires memory to be allocated and disposed of at run time it may be slower than the use of a statically maintained list. However, with dynamic implementation the address of a node is given by the pointer that points to it, whereas with static representation there is the overhead of adding the base address of the array to the address of the node if the machine code does not have an indexed addressing mode. With static implementation there is also the overhead of copying the original list before alterations are made to it.

GENERALIZED LISTS

Our implementations of lists always used the type InfoType to denote the type of information that the items in the list hold. There is no reason why this InfoType should not be of type List. This would allow us to develop lists of greater generality: lists of lists.

Definition

A *generalized list* is either empty or of the form Cons (h, t) where t is a generalized list and h is either an atom or a generalized list.

The word 'atom' in this context is used to refer to any basic, indivisible data type (such as CHAR or CARDINAL or some user-defined type). Note that this definition is recursive. It states that the item at the head of a list is either an atom or a generalized list. In the second case the item is called a *sublist*. As with the abstract data type list, all atoms must be of the same type. The following are examples of generalized lists of names:

    List1 = ( )
    List2 = (Beth, (Kim, Ann, Zoe))
    List3 = (List2, List1)

Applications

Their very generality ensures the usefulness of generalized lists. For example, consider writing a program to manipulate sentences. Each sentence is a list of words, and each word is a list of characters. Alternatively, matrices: each row is a list of items and a matrix is a list of rows.

Blocks of memory consist of lists of memory cells. Generalized lists can also be used to implement the abstract data types *priority queue*, (which will be discussed in the next chapter), and *tree*, which will be discussed later in the book.

Access procedures

We must now consider what access procedures we need for the abstract data type generalized list. Many functional languages (such as Hope) allow data types to be *polymorphic* or *generic*. This means that the type of the objects that are held in a data type such as a list is immaterial: only one set of procedures need ever be written to handle all types of items. In such languages implementing generalized lists is trivial, since the access procedures are exactly the same. Unfortunately, Modula-2 does not allow polymorphic types but in fact has strong type checking, which means that we cannot have a procedure which takes either a list or an atom as a parameter. Consequently, as well as the five access procedures we had before, we will need a new constructor function:

```
PROCEDURE ConsList ( i, l : List ) : List;
(* Precondition: takes two generalized lists
   Postcondition: returns a generalized list  which has  list
   i as its head and l as its tail *)
```

Now we can give a more precise definition of the abstract data type:

A *generalized list* is either empty or of the form Cons (h, t) where t is a generalized list and h is an atom, or of the form ConsList (l, t) where both l and t are generalized lists.

We will also need an extra selector function to return the head of a list if the head is itself a list:

```
PROCEDURE ListHead (l : List) : List;
(* Precondition: takes a generalized list which has a list
   at its head
   Postcondition: returns the list which is at the head of
   l *)
```

Finally we will need an extra predicate function to determine whether the item at the head of a list is an atom or a list:

```
PROCEDURE ContainsData (i : List) : BOOLEAN;
(* Precondition: takes a generalized list
   Postcondition: returns TRUE if the item at the head of i
   is an atom, FALSE if it is a list *)
```

The definition module for the abstract data type is given below:

```
DEFINITION MODULE GeneralizedLists;
(* Access procedures for the abstract data type generalized
   list *)
```

```
    FROM Atoms IMPORT AtomType ;

TYPE
    List ; (* an opaque type *)

    PROCEDURE Empty( ) : List;
    PROCEDURE Cons (i : AtomType; l : List) : List;
    PROCEDURE ConsList (i : List; l : List) : List;
    PROCEDURE Head (l : List) : AtomType;
    PROCEDURE ListHead (l : List) : List;
    PROCEDURE Tail (l : List) : List;
    PROCEDURE IsEmpty (l : List) : BOOLEAN;
    PROCEDURE ContainsData (i : List) : BOOLEAN;
END GeneralizedLists.
```

For example, for the lists we had earlier:

    List1 = ( )
    List2 = (Beth, (Kim, Ann, Zoe))
    List3 = (List2, List1)

we have:

    Head (List2)   = 'Beth'
    Tail (List2)   = ((Kim, Ann, Zoe))
    ListHead (List3) = List2
    Tail (List3)   = (List 1)

Semantics

For a full algebraic specification of the abstract data type we will need to supply more axioms to describe the semantics of the new access procedures. A list can now have one of three forms:

(1) `Empty ( );`
(2) `Cons ( h, t )` where h is an atom and t is a generalized list;
(3) `ConsList ( l, t )` where both l and t are generalized lists.

The semantic specification must now include axioms for the third form and is as follows:

1.   IsEmpty (Empty ( )) = TRUE
2.   IsEmpty (Cons (h, t)) = FALSE
2.   IsEmpty (ConsList (l, t)) = FALSE
4.   Head (Empty ( )) = error
5.   Head (Cons (h, t)) = h
6.   Head (ConsList (l, t)) = error
7.   Tail (Empty ( )) = error
8.   Tail (Cons (h, t)) = t
9.   Tail (ConsList (l, t)) = t
10. ListHead (Empty ( )) = error
11. ListHead (Cons (h, t)) = error

12. ListHead (ConsList (l, t)) = l
13. ContainsData (Empty ( )) = FALSE
14. ContainsData (Cons (h, t)) = TRUE
15. ContainsData (ConsList (l, t)) = FALSE

We also want the access procedures to be strict, that is, to return an error if any argument is an error value.

We can now use these access procedures to construct and manipulate generalized lists.

EXERCISES

1. Write the procedure below:

```
PROCEDURE Append ( l1, l2 : List ) : List ;
(* Precondition l1 and l2 are generalized lists
   Postcondition: returns l2 appended to l1 *)
```

Solution

Now there are three cases to consider: either a list is empty, or of the form Cons (h, t) or ConsList (l, t).

The first case is trivial:

```
IF IsEmpty ( l1 ) THEN
    RETURN l2
```

Now we have to check the head of list l1 to determine whether it contains data or a list:

```
IF ContainsData ( l1 ) THEN
    RETURN Cons (Head(l1), Append(Tail(l1), l2))
```

otherwise the head is a list and so we must use ConsList :

```
ELSE
    RETURN ConsList ( ListHead ( l1 ) , Append ( Tail ( l1 ),
                                                    l2 ))
```

giving us the procedure below:

```
PROCEDURE Append (l1,l2 : List ) : List ;
(* Precondition: l1 and l2 are generalized lists
   Postcondition: returns l2 appended to l1 *)

BEGIN
    IF IsEmpty (l1) THEN
        RETURN l2
    ELSE
        IF ContainsData ( l1 ) THEN
```

```
            RETURN Cons(Head(l1), Append(Tail(l1), l2))
        ELSE
            RETURN ConsList ( ListHead ( l1 ) ,
                                        Append ( Tail (l1), l2 ))
        END
    END
END Append ;
```

2. Write a procedure which will reverse a generalized list without reversing its sublists.

Solution

The procedure can be written by analysing the form of a generalized list (as above):

```
PROCEDURE Reverse (l: List) : List ;
(* Precondition: l is a generalized list
    Postcondition: returns a list consisting of the items in
    l reversed *)

BEGIN
    IF IsEmpty (l) THEN
        RETURN l
    ELSE
        IF ContainsData ( l ) THEN
            RETURN Append ( Reverse(Tail(l)), Cons(Head
                            (l),Empty()) )
        ELSE
            RETURN Append ( Reverse ( Tail ( l )),
                            ConsList ( ListHead ( l), Empty
                            ()))
        END
    END
END Reverse ;
```

3. Write a procedure which returns the last item in a list.

Solution

```
PROCEDURE Last ( l: List ) : AtomType ;
(* Precondition: l is a non-empty list
    Postcondition: returns the last element of l *)

BEGIN
    IF IsEmpty (l) THEN
        WriteString ("trying to find the last item of an
                                        empty list!");
        HALT
    ELSIF IsEmpty ( Tail ( l ) ) THEN
        IF ContainsData ( l ) THEN
            RETURN Head(l)
        ELSE
            RETURN ListHead ( l )
```

```
        END
    ELSE
        RETURN Last (Tail(l))
    END
END Last ;
```

Exercises 2.3

1. Write a procedure which returns the length of a generalized list.
2. Write a procedure which will reverse a generalized list and also reverses its sublists.
3. Write a procedure which will print a generalized list and show its structure by separating items by commas and enclosing each list in brackets, for example:

(((A, B, C), D), E, F)

which is a generalized list of length three, the head of which is a list of length 2, the head of which is a list of length 3.

IMPLEMENTATION OF GENERALIZED LISTS

How can these lists be represented diagrammatically? We will use nodes which are similar to those we used earlier, in that each will have two sections. However the data field will now contain either an atom or a list.

List1 is the empty list.

List2 is a list of length two, whose second element is a list of length three. List3 is also of length two and has List2 as its first element. Its second element is List1.

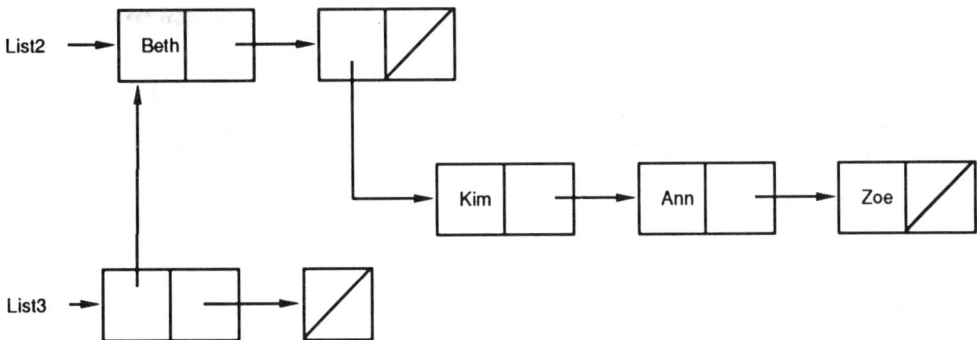

How can generalized lists be implemented? Since the data field of the nodes can be either an atom or a pointer, this suggests the use of a variant record. The implementation could be either dynamic or static. The dynamic implementation is given below:

```
IMPLEMENTATION MODULE access;
(* Access Procedures for generalized Lists *)

    FROM Atoms IMPORT AtomType ;
    FROM InOut IMPORT WriteString, WriteLn ;
    FROM Storage IMPORT ALLOCATE ;

    TYPE
        String = ARRAY [1..200] OF CHAR ;
        List = POINTER TO NODE;
        NodeType = (Data, Pointer);
        Node = RECORD
                    CASE Contents : NodeType OF
                        Data : Atom : AtomType|
                        Pointer : Link : List;
                    END ;
                    Next : List
                END;

PROCEDURE Error (Message : String);
(* Postcondition: writes an error message to the screen *)

BEGIN
    WriteString (Message);
    WriteLn ;
END Error;

PROCEDURE Empty (): List ;
(* Postcondition: returns an empty list *)

BEGIN
    RETURN NIL
END Empty;

PROCEDURE IsEmpty (l : List) : BOOLEAN ;
(* Postcondition: returns TRUE if l is empty, otherwise
    FALSE *)

BEGIN
    RETURN (l = NIL)
END IsEmpty;

PROCEDURE Cons (i : AtomType ; l : List) : List ;
(* Postcondition: returns a list with i as its head and
    l as its tail *)

VAR
    Temp : List;

BEGIN
    NEW(Temp);
    Temp^.Contents := Data;
    Temp^.Atom := i;
    Temp^.Next := l;
    RETURN Temp
END Cons;
```

```
PROCEDURE ConsList ( i : List; l : List) : List ;
(* Precondition: takes two generalized lists
   Postcondition: returns a generalized list which has
   list i as its head and l as its tail *)

VAR
   Temp : List;

BEGIN
   NEW(Temp);
   Temp^.Contents := Pointer ;
   Temp^.Link := i ;
   Temp^.Next := l;
   RETURN Temp
END ConsList;

PROCEDURE Head (l : List) : AtomType ;
(* Postcondition: returns the item at the head of the list
   L *)

BEGIN
   IF ContainsData ( l ) THEN
     RETURN l^.Atom
   ELSE
     Error ("Error in procedure Head - the head of this list
                             does not contain data !" );
   HALT
   END
END Head;

PROCEDURE ListHead (l : List) : List ;
(* Precondition: takes a generalized list which has a list
   at its head
   Postcondition: returns the list which is at the head of
                                                     l *)

BEGIN
   IF NOT ContainsData ( l ) THEN
      RETURN l^.Link
   ELSE
      Error ("Error in procedure ListHead - the head of this
                             list contains data ! " ) ;
      HALT ;
   END
END ListHead;

PROCEDURE Tail (l : List) : List ;
(* Postcondition: returns the tail of the list L *)

BEGIN
   IF IsEmpty (l) THEN
      Error("Can't take TAIL of empty list")
   ELSE
      RETURN l^.Next
   END
END Tail;
```

```
    PROCEDURE ContainsData ( i : List ) : BOOLEAN ;
    (* Precondition: takes a generalized list
       Postcondition: returns TRUE if the item at the head of
       i is an atom, FALSE if it is a list *)

    BEGIN
        IF IsEmpty ( i ) THEN
            RETURN FALSE
        ELSE
            RETURN (i^.Contents = Data)
        END ;
    END ContainsData;

    END access.
```

Then we can write a simple test harness:

```
    MODULE listtest ;

    FROM InOut IMPORT WriteString,Write, Read, WriteLn,
    ReadCard, WriteCard ;
    FROM ListIO IMPORT ReadList ;
    FROM access IMPORT List, Empty, IsEmpty, Cons,
    Head, Tail, ContainsData, ListHead, ConsList;

    PROCEDURE Makelist( ) : List ;
    (* Postcondition: returns a list with 5 items in it
       for testing purposes *)

    VAR
        Newlist : List ;
        i : CARDINAL ;

    BEGIN
        Newlist := Empty ( ) ;
        WriteString (" please enter 5 items " ) ;
        FOR i := 1 TO 5 DO
            Newlist := Cons( ReadList (), Newlist ) ;
        END ; (*FOR*)
        RETURN Newlist
    END Makelist ;


    PROCEDURE PrettyPrintlist ( L : List);
    (* Postcondition: prints the generalized list L,
       separating lists with brackets and items by commas *)

    PROCEDURE Printlist ( L : List);

    BEGIN
        IF NOT IsEmpty (L) THEN
            IF ContainsData ( L ) THEN
                Write (Head(L) ) ;
            ELSE
                    PrettyPrintlist ( ListHead ( L)) ;
            END ;
```

```
        IF NOT IsEmpty ( Tail (L)) THEN
            Write(",") ;
            Printlist(Tail(L)) ;
        END ;
    END; (*IF *)
END Printlist ;

BEGIN
    Write ( '(' ) ;
    Printlist(L) ;
    Write (')') ;
END PrettyPrintlist;

PROCEDURE TestCons () ;
(* Postcondition: tests Cons and ConsList *)

VAR thelist : List ;
BEGIN
    thelist := Makelist () ;
    PrettyPrintlist ( ConsList ( thelist, Empty () ));
    WriteLn ;
    PrettyPrintlist ( Cons (ReadList(),ConsList
                             (thelist,Empty()))));
    WriteLn ;
END TestCons ;

BEGIN
    WriteString (" welcome to list test " ) ;
    PrettyPrintlist ( Makelist ());
    WriteLn ;
    TestCons () ;
    WriteLn ;
END listtest.
```

SUMMARY

The abstract data type *list* is a linear sequence of an arbitrary number of items of the same type together with a number of access procedures.

The five access procedures are: Empty, Cons, IsEmpty, Head and Tail. Of these, Empty and Cons are *constructor* functions, IsEmpty is a *predicate* function and Head and Tail are *selector* functions.

The specification of the abstract data type list consists of a definition module, which gives the syntax of the access procedures, and six axioms which define their semantics.

Using the access procedures we can construct higher-level procedures which are independent of the implementation of the access procedures.

A procedure which takes a procedure as a parameter or returns one as a result is called a *higher-order function*. Modula-2 allows us to write higher-order functions by means of *procedure types* and *procedure variables*. Higher-order functions offer greater generality.

We have shown how the abstract data type list can be implemented dynamically in a functional style, and verified that the implementation conformed to the algebraic specification. A truly static implementation uses an array to hold the items in the list. However, such an implementation does not allow us to use opaque types and some Modula-2 compilers do not allow structured types (such as arrays) to be returned from functions. Consequently we discussed an implementation which used a pointer to an array. Finally, another truly static implementation was discussed, which had the advantage of allowing nodes to be garbage collected.

A *generalized list* is either empty or of the form Cons (h, t) where t is a generalized list and h is either an atom or a generalized list.

Due to the fact that Modula-2 does not support polymorphic data types, the algebraic specification of a generalized list is not the same as that of a list. For example, extra procedures are needed to deal with the fact that the head of a list may be either a list or an atom.

CHAPTER 3

The Abstract Data Type Queue

INTRODUCTION

In this chapter we discuss the abstract data type *queue*. After giving its definition and algebraic specification we go on to consider possible static and dynamic implementations. We end the chapter by looking at two different variations of the type queue, *priority queues* and *dequeues*.

DEFINITION

The abstract data type *queue* is a linear sequence of an arbitrary number of items (of the same type) together with a number of access procedures.

Note that the definition of the abstract data type queue is actually the same as that of a list, the only difference being the access procedures which are provided. These are such that additions are only allowed at the back of the queue, in contrast with lists which only allowed additions at the front. Note that the item at the front of the queue:

(Bobby, Pam, Sue)

is 'Bobby', and the item at the back of the queue is 'Sue'.

Consequently the abstract data type queue is known as a FIFO (First-In–First-Out) structure. Applications for this type include allocation of resources (such as printers, disk access, CPU time) by operating systems on multi-user machines and simulation of real-world queuing.

ALGEBRAIC SPECIFICATION

We will start by giving the algebraic specification for the abstract data type queue. This consists of the syntax and semantics of the access procedures.

Syntax of the access procedures

1. Constructor functions

```
PROCEDURE Empty ( ) : Queue ;
(* Postcondition: returns an empty queue *)
```

```
PROCEDURE Add ( Q : Queue ; I : InfoType ) : Queue ;
(* Postcondition: returns a queue with item I added
   at the back, the rest being queue Q *)
```

2. Predicate function

```
PROCEDURE IsEmpty ( Q : Queue ) : BOOLEAN ;
(* Postcondition: returns TRUE if Q is empty, FALSE
   otherwise *)
```

3. Selector functions

```
PROCEDURE Front ( Q : Queue ) : InfoType ;
(* Postcondition: returns the item at the front of Q *)

PROCEDURE Back ( Q : Queue ) : Queue ;
(* Postcondition: returns a queue with the item
   at the front of Q removed *)
```

These access procedures are collected together in the following definition module. The type of the items in the queue (InfoType) must be imported from the module in which it is declared (which in the following example is called 'Items').

```
DEFINITION MODULE Queues ;
(* Access procedures for the abstract data type queue *)

FROM Items IMPORT InfoType ;

TYPE Queue ;
(* an opaque type: see implementation module for details *)

PROCEDURE Empty ( ) : Queue ;
(* Postcondition: returns an empty queue *)

PROCEDURE IsEmpty ( Q : Queue ) : BOOLEAN ;
(* Postcondition: returns TRUE if Q is empty, otherwise
   FALSE *)

PROCEDURE Add ( Q : Queue ; I: InfoType ) : Queue ;
(* Postcondition: returns a queue with item I added
   at the back, the rest being queue Q*)

PROCEDURE Front ( Q : Queue ) : InfoType ;
(* Postcondition: returns the item at the front of Q *)

PROCEDURE Back ( Q : Queue ) : Queue ;
(* Postcondition: returns a queue with the item at
   the front of Q removed *)

END Queues.
```

Semantics of the access procedures

The first three axioms are self-explanatory.

1. IsEmpty (Empty ( )) = TRUE
2. IsEmpty (Add (q, i)) = FALSE
3. Front (Empty ( )) = error

The fourth axiom specifies the behaviour of the access procedure Front with a non-empty queue:

4. Front (Add (q, i)) = if IsEmpty (q) then i else Front (q)

This axiom can be explained as follows. If we add an item i to the back of an empty queue, then it must also be at the front of the queue, and so we can return that item. Otherwise, we ignore the item i (since it is at the back of the queue) and ask what item is at the front of q. Now since q is not empty, it is of the form Add (q′, i′), where q′ is a queue and i′ is an item. Now if q′ is empty, then i′ is the item at the front of q and we are finished. Otherwise we must ask what item is at the front of q′, and so on.

The final two axioms specify the behaviour of the access procedure Back.

5. Back (Empty ( )) = error
6. Back (Add (q, i)) = if IsEmpty (q) then Empty ( ) else Add (Back (q), i)

We can paraphrase axiom 6: if we add an item i to a queue which is empty, then i becomes the front, and so the back of the queue, being the result of removing the item at the front of the queue, is the empty queue. Otherwise we must add i to the result of finding the back of q. Now, as before, q is of the form Add (q′, i′). If q′ is empty, then we return the empty queue (because i′ is the item at the front of q), and so the result is the item i. Otherwise we must add i′ to the result of finding the back of q′, and so on.

For example, rewriting a call to determine the back of a queue with three numbers in it, Back ((1, 2, 3)):

Back ((1, 2, 3)) → Back (Add ((1, 2), 3))
                    → Add (Back ((1, 2)), 3)
                    → Add (Add (Back ((1)), 2), 3)
                    → Add (Add (Back (Add (( ), 1)), 2), 3)
                    → Add (Add (( ), 2), 3)
                    → Add ((2), 3)
                    → (2, 3)

We also require the access procedures to be strict, that is, to return an error value if an error is passed to them as a parameter.

HIGHER-LEVEL PROCEDURES

We can now use the access procedures to write procedures which manipulate queues. For example, we could write a procedure to check a queue for the presence of a particular item. This could then be used if we wanted to make sure that no item is inserted into the queue twice.

```
PROCEDURE IsIn ( I : Infotype; Q : Queue) : BOOLEAN ;
(* Postcondition: returns TRUE if item I is in
   queue Q, otherwise FALSE *)

BEGIN
    IF IsEmpty (Q) THEN
        RETURN FALSE
    ELSIF IsEqual (I, Front (Q)) THEN        (* see below *)
        RETURN TRUE
    ELSE
        RETURN IsIn (I, Back (Q))
    END (* if *)
END IsIn ;
```

IsEqual is a boolean-valued procedure which takes two items and returns TRUE if they are equal and FALSE otherwise. This procedure is used for generality, as we do not want to restrict our higher-level functions to a particular type of item. IsEqual should be implemented in a separate module when the type of the items to be held in the queue is known.

Now consider a procedure to append two queues. This could be of use, for example, if there are two queues for one resource, and one queue has higher priority than the other.

```
PROCEDURE Append ( q1,q2 : Queue ) : Queue ;
(* Postcondition: returns q2 appended to q1 *)

BEGIN
    IF IsEmpty (q2) THEN
        RETURN q1
    ELSE
        RETURN Append ( Add ( q1, Front ( q2 )), Back (q2))
    END
END Append ;
```

IMPLEMENTATION METHODS

As with the type list, the implementation of the abstract data type queue can be either static (using an array) or dynamic (using pointer variables). For both implementations we need rapid access to the front and back of the queue.

Dynamic implementation

The dynamic implementation is also called a *linked* or *chained* implementation. Nodes for the items in the queue are allocated dynamically when the program is executed by calls to the procedure NEW and linked together by pointers.

If there is only one pointer to the queue, for example at the front, then every time an item is inserted at the back of the queue the entire queue must be traversed. An alternative which is more efficient is to have two pointers to the queue, one for the front and one for the back. This suggests the use of a node containing two pointers, one that points to the front and one that points to the rear of the queue. Such a node is called a **header** node (see figure 3.1). `Last` now points to the last item placed in the queue. If the queue is empty then both `First` and `Last` have the value `NIL` (figure 3.2).

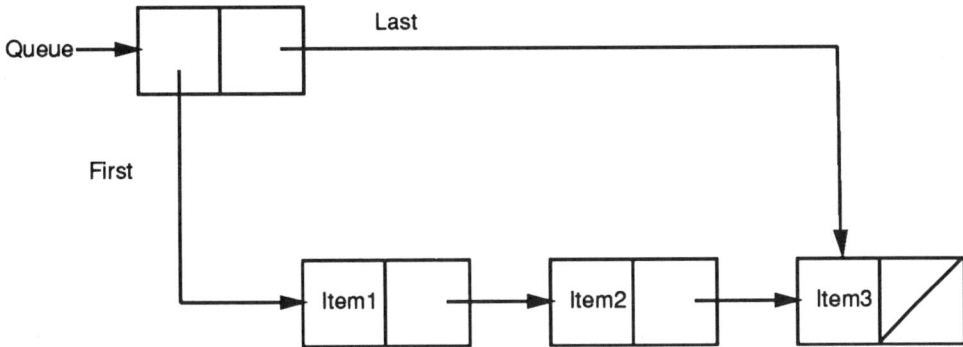

Figure 3.1 Dynamic implementation of a queue

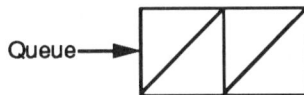

Figure 3.2 An empty queue

Thus the declaration of the data structure in Modula-2 could be:

```
TYPE
    QueuePointer = POINTER TO QueueRecord ;

    QueueRecord = RECORD
                    Item : InfoType ;
                    Next : QueuePointer
              END ;

    Queue = POINTER TO RECORD
                    First : QueuePointer ;
                    Last  : QueuePointer
              END ;
```

Note the use of the pointer in the declaration of the type `Queue`. As explained in the discussion of the static implementation of a list (Chapter 2) this is for two reasons:

(1) So that its declaration in the definition module can be opaque (many implementations of Modula-2 restrict opaque types to be pointer variables);
(2) So that variables of type `Queue` can be returned from functions (older versions of Modula-2 did not allow functions to return variables which were structured types).

Another reason for the decision is efficiency. When a value parameter is passed to a procedure a copy of it is made. It is takes less time and space to copy a pointer than it does to copy a record which may have several fields of data.

As with the abstract data type list, we will implement the access procedures in a functional style, without using side-effects and variable parameters.

1. The constructor function `Empty` is implemented by setting the pointers `First` and `Last` to `NIL`.

```
PROCEDURE Empty ( ) : Queue ;
(* Postcondition: returns an empty queue *)

VAR Temp : Queue ;

BEGIN
    NEW ( Temp) ;
    Temp^.First := NIL ;
    Temp^.Last := NIL ;
    RETURN Temp
END Empty ;
```

2. For the predicate function `IsEmpty` we note that as soon as an item is added to a queue, the pointer `First` will no longer be `NIL`, and so this is all we need to check:

```
PROCEDURE IsEmpty ( Q : Queue ) : BOOLEAN ;
(* returns TRUE if Q is empty, otherwise FALSE *)

BEGIN
    RETURN Q^.First = NIL
END IsEmpty ;
```

We can now easily verify that the first of the axioms describing the behaviour of the access procedures is correct, i.e. that `IsEmpty ( Empty ())` is `TRUE`.

3. The implementation of the constructor function `Add` is slightly more complicated. This procedure first allocates a queue node and sets the data field to contain the item which is to be added. It must then set the `Last` pointer of the queue's header node to point to the new queue node (which is now the last node in the queue) and adjust the pointer of the last node in the old queue so that it points to the new node—of course, we also have to take into account the fact that the queue may be empty initially. Each step is explained below with the help of diagrams.

(a) We need to create a new node to hold the new item. So we need to declare:

```
VAR Temp : QueuePointer ;
```

then we can say:

```
NEW (Temp) ;
Temp^.Item := I ;
Temp^.Next := NIL
```

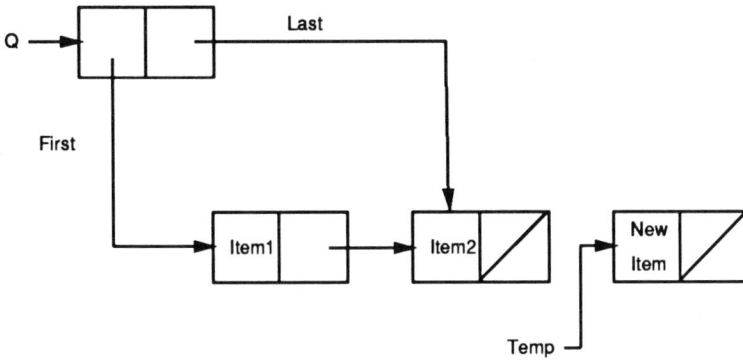

(b) Now we must change the pointer from the previous item to point to the new one (assuming that Q is non-empty):

```
Q^.Last^.Next := Temp ;
```

Q^ takes us to the node which is pointed to by Q, and Last^.Next gives us the Next field of the node to which Last points.

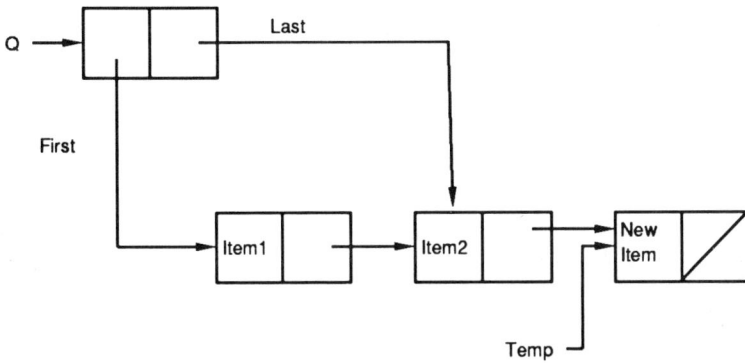

(c) Finally, we want to return this new structure. In order to do this without side-effecting the original queue we declare another variable of type Queue:

```
VAR TempAdd : Queue ;
```

We will make the First and Last pointers of this queue refer to our new queue, so leaving the original queue unchanged. We will then return TempAdd. If Q is not empty this gives us:

```
NEW (TempAdd) ;
TempAdd^.First := Q^.First ;
TempAdd^.Last := Temp ;
RETURN (TempAdd) ;
```

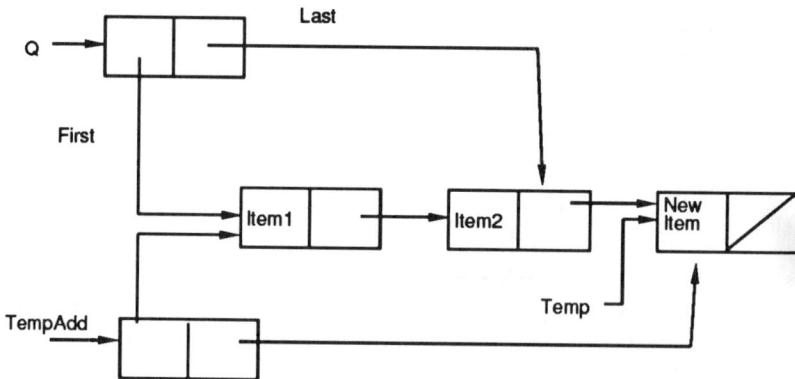

To summarize, the entire procedure is:

```
PROCEDURE Add ( Q : Queue ; I : InfoType ;) : Queue ;
(* Postcondition: returns a queue with item I added to
   the Last of Q *)

VAR Temp : QueuePointer ;
    TempAdd : Queue ;

BEGIN
    NEW (Temp) ;
    Temp^.Item := I ;
    Temp^.Next := NIL ;
    NEW (TempAdd) ;
    IF NOT IsEmpty (Q) THEN
        Q^.Last^.Next := Temp ;
        TempAdd^.First := Q^.First
    ELSE
        TempAdd^.First := Temp
    END ; (* if *)
    TempAdd^.Last := Temp ;
    RETURN (TempAdd)
END Add ;
```

Now we can verify the second axiom, IsEmpty (Add (q, i)) = FALSE. We can see from the procedure Add that the queue which is returned has its First pointer set to point to the node Temp, where Temp contains the new item. IsEmpty checks the queue's First pointer and returns FALSE because it is not NIL.

Note: The reader may have noticed that the procedure Add has a side-effect. Suppose that we have a queue, q, which contains 3 items, a, b, and c. Let us denote this queue using the same notation that we used for lists. Thus q = (a, b, c) denotes a queue with the item a at the front and c at the back. Now consider:

```
q1 := Add ( q, d ) ;
PrintQ ( q1 ) ;
q2 := Add ( q, e ) ;
PrintQ ( q2 ) ;
PrintQ ( q1 ) ;
```

where PrintQ is a procedure which outputs the contents of a queue surrounded by parentheses. The result of executing this code is:

q1: (a, b, c, d)
q2: (a, b, c, e)
q1: (a, b, c, e)

Thus q1 has been affected by the addition of e to q. However, the style of coding shown in this example is not functional and so should be avoided. It is preferable to declare one variable which is a data type, and then use this to build up the solution to the problem under consideration. For example, we could add two more items to q with a statement of the form

```
q := Add ( Add ( q, d ), e )
```

One way to avoid the side-effect in the procedure Add is to *copy all the contents of* q before inserting an item: however, this has the drawback of being inefficient. Alternatively, we could implement Add as a procedure rather than a function, making the side-effect more obvious by returning the result as a VAR parameter.

(4) When implementing the selector function Front we must remember that the semantics of the algebraic specification stated that an attempt to find the item at the front of an empty queue results in an error. The first part of the function below ensures that this axiom is fulfilled.

```
PROCEDURE Front ( Q : Queue ) : InfoType ;
(* Postcondition: returns the item at the front of the
      queue Q *)

BEGIN
    IF IsEmpty(Q) THEN
        WriteString (" attempt to use Front on an empty
                                            queue ! " ) ;
        HALT;
    ELSE
        RETURN Q^.First^.Item ;
    END ;
END Front ;
```

Therefore we can verify axiom 3, i.e. Front (Empty ( )) = error. Similarly, we can verify axiom 4, since Front (Add (q, i)) will return i if q is empty, and otherwise returns whatever the First pointer of q points to, i.e. Front (q).

(5) According to the semantics for the access procedure Back, if Q is empty an attempt to remove an item from it should result in an error. Also, if Q only has one item the resulting queue will be empty.

The returned queue is pointed to by the pointer Temp given in the following diagram.

The procedure is given below. Note that the queue which is returned has been created by sharing all but the first of Q's nodes, so minimizing the amount of space which needs to be allocated for the new queue.

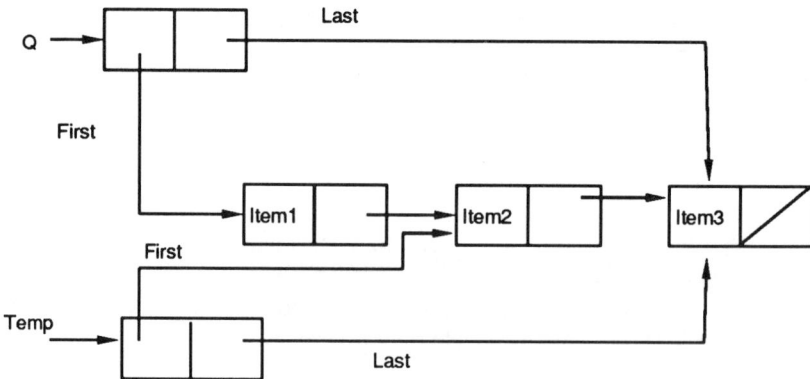

```
PROCEDURE Back ( Q : Queue ) : Queue ;
(* Postcondition: returns a queue with the item at the
   front of Q removed *)


VAR Temp : Queue ;

BEGIN
    IF IsEmpty(Q) THEN
        WriteString (" attempt to use Back on an empty
                                               queue ! " ) ;
        HALT
    ELSE
        IF Q^.First = Q^.Last THEN
            Temp := Empty ( ) (* there is only one item in
            the queue *)
        ELSE
            NEW (Temp) ;
            Temp^.First := Q^.First^.Next ;
            Temp^.Last := Q^.Last
        END ; (* if *)
        RETURN Temp
    END (* if *)
END Back ;
```

Thus we can see that Back (Empty ( )) = error, which agrees with axiom 5. To check axiom 6,

Back (Add (q, i)) = *if* IsEmpty (q) *then* Empty ( ) *else* Add (Back (q), i)

we note that if q is empty, then adding one item to it results in a queue in which both First and Last point to the same node (see the procedure Add to verify this). Consequently Back will return an empty queue, as specified. If q contains one item, then the axiom states that we should add the item i to the result of finding the back of q. This is precisely what the function Back will return. The entire implementation is given below:

```
IMPLEMENTATION MODULE Queues ;

(* This module contains the implementation of the
   access procedures for the abstract data type queue *)

FROM InOut IMPORT WriteString ;
FROM Item IMPORT InfoType ;

TYPE
   QueuePointer = POINTER TO QueueRecord ;

   QueueRecord = RECORD
                     Item : InfoType ;
                     Next : QueuePointer
                 END ;

   Queue = POINTER TO RECORD
                     First : QueuePointer ;
                     Last  : QueuePointer
                 END ;

PROCEDURE Empty ( ) : Queue ;
(* Postcondition: returns an empty queue *)

VAR Temp : Queue ;

BEGIN
   NEW ( Temp) ;
   Temp^.First := NIL ;
   Temp^.Last := NIL ;
   RETURN Temp
END Empty ;

PROCEDURE IsEmpty ( Q : Queue ) : BOOLEAN ;
(* Postcondition: returns TRUE if Q is empty, otherwise
   FALSE *)

BEGIN
   RETURN Q^.First = NIL
END IsEmpty ;

PROCEDURE Add( Q : Queue ; I : InfoType ) : Queue ;
(* Postcondition: returns a queue which has item
   I at the back, the rest being queue Q*)

VAR Temp : QueuePointer ;
TempAdd : Queue ;

BEGIN
   NEW (Temp) ;
   Temp^.Item := I ;
   Temp^.Next := NIL ;
   NEW (TempAdd) ;
   IF NOT IsEmpty (Q) THEN
```

```
        Q^.Last^.Next := Temp ;
        TempAdd^.First := Q^.First
    ELSE
        TempAdd^.First := Temp
    END ;(* if *)
    TempAdd^.Last := Temp ;
    RETURN (TempAdd)
END Add ;

PROCEDURE Front ( Q : Queue ) : InfoType ;
(* Postcondition: returns the item at the front of Q *)

BEGIN
    IF IsEmpty(Q) THEN
        WriteString (" attempt to use Front on an empty
                                        queue ! " ) ;
        HALT;
    ELSE
        RETURN Q^.First^.Item ;
    END ;
END Front ;

PROCEDURE Back ( Q : Queue ) : Queue ;
(* Postcondition: returns a queue with the item at the
    front of Q removed *)

VAR Temp : Queue ;

BEGIN
        IF IsEmpty(Q) THEN
            WriteString (" attempt to use Back on an empty
                                            queue ! " ) ;
            HALT;
        ELSE
            IF Q^.First = Q^.Last THEN
                Temp := Empty ( )  (* there is only one item in
                                            the queue *)
            ELSE
                NEW (Temp) ;
                Temp^.First := Q^.First^.Next ;
                Temp^.Last := Q^.Last
        END ;  (* if *)
        RETURN Temp
    END (* if *)
END Back ;

END Queues ;
```

Static implementation

Static implementations which use successive slots of an array are also called **contiguous**. Of course, with this implementation there is a limit to the maximum number of items that can be held in the queue. We will use the two variables First and Last to denote the limits of the queue. First points to the first item in the queue and Last to the first free space. In figure 3.3 Max is used to represent the maximum number of items that can be held in the queue.

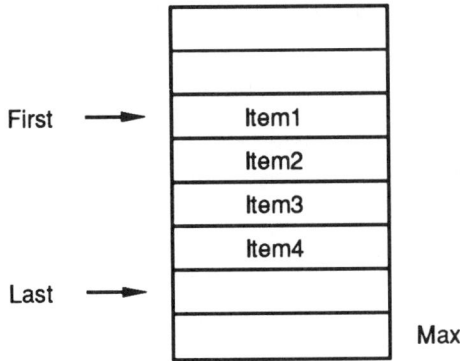

Figure 3.3 Static implementation of a queue

As items are added to the queue the pointer Last moves down the array. As items are removed from the queue the pointer First moves down as well. When Last reaches the end of the array the queue is allowed to wrap around the array, making it a **cyclic buffer** (figure 3.4).

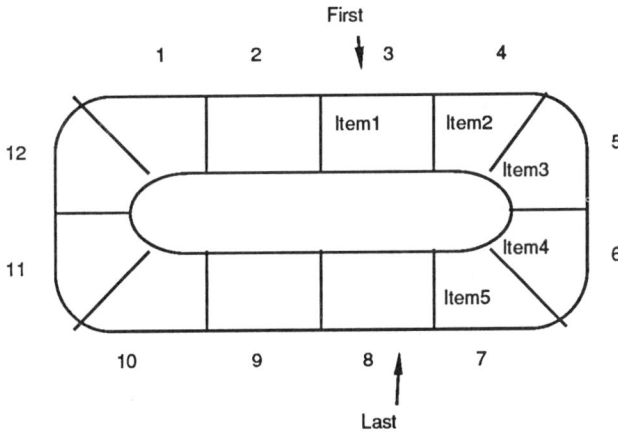

Figure 3.4

In this implementation First and Last both have the value one initially. When the queue becomes full First and Last will have the same value again (one if no removals have taken place). This makes it difficult to distinguish between empty and full queues. To resolve this difficulty we could have an additional variable, Length, to record the number of items currently in the queue. Alternatively, we could implement a predicate function which returns true if every space but one in the buffer is full. The implementor should try to ensure that the array is large enough to prevent this error ever occurring. This is the approach we have taken. Possible type declarations are given below:

```
TYPE
    Size = [ 1..Max ] ;
    Length = [ 0..Max ] ;
```

```
        Queue = POINTER TO QueueRecord ;

        QueueRecord = RECORD
                          Buffer : ARRAY Size OF InfoType ;
                          First, Last : Size ;
                          Len : Length
                      END
    (*or*)
        QueueRecord = RECORD
                          Buffer : ARRAY Size OF InfoType ;
                          First, Last : Size ;
                      END ;
```

The procedure `IsFull` must return true if the difference between `First` (which points to the first item in the queue), and `Last` (which points to the position in which the next item will be inserted) is one. However, the boolean expression

```
    Q^.First - Q^.Last = 1
```

is not sufficient, because the buffer is circular. Instead we will need:

```
    Q^.First - ( Q^.Last MOD Max ) = 1
```

to take care of the case which will arise if `First` has the value 1 and the value of `Last` is equal to `Max`.

Note that the type `Queue` has been declared as a pointer to an array, rather than declaring it as an array, as might have been expected. The main reasons for doing this are (as explained in a similar implementation of the data type list) so that the type `Queue` can be declared to be opaque in the definition module and also so that variables of type `Queue` can be returned as a result from functions. The implementation module is given below:

```
    IMPLEMENTATION MODULE Queues ;

    (* This module contains the implementation of the
       access procedures for the abstract data type queue *)

    FROM InOut IMPORT WriteString ;
    FROM Item IMPORT InfoType ;

    CONST Max = 100 ;
    TYPE
        Size = [ 1..Max ] ;
        Queue = POINTER TO QueueRecord ;
        QueueRecord = RECORD
                          Buffer : ARRAY Size OF InfoType ;
                          First, Last : Size ;
                      END ;

    PROCEDURE Empty ( ) : Queue ;
    (* Postcondition: returns an empty queue *)

    VAR Temp : Queue ;
```

```
BEGIN
   NEW ( Temp) ;
   Temp^.First := 1 ;
   Temp^.Last := 1 ;
   RETURN Temp
END Empty ;

PROCEDURE IsEmpty ( Q : Queue ) : BOOLEAN ;
(* Postcondition: returns TRUE if Q is empty, otherwise
   FALSE *)

BEGIN
   RETURN Q^.First = Q^.Last
END IsEmpty ;

PROCEDURE IsFull ( Q : Queue ) : BOOLEAN ;
(* Postcondition: returns TRUE if Q is full, otherwise
   FALSE *)

BEGIN
   RETURN (Q^.First - ( Q^.Last MOD Max ) = 1 )
END IsFull ;

PROCEDURE Add ( Q : Queue ; NewItem : InfoType ) : Queue ;
(* Postcondition: returns a queue with NewItem
   added to the back, the rest being queue Q *)

VAR Temp : Queue ;

BEGIN
   IF IsFull ( Q ) THEN
      WriteString (" The queue is full ! " ) ;
      HALT ; (* tidy exit *)
   ELSE
      NEW (Temp ) ;
      Temp^ := Q^ ;
      Temp^.Buffer[Temp^.Last] := NewItem ;
      IF (Temp^.Last = Max) THEN
         Temp^.Last := 1
      ELSE
         Temp^.Last := Temp^.Last + 1 ;
      END ;
      RETURN (Temp)
   END ;
END Add ;

PROCEDURE Front ( Q : Queue ) : InfoType ;
(* Postcondition: returns the item at the front of Q *)

BEGIN
   IF IsEmpty(Q) THEN
      WriteString (" attempt to use Front on an empty
      queue ! " ) ;
      HALT; (* tidy exit *)
```

```
    ELSE
        RETURN Q^.Buffer[Q^.First] ;
    END ;

END Front ;

PROCEDURE Back ( Q : Queue ) : Queue ;
(* Postcondition: returns a queue with the item at the
 front of Q removed *)

VAR Temp : Queue ;

BEGIN
    IF IsEmpty(Q) THEN
        WriteString (" attempt to use Back on an empty queue
                                                ! " ) ;
        HALT; (* tidy exit *)
    ELSE
        NEW (Temp) ;
        Temp^ := Q^ ;
        Temp^.First := (Temp^.First) MOD Max + 1;
    END ; (* if *)
    RETURN Temp
END Back ;

END Queues .
```

The static implementation of the abstract data type queue is most appropriate if the maximum number of items to be held in the queue is known in advance. Of course, the array implementation does have the disadvantage that the number of items that can be inserted into the queue is limited by the size of the array. However, the dynamic implementation is also restricted by the amount of space which is available for use in the computer's run-time heap.

THE ABSTRACT DATA TYPE PRIORITY QUEUE

Sometimes the abstract data type queue is not sufficiently structured. Some problems require different items to be given different priorities, depending on some notion of their merit.

Definition

The abstract data type *priority queue* is a linear sequence of an arbitrary number of *ordered* items, all of the same type, together with a number of access procedures.

Such a queue is also called an **ordered** queue. A priority queue is similar in functionality to a queue except in the case of insertion: an item is inserted in the queue according to its priority, and not (in general) at the back of the queue. When an item is inserted it is placed after all items of the same priority, but before any item of lower priority. For example, if we have data items X, Y and Z, with respective priorities 29, 14 and 26, the priority queue could be written as:

$$((X, 29) , (Z, 26) , (Y, 14))$$

This abstract data type does not really qualify to be called a queue, since insertion is not necessarily at the back of the sequence. It is more similar to the data type list that we discussed in Chapter 2. The algebraic specification of the priority queue is left as an exercise for the reader.

Implementation

Note that we no longer need fast access to the end of the queue, since items are not automatically added to the end. Consequently we only need one pointer to the front of the queue and so do not need to have a header node. Therefore the priority queue above could be represented figure 3.5. When inserting an item into a priority queue we must ensure that it is inserted in the correct position according to its merit.

Figure 3.5 A priority queue

Implementation can be either dynamic (using pointer variables) or static (using an array). In fact we already have a good implementation: as we now only need one pointer to the front of the queue, we could use the implementation of the abstract data type list, where 'front' corresponds to 'head'. Only a few alterations are necessary. First, the access procedure Cons should no longer be exported, and must be removed from the definition module so that it is not visible to the user of the abstract data type priority queue. In place of Cons we need to implement a procedure ('InsertInOrder') which, given an item and a priority queue, will place the item in its correct position in the queue. This is easy to implement using the access procedures Cons, Empty, IsEmpty and Head that we have already implemented for the abstract data type list. For generality we will also need a procedure IsGreater which takes two items and returns true if the first is greater than the second. This procedure can only be implemented when the type of the items to be held in the queue is known.

```
PROCEDURE InsertInOrder (i : InfoType ; l : List) : List ;
(* Precondition: the items in the list l are in order
    Postcondition: returns l with i inserted so as to
    maintain the order *)

BEGIN
    IF IsEmpty(l) THEN
        RETURN Cons ( i, Empty() )
    ELSIF IsGreater ( i , Head (l)) THEN
        RETURN Cons (i, l)
    ELSE
        RETURN Cons ( Head(l), InsertInOrder(i, Tail(l)))
    END
END InsertInOrder ;
```

Our declaration of InfoType must also be altered. Now we require InfoType to consist of a pair of objects of different types, one being a number which indicates the priority of the item. This suggests that we declare `InfoType` to be a record. Since some Modula-2 compilers do not allow us to return structured types from functions we will declare `InfoType` as a pointer to a record. This is also slightly more efficient: every time we pass a value parameter of type `InfoType` to a procedure a copy of it is made and it is more efficient to copy a pointer than it is to copy a record.

```
TYPE
    InfoType = POINTER TO RECORD
                          Info : DataType ;
                          Priority : CARDINAL
                          END ;
```

Where `DataType` has been defined in another module to be the type of the items in the priority queue, for example:

```
TYPE
    DataType = ARRAY OF CHAR;
```

This means that figure 3.5 should be redrawn as figure 3.6.

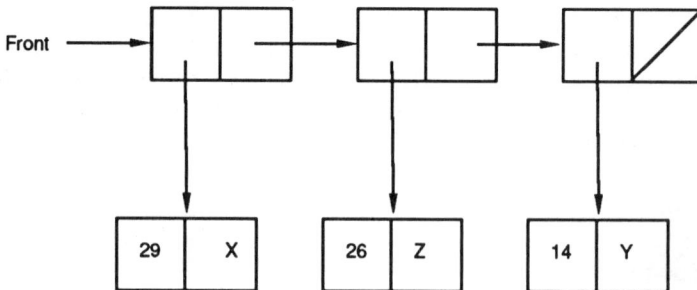

Figure 3.6

The only other alterations that are necessary are to any procedures which are type dependent, such as input and output of items of type `InfoType`, comparison of two items for equality and inequality, and so on. If all these procedures have been kept together in one module the task will be straightforward.

Note that this implementation also suggests an alternative implementation for lists of lists, by replacing the field `Priority` by a pointer to another node of type `InfoType`.

The number of different values of priority depends on the problem being solved. For some applications (such as the queue for a central processing unit) it may be best to have a large number of different priorities. In more complicated schedulers the priority may be a function of the time the item has spent in the queue as well as its importance.

In some applications (queues for printers) it may be enough to have only a few priorities (for example, High, Medium and Low). In this case it may be best to have several subqueues, each of which holds items which have the same priority. Items are added to the end of the appropriate subqueue and removed from the front. Consequently pointers are needed to the front and rear of the subqueues. Figure 3.7 shows a priority queue with three priorities.

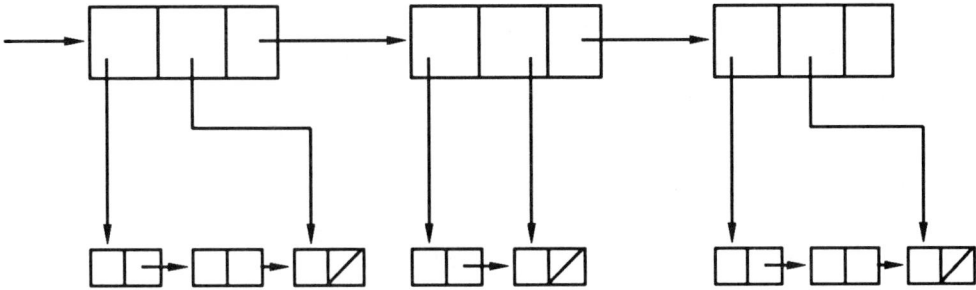

Figure 3.7

There are many applications for priority queues in the area of resource allocation for multi-user operating systems. For example, the items may be processes (programs in execution) which must be scheduled for processor time. There are several well-known algorithms which have been implemented using the abstract data type queue. For example, the Round-Robin scheduling algorithm for items which are competing for a resource uses a circular queue, in which an item is taken from the front of a queue, given a certain amount of time and is then returned to the back. Short jobs will finish quickly and be removed from the queue, whereas longer ones will need several cycles to complete.

A multi-level queue has a top-priority one which all jobs join initially. Jobs which are not completed within a certain amount of time are then relegated to a second queue which is served less frequently and are then only given limited amounts of time. Such queues are common in schedulers for timesharing systems.

THE ABSTRACT DATA TYPE DEQUEUE

The last and most flexible abstract data type we discuss in this chapter is called a *double-ended* queue, or *dequeue* for short. Such queues allow insertion and deletion at both ends of the sequence. The algebraic specification for the abstract data type dequeue is given below.

Syntax

```
DEFINITION MODULE Dequeues ;

TYPE Dequeue ;
            (* an opaque type; see implementation module
                                        for details *)

PROCEDURE Empty ( ) : Dequeue ;
(* Postcondition : returns an empty queue *)

PROCEDURE IsEmpty ( D : Dequeue ) : BOOLEAN ;
(* Postcondition : returns TRUE if the dequeue D is empty *)

PROCEDURE Left ( D : Dequeue ) : InfoType ;
(* Postcondition : returns the leftmost item in the dequeue
    D *)
```

```
PROCEDURE Right ( D : Dequeue ) : InfoType ;
(* Postcondition : returns the rightmost item in the
   dequeue D *)

PROCEDURE LeftCons( I : InfoType ; D : Dequeue ) : Dequeue ;
(* Postcondition: returns a dequeue with item I
   added on the left of the dequeue D *)

PROCEDURE RightCons (I : InfoType ; D : Dequeue ) :Dequeue ;
(* Postcondition: returns a dequeue with item I
   added on the right of the dequeue D *)

PROCEDURE LeftTail ( D : Dequeue ) : Dequeue ;
(* Postcondition: returns a dequeue without the leftmost
   item of D *)

PROCEDURE RightTail ( D : Dequeue ) : Dequeue ;
(* Postcondition: returns a dequeue without the rightmost
   item of D *)

END Dequeues.
```

Semantics

1. IsEmpty (Empty ( )) = TRUE
2. IsEmpty (RightCons (i, q)) = FALSE
3. IsEmpty (LeftCons (i, q)) = FALSE
4. Right (Empty ( )) = error
5. Right (RightCons (i, q)) = i
6. Right (LeftCons (i, q)) = if IsEmpty (q) $then$ i
    $else$ Right (q)
7. Left (Empty ( )) = error
8. Left (LeftCons (i, q)) = i
9. Left (RightCons (i, q)) = if IsEmpty (q) $then$ i
    $else$ Left (q)
10. RightTail (Empty ( )) = error
11. RightTail (RightCons (i, q)) = q
12. RightTail (LeftCons (i, q)) = if IsEmpty (q) $then$ Empty ( )
    $else$ LeftCons (i, RightTail (q))
13. LeftTail (Empty ( )) = error
14. LeftTail (LeftCons (i, q)) = q
15. LeftTail (RightCons (i, q)) = if IsEmpty (q) $then$ Empty ( )
    $else$ RightCons (i, LeftTail (q))

As usual we assume that the access procedures are strict, that is, they return an error if passed an error parameter.

Dequeues may be input-restricted, allowing input only at one end, or output-restricted, allowing output also at one end only.

Some applications that use this abstract data type may not need the full power of a dequeue but simply the ability to put some items at the front of the queue. Note that this structure does not really qualify to be called a queue because it does not exhibit FIFO behaviour.

Implementation of dequeues

Implementation of dequeues is similar to that of queues. It can be either static, using an array, or dynamic, using pointer variables. One possibility with a dynamic implementation is to have a doubly linked list with a header node. This would allow efficient insertion and deletion at both ends of the queue (see figure 3.8).

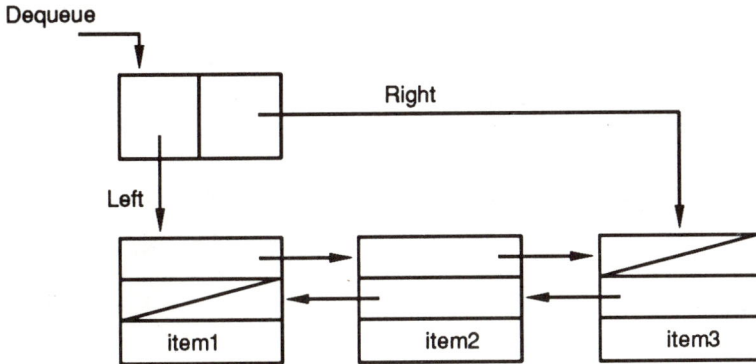

Figure 3.8 Dynamic implementation of a dequeue

The declarations for this implementation are similar to those of the queue we had earlier:

```
TYPE
DeQPointer = POINTER TO DeQRecord ;


DeQRecord = RECORD
               Item : InfoType ;
              Next, Previous : DeQPointer
          END ;


DeQueue = POINTER TO RECORD
                        Left : DeQPointer ;
                        Right : DeQPointer
                    END ;
```

The implementation of the access procedures is left as an exercise for the reader.

Exercises 3.1

1. Implement the access procedures for queues using the access procedures for lists.
2. Write the routines for input, output and comparison of items held in a priority queue assuming that the items are words of up to ten characters.
3. Give the algebraic specification of the abstract data type priority queue.
4. Implement a dequeue (a) statically and (b) dynamically.

SUMMARY

The abstract data type *queue* is a linear sequence of an arbitrary number of items (of the same type) together with a number of access procedures.

The access procedures (`Empty, Add, IsEmpty, Front` and `Back`) are such that additions are only allowed at the back of a queue. Consequently the semantics of the algebraic specification is different to that given for the abstract data type list.

The implementation can be either static, using an array, or dynamic, using pointer variables. The static implementation does not have the time overheads of pointer manipulation but obviously limits the number of items that can be held in the queue.

The abstract data type priority queue is a linear sequence of an arbitrary number of *ordered* items, all of the same type, together with a number of access procedures. Such a queue is also called an *ordered* queue.

The abstract data type dequeue is a double-ended queue in which insertion and deletion are allowed at both ends of the sequence.

CHAPTER 4

The Abstract Data Type Stack

INTRODUCTION

In this chapter we consider the abstract data type *stack*. Since the types stack and list are isomorphic, rather than manipulating expressions using the type stack we will concentrate on the role that it plays in the allocation of run-time memory for programs written in block-structured languages. This leads us into a discussion of the use of stacks in the removal of *tail recursion*. We start by defining the abstract data type stack and giving its algebraic specification.

DEFINITION

The abstract data type *stack* is a linear sequence of an arbitrary number of items (all of the same type) together with a number of access procedures.

Note that the definition of the abstract data type stack, like that of a queue, is actually the same as that of the list. The access procedures are such that all insertions and deletions take place at one end of the sequence, called the *top*. The item most recently inserted on a stack is always the first to be removed. Consequently the abstract data type stack has come to be known as a LIFO structure (Last-In–First-Out).

NOTATION

We can use the same representation for stacks as we did for lists: for example:

    The empty stack: ( )
    A stack of vowels: ('a', 'e', 'i')
    A stack of words: ("hello", "world", "nice", "day")

In the second example, the character 'a' is at the top, and similarly, in the third example, the word "hello" is at the top. If we *pop* the third stack we will have a stack containing the words ("world", "nice", "day"). If we then push a new item on the stack (the word "bye" say) we would have the stack ("bye", "world", "nice", "day").

77

ALGEBRAIC SPECIFICATION

The algebraic specification of the abstract data type stack is equivalent (or *isomorphic*) to that of the list, the only difference being that the access procedure Cons has been renamed Push, Head has become Top and Tail has been renamed as Pop.

Syntax of the access procedures

1. Constructor functions

```
PROCEDURE Empty ( )  : Stack ;
(* Postcondition : returns an empty stack *)
```

We need a procedure that will add an item to the top of a stack. This function, which is generally known as Push, corresponds to the function Cons which we had for the abstract data type list.

```
PROCEDURE Push ( I : InfoType ; S : Stack ) : Stack ;
(* Postcondition: returns a stack with item I at
     the top, the rest being the stack S *)
```

2. Predicate function

```
PROCEDURE IsEmpty ( S : Stack ) : BOOLEAN ;
(* Postcondition: returns TRUE if S is empty, otherwise
     FALSE *)
```

3. Selector functions

```
PROCEDURE Top ( S : Stack ) : InfoType ;
(* Postcondition: returns the item at the top of S *)
```

This is equivalent to the procedure Head.

```
PROCEDURE Pop ( S : Stack ) : Stack ;
(* Postcondition: returns the stack obtained by
     removing the item at the top of S *)
```

This corresponds to the procedure Tail.

Semantics of the access procedures

The access procedures must satisfy the following axioms, where i is an item and s is a stack:

1. IsEmpty (Empty ( )) = TRUE
2. IsEmpty (Push (s, i)) = FALSE
3. Top (Empty ( )) = error

4. Top (Push (s, i)) = i
5. Pop (Empty ( )) = error
6. Pop (Push (s, i)) = s

The proof of consistency and sufficient completeness is the same as was given for lists.

Applications

The applications of stacks in computing are many and varied. Two examples are allocation of run-time memory and parsing of expressions.

IMPLEMENTATION

As the abstract data type stack is considered to have a 'top' it is usual to represent it diagrammatically as shown in figure 4.1. The items are numbered according to the order they were put on the stack.

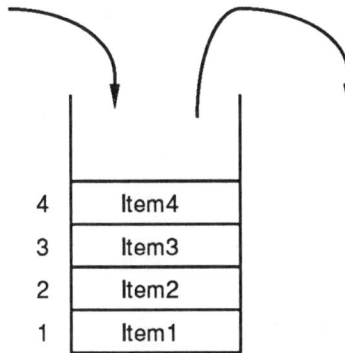

4	Item4
3	Item3
2	Item2
1	Item1

Figure 4.1 A stack

Since the types list and stack are equivalent, their possible implementations are also identical, and we will merely repeat the type declarations here with the appropriate function names.

Dynamic implementation

```
TYPE
     Stack =  POINTER TO Node ;
     Node =   RECORD
                  Info : InfoType ;
                  Next : Stack
              END ;
```

Static implementation

```
TYPE
    Size = [ 1.. Max ] ;
    PointerRange = [ 1.. (Max + 1) ] ;

    Stack = POINTER TO Node ;
    Node = RECORD
              Buffer : ARRAY Size OF InfoType ;
              TopPtr : PointerRange
           END ;
```

As with the static implementation of the list, we declare the type Stack as a *pointer* to a node so that it can be declared as opaque in the definition module and so that variables of type Stack can be returned from functions.

Block-structured languages which support the use of recursive procedures (such as Modula-2 and Pascal) use stacks to implement the run-time representation of data. We describe how stacks are used by compilers of these languages and later in the chapter use our abstract data type stack to simulate the same effect without relying on compiler-provided recursion.

STACKS AND RECURSIVE PROCEDURES

The rules of block-structured languages determine the lifetime (or **scope**) of variables in such a way that:

(1) A representation of each variable declared within a procedure (or program) is created on entry to that procedure and destroyed on exit from it.

(2) Distinct representations for each of these variables are created on each re-entry to a procedure.

These rules enable Modula-2, Pascal and other *stack-based* languages to permit recursive calls to procedures.

For example, consider the module ScopeExample in figure 4.2. On the right-hand side of the module boxes have been drawn which represent the storage location which has been allocated for variable x. At the beginning of the main program the value assigned to x is 0. The procedure Change is then invoked, the value 1 is assigned to x and the procedure Change-Again is called. In this procedure a local variable, which is also called x, is declared and another storage location is allocated for this local variable. Within ChangeAgain, this local x is assigned the value 3. However, as soon as we return to the main program the local x is destroyed, leaving the global x with the value 1, and consequently this is the value that the statement WriteCard (x, 4) writes to the screen. (Details of the library module InOut are given in Appendix 3.)

This illustrates two procedures which should be avoided when programming because of the confusion they can cause: the use of a global variable, and the use of a local variable of the same (rather meaningless) name. Although this will not cause any confusion for the computer it may do so for the programmer.

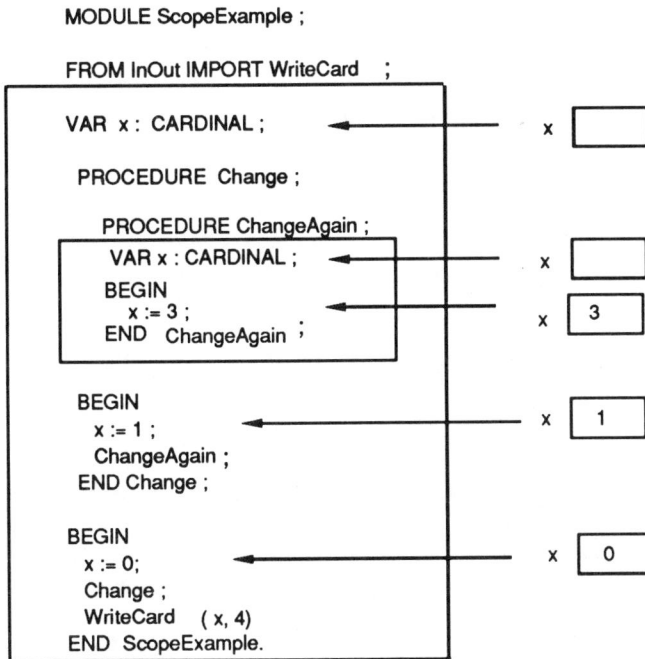

```
MODULE ScopeExample ;

FROM InOut IMPORT WriteCard   ;

    VAR x : CARDINAL ;                          x  ☐

    PROCEDURE  Change ;

       PROCEDURE ChangeAgain ;
          VAR x : CARDINAL ;                     x  ☐
          BEGIN
             x := 3 ;                            x  3
          END  ChangeAgain ;

       BEGIN
          x := 1 ;                               x  1
          ChangeAgain ;
       END Change ;

    BEGIN
       x := 0;                                   x  0
       Change ;
       WriteCard   ( x, 4)
    END  ScopeExample.
```

Figure 4.2

As another example of run-time memory management consider the recursive version of the factorial function:

```
PROCEDURE Fact ( n: CARDINAL ) : CARDINAL ;
(* Precondition: n is a CARDINAL
   Postcondition: returns factorial n *)

BEGIN
   IF n = 0 THEN
       RETURN 1
   ELSE
       RETURN n* Fact(n -1)
   END (* if *)
END Fact ;
```

Suppose that $n = 3$. Then Fact (3) is evaluated in the following way:

$$
\begin{aligned}
\text{Fact (3)} &= 3 * \text{Fact (2)} \\
&= 3 * 2 * \text{Fact (1)} \\
&= 3 * 2 * 1 * \text{Fact (0)} \\
&= 3 * 2 * 1 * 1 \\
&= 6
\end{aligned}
$$

Each time the procedure `Fact` is entered, a new storage location is allocated for its parameter *n*. The recursion terminates when *n* has the value zero, at which point the value one can be returned for `Fact ( 0 )`, which in turn enables the value one to be returned for `Fact ( 1 )`, which in turn enables a value to be returned for `Fact ( 2 )`, and finally a value can be returned for `Fact ( 3 )`.

The function calls are put on a stack, with the call to `Fact ( 3 )` going on the stack first, followed by the call to `Fact ( 2 )`, etc. Consequently a value cannot be returned for `Fact ( 3 )` until all the other function calls on the stack have been removed.

During execution of a program, storage is allocated dynamically by means of a stack as follows:

(1)   The first locations are allocated to the global variables of the program (i.e. those declared in the outermost block).

(2)   On entry to any procedure, an area of memory known as a *stack frame* is set up on the stack. On this go:

    (a)   Some control information necessary for control of the stack and the program. For example, the *return address*, which is the address of the instruction to be executed immediately upon exit from the procedure (see figure 4.3).

    (b)   All parameters passed to the procedure. If a parameter is passed by value, a copy of it is made and this value goes on the stack frame. The only alternative to this (in Modula-2) is to pass a parameter by reference, in which case it is a variable parameter, indicated by the reserved word VAR in the procedure heading. In this case the *address* of the variable is placed on the stack frame.[1]

    (c)   All local variables declared in the procedure.

    (d)   The *stack link*, which points to the base of the stack frame and is used to ensure that the stack returns to its original state on exit from a procedure.

Space may also be reserved for the return value of the procedure.

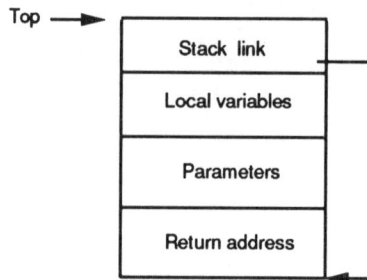

Figure 4.3

---

1   Other methods of parameter passing include pass by *name* and pass by *need*. With pass by name, each time a reference to a formal parameter is encountered during execution of the procedure body the argument expression is evaluated and its value substituted into the body. The address of code to perform this evaluation of the argument is placed in the stack frame. For purely functional languages (such as Hope) yet another alternative is to pass a parameter by need. This is the same as pass by name for the first occurrence of a parameter, but the value of the argument is re-used for any subsequent occurrences—this value is guaranteed to be the same by referential transparency. Parameter passing by need is clearly more efficient than by name, but cannot be used in an imperative language as such languages are not referentially transparent.

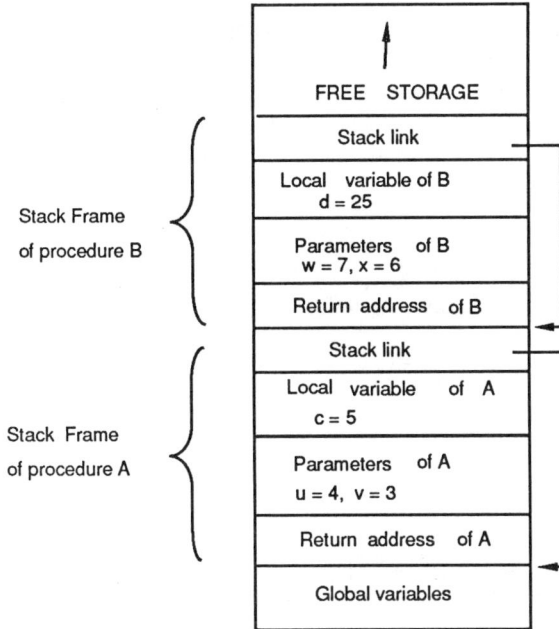

Figure 4.4

The data stack of a program will consist of several of these stack frames. Figure 4.4 shows the data stack of a program which has two procedures, A and B. Procedure A calls procedure B:

```
MODULE Example;

VAR Global : ARRAY [1..Max] OF CHAR ;

PROCEDURE A (u,v : CARDINAL ) ;
VAR c : CARDINAL ;

    PROCEDURE B (w,x : CARDINAL ) ;

    VAR d : CARDINAL ;
    BEGIN
        d := 25 ;
        (* rest of procedure B *)
    END B;

BEGIN
    c := 5 ;
    B ( u+v, u-v+c )
END A;


BEGIN
    A ( 4, 3 ) ;
END Example ;
```

During execution of procedure B, the data stack as shown in figure 4.4. On exit from a particular procedure the corresponding stack frame is popped off the stack, and so becomes available for use on entry to the next procedure.

Another example of a recursive function is one which calculates Fibonacci numbers. As was mentioned in Chapter 1, these are defined by the recurrence relation:

if n ≤ 2 *then* Fib (n) = 1
else Fib (n) = Fib(n −1) + Fib(n − 2)

which immediately suggests a recursive solution for production of the nth Fibonacci number:

```
PROCEDURE Fib (n : CARDINAL ) : CARDINAL ;
(* Precondition: n > 0
   Postcondition: returns the nth Fibonacci number *)

BEGIN
    IF n <= 2 THEN
        RETURN 1
    ELSE
        RETURN (Fib(n −1) + Fib(n − 2))
    END (* if *)
END Fib ;
```

To illustrate the action of Fib we will rewrite a call to calculate the fifth Fibonnacci number:

$$
\begin{aligned}
\text{Fib}(5) &= \text{Fib}(4) + \text{Fib}(3) \\
&= \text{Fib}(3) + \text{Fib}(2) + \text{Fib}(2) + \text{Fib}(1) \\
&= \text{Fib}(2) + \text{Fib}(1) + 1 + 1 + 1 \\
&= 1 + 1 + 1 + 1 + 1 \\
&= 5
\end{aligned}
$$

Note that each recursive step involves calling the function *twice*. In the calculation of Fib (5), Fib (4) was called once, Fib (3) was called twice, Fib (2) was called three times and Fib (1) was called twice. The number of calls is said to explode exponentially with n. Alternatively, we could say that the algorithm is O (2^n), using *order notation* which is explained below. With all the overhead of stack manipulation that this will involve we may be prompted to look for an alternative implementation.

Note: A function which is O (n) for some integer n is said to be of *order n*. More formally, a function g with formal parameter n is said to be O (f (n)) if there exists a constant c such that

$$g(n) \le c\, f(n)$$

for all but some finite (possibly empty) set of non-negative values for n.

This notation is called *order* notation: it helps us to give an approximation for the number of operations that an algorithm requires.

The alternative to recursion is *iteration*, that is, repetition which is controlled by a FOR, WHILE or REPEAT loop. This avoids the overhead of passing arguments and returning values from functions. For the Fibonacci function it will also remove duplication of effort. The iterative version of Fibonacci given below uses four local variables:

```
PROCEDURE IterativeFib ( n: CARDINAL ) : CARDINAL ;
(* Precondition: n > 0
   Postcondition: return the nth Fibonacci number *)


VAR First, Result, Count, Temp : CARDINAL;

BEGIN
   First := 1 ;
   Result := 1 ;
   FOR Count := 3 TO n DO
      Temp := Result ;
      Result := First + Result ;
      First := Temp
   END (* for *)
   RETURN Result
END IterativeFib ;
```

However, we could write a more efficient recursive version of the Fibonacci function by using an accumulating parameter. This is an extra parameter to the procedure which is used to store the partial result as it is being produced. The procedure below is a recursive version of the function Fib, which is O (n) : that is, the number of operations which will be carried out is proportional to the number supplied as an argument.

```
PROCEDURE Fib ( n : CARDINAL ) : CARDINAL ;
(* Precondition: n > 0
   Postcondition: return the nth Fibonacci number *)


PROCEDURE F ( count, temp, accumulator : CARDINAL ) :
                                          CARDINAL ;

   BEGIN
      IF count = 1 THEN
         RETURN accumulator
      ELSE
         RETURN ( F ( count - 1, accumulator, accumulator +
                                                    temp ))
      END
   END F ;


BEGIN
   RETURN F ( n, 0, 1 )
END Fib ;
```

The accumulating parameter could be an abstract data type if necessary. For example, the procedure below uses an accumulating parameter to reverse a list. It assumes the existence of the access procedures IsEmpty, Tail, Head and Cons. This procedure is also an O (n) procedure, so the number of Cons operations is proportional to the number of items in the list. This is in contrast with the Reverse function we had in Chapter 2, which was O (n^2).

Example

```
PROCEDURE Reverse ( L, Acc : List ) : List ;
(* Precondition: Acc should be empty initially
   Postcondition: returns a list consisting of the items
   in the list L reversed *)

BEGIN
    IF IsEmpty ( L ) THEN
        RETURN Acc
    ELSE
        RETURN Reverse ( Tail(L), Cons( Head(L), Acc ))
    END (*IF *)
END Reverse ;
```

Since recursion and iteration are just two syntaxes for expressing some form of repetition, we might suspect that they could be mechanically converted from one to the other. Although any iterative procedure has an equivalent recursive form which can be devised quite simply the converse is not so straightforward in general. The rest of this chapter is devoted to a discussion of the conversion of recursive functions into iterative equivalents.

RECURSION TO ITERATION

Recursion often provides the simplest and most natural solution to a problem. In some languages, however, procedure calls are much more costly in terms of both time and space than the assignment statements used in iterative solutions. A program may run significantly faster if recursive procedure calls are eliminated from it. Consequently, if efficiency is important it may be necessary to investigate the possible elimination of recursion from those parts of the code that are executed most frequently. However, it must be said that the simplicity of expression that recursion gives to a problem is often well worth the increased run time.

The elimination of recursion becomes even more necessary, of course, if a language does not have any provision for recursive calls (for example, Cobol and some versions of Fortran). An understanding of the run-time storage allocation scheme helps us to see how recursive procedures can be written without using recursion. There is one pattern of recursion which is particularly easy to convert: *tail recursion*.

Tail recursion

A procedure is *tail recursive* if there is no code to be executed after the recursive call. For example, the procedure below prints out a list of numbers. It assumes the existence of the access procedures `IsEmpty`, `Head` and `Tail`, and a procedure for output, `WriteItem`. The procedure is referentially transparent in that the parameter (`AList`) is unchanged by its execution, because it is passed as a value parameter. Note that the recursive call to `PrintList` is the last command to be executed in the procedure.

```
PROCEDURE PrintList ( AList : list ) ;
(* Postcondition: outputs the contents of AList *)
```

```
BEGIN
    IF NOT IsEmpty ( AList ) THEN
        WriteItem ( Head ( AList )) ;
        PrintList ( Tail ( AList ))
    END (* IF *)
END PrintList ;
```

Rule

To transform a tail-recursive procedure into an iterative one the IF statement is changed to a WHILE loop and the procedure call is replaced by an assignment which explicitly evaluates the parameter list of the recursive procedure call.

Using this rule, our PrintList procedure can be written iteratively as follows:

```
PROCEDURE PrintList ( AList : list ) ;
(* Postcondition: outputs the contents of AList *)

BEGIN
    WHILE NOT IsEmpty ( AList ) DO
        WriteItem ( Head ( AList )) ;
        AList := Tail ( AList ) (* explicit evaluation *)
    END (* while *)
END PrintList ;
```

Note that the assignment statement

```
AList := Tail ( AList )
```

does not affect the transparency of this procedure because AList is passed as a value parameter. Also note that the factorial function we used earlier:

```
IF n = 0 THEN
    RETURN 1
ELSE
    RETURN n* Fact (n -1)
```

is *not* tail recursive, because of the multiplication by n which takes place *after* the recursive call to *Fact*.

Elimination of recursion in general

We have discussed a method of converting a tail-recursive procedure into an equivalent iterative one. There is a more general approach that similarly converts **any** recursive procedure (or function). The general solution is to simulate the stack mechanism that a compiler uses and hence the recursion itself. The stack will hold:

(1) The current values of the parameters of the procedure;
(2) The current values of any local variables of the procedure.

Note that we do not need an indication of the return address (i.e. the statement that control returns to after completion of the procedure call), because the recursive call will be removed. To illustrate the method we will look at the Towers of Hanoi problem.

The Towers of Hanoi

The problem of the Towers of Hanoi or The Emperor's Puzzle became well known in the nineteenth century. The story accompanying the puzzle involved some priests in the oriental city of Hanoi working on a puzzle which, when solved, would signify the end of the world.

There are three wooden towers or poles which we will call left, middle and right. There are also 64 golden disks of increasing sizes. There is a hole in the centre of each disk so that it can be placed on a pole. Initially the disks are all placed in order of size on the left pole, with the largest at the bottom and the smallest at the top. The diagram below shows three such disks:

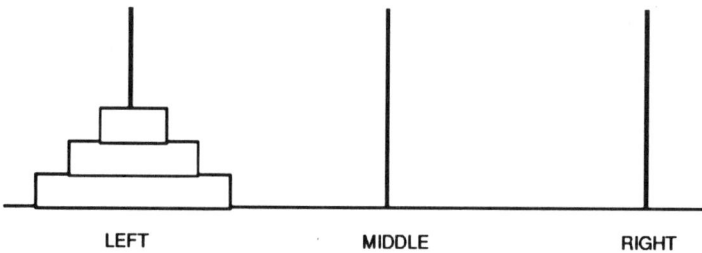

LEFT   MIDDLE   RIGHT

The problem is to move all the disks from the left pole to the right pole according to the following rules :

(1) Only one disk may be moved at a time (which must be the top one on one of the poles);
(2) A disk must never be placed on top of a smaller one;
(3) Each disk must always be on one of the poles or in transit between them.

The way to solve this problem is not to think about a solution for the 64 disks but rather to concentrate on the largest disk at the bottom. We know that this must be moved from the left pole to the right one. While that move is taking place the 63 other disks must be somewhere else, and the only other place they can be is on the middle pole. Suppose we have a procedure MoveTower:

```
MoveTower (NumberOfDisks, Source, Destination)
(* Postcondition: moves NumberOfDisks from the top
   of the Source pole to the Destination pole *)
```

Then we can write our solution in pseudocode:

MoveTower (63, Left, Middle)
(* move 63 disks to the
Middle pole *)
Move a disk from the Left pole to the Right pole
(* move the largest disk *)
MoveTower (63, Middle, Right)
(* move the first 63 disks to
the Right pole *)

The diagrams below show how this works for three disks. First, move two of the disks to the middle pole:

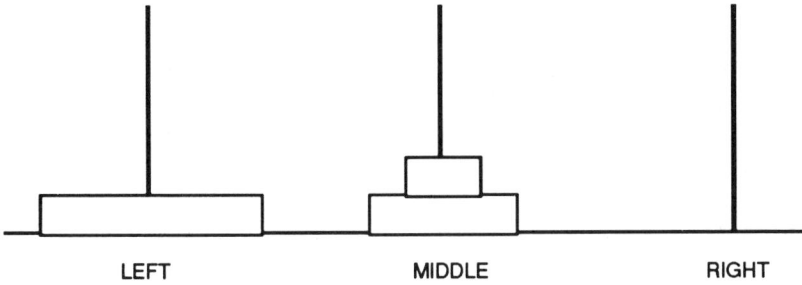

Then move the largest disk to the right pole.

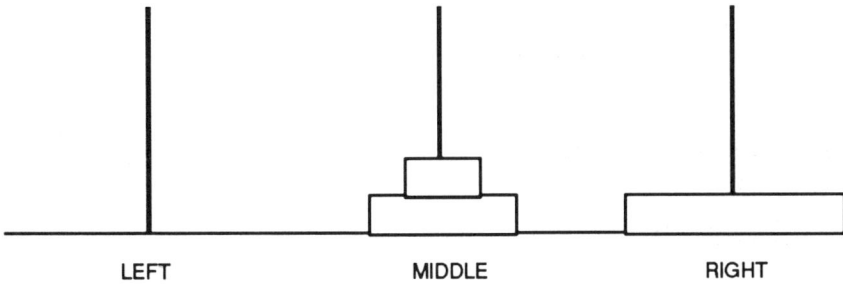

Then move the two disks on the middle pole on top of it:

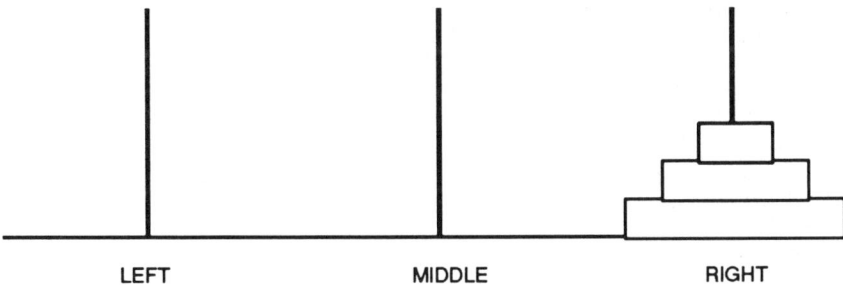

Now we have to solve the problem of moving 63 disks from the left pole to the middle pole. But this is precisely the problem we have already solved. All we have to do is to concentrate on moving the bottom one of these disks from the left to the middle pole. While that move is taking place the other 62 disks will have to be on the right pole. So we can use MoveTower again, this time to move 63 disks from the left to the middle pole.

MoveTower (62, Left, Right)
                                                   (* move 62 disks to the Right
                                                       pole *)
Move a disk from the Left pole to the Middle pole
                                                   (* move the largest disk *)
MoveTower (62, Right, Middle)
                                                   (* move 62 disks to the Middle
                                                       pole *)

Similarly for the move from the middle to right pole, and so on for 61, 60, disks and so on down to 1 disk, suggesting a simple recursive solution.

The source and destination poles are switched from one call to the next, using the remaining pole as a temporary resting place for the other disks. The solution can be expressed by a call to the procedure Move, as shown below, in which this temporary pole is given as one of the parameters:

```
Move  (Num,  Left,  Middle,  Right )
```

where Num is the number of disks to be moved from the Left pole to the Right using the Middle pole for the temporary tower. The procedure is given below. The procedure Move-Disk moves a single disk from the source to the destination pole.

```
TYPE
   Pole = ( Left, Middle, Right );

PROCEDURE Move ( DiskNum : CARDINAL ; Source, Temp, Dest :
Pole ) ;
(* Postcondition: Moves DiskNum disks from Source to Dest
   *)

BEGIN
   IF DiskNum = 1 THEN
      MoveDisk ( Source, Dest )
   ELSE
      Move ( DiskNum - 1, Source, Dest, Temp) ;
      MoveDisk ( Source, Dest ) ;
      Move ( DiskNum - 1, Temp, Source, Dest )
   END (* if *)
END Move ;
```

By induction we can prove that the time required to move N disks is proportional to

$$2^N - 1.$$

Assuming that one move takes one second, this means that it will be six hundred thousand million years before the end of the world. Even working at one move per microsecond it would take half a million years.

How can the procedure be written without using recursion? One way is to try to simulate the use of the recursion stack for holding parameters of the procedure Move. Each recursive call leads to either a simple single disk move or else the call is replaced by three other sets of moves. Therefore the effect of the initial procedure call:

```
Move ( Num, Left, Middle, Right )
```

can be obtained non-recursively by first pushing the four parameters onto a stack which has been created to simulate the recursion stack.

To simulate the effect of the recursive call, the parameters are popped off the stack and the value of `DiskNum` is checked. If it is one, then a single disk move is performed between the poles `Source` and `Dest`. Otherwise, three new groups of parameters are pushed onto the stack, where the value of each group corresponds to the parameters of the corresponding call in the recursive procedure.

To obtain the correct order of simulated calls, these groups are pushed onto the stack in the reverse order to that in which the recursive calls appear. The process continues by repeatedly popping the top set of parameters off the stack and interpreting their effect, as above, until the stack is empty. At this stage all the recursive calls have been interpreted and so the sequence of required moves has been generated. In Modula-2 the intermediate step towards an iterative solution is:

```
PROCEDURE Move ( DiskNum : CARDINAL ; Source, Temp, Dest :
                                                  Pole ) ;
(* Postcondition: Moves DiskNum disks from Source to Dest *)


VAR
    S : Stack ;                      (* used to simulate recursion *)


BEGIN
    S := Push ( DiskNum, Push ( Source, Push ( Temp,
                          Push ( Dest, Empty ( ) ) ) ) ) ;
    WHILE NOT ( IsEmpty ( S )) DO
        DiskNum := Top ( S ) ;
        S := Pop ( S ) ;
        Source := Top ( S ) ;
        S := Pop ( S ) ;
        Temp := Top ( S ) ;
        S := Pop ( S ) ;
        Dest := Top ( S ) ;
        S := Pop ( S ) ;
        IF DiskNum = 1 THEN
            MoveDisk ( Source, Dest )
        ELSE
            S := Push ( DiskNum - 1, Push ( Temp, Push (Source,
                                     Push ( Dest, S )))) ;
                    (* parameters of third sub-move *)
          S := Push ( 1, Push (Source, Push ( Temp,
                                     Push ( Dest, S )))) ;
                    (* parameters of second sub-move *)
            S := Push ( DiskNum - 1, Push ( Source, Push (Dest
                                     Push ( Temp, S ))))
                    (* parameters of first sub-move *)
        END (* if *)
    END (* while *)
END Move ;
```

where we assume that

```
TYPE Pole = CARDINAL ; (* 1 = Left, 2 = Middle, 3 = Right *)
```

because our abstract data type stack is not generic, i.e. it can only hold one type of item.

The final step is to remove the recursive calls to Push. This can be achieved by writing a short auxiliary function HPush (Hanoi Push) which takes four items and a stack and returns a stack with the items pushed on it. The final iterative solution thus arrived at is given below:

```
PROCEDURE Move ( DiskNum : CARDINAL ; Source, Temp, Dest :
Pole ) ;
(* Postcondition: Moves DiskNum disks from Source to Dest *)


VAR
    S : Stack ;                        (* used to simulate recursion *)


BEGIN
    S := HPush ( DiskNum, Source, Temp, Dest, Empty ( ) ) ;
    WHILE NOT ( IsEmpty ( S )) DO
        DiskNum := Top ( S ) ;
        S := Pop ( S ) ;
        Source := Top ( S ) ;
        S := Pop ( S ) ;
        Temp := Top ( S ) ;
        S := Pop ( S ) ;
        Dest := Top ( S ) ;
        S := Pop ( S ) ;
        IF DiskNum = 1 THEN
            MoveDisk ( Source, Dest )
        ELSE
            S := HPush ( DiskNum - 1, Temp, Source, Dest, S ) ;
                                    (* parameters of third
                                                sub-move *)
            S := HPush ( 1, Source, Temp, Dest, S ) ;
                                    (* parameters of second
                                                sub-move *)
            S := HPush ( DiskNum - 1, Source, Dest, Temp, S )
                                    (* parameters of first
                                                sub-move *)
        END (* if *)
    END (* while *)
END Move ;
```

where the procedure HPush is:

```
PROCEDURE HPush ( N : CARDINAL ; A, B, C : Pole ; S : Stack
                                          ) : Stack ;

(* Postcondition: returns the stack which results
    from pushing C, B, A and N (in that order) onto S *)

VAR T : Stack ;
```

```
BEGIN
    T := Push ( S, C ) ;
    T := Push ( T, B ) ;
    T := Push ( T, A ) ;
    T := Push ( T, N ) ;
    RETURN T
END HPush ;
```

Exercises 4.1

1. Transform the following tail-recursive procedures to iterative ones:

(a)
```
PROCEDURE Last (L: List) : InfoType ;
(* Precondition: L should not be empty
    Postcondition: returns the last item of the list L *)

BEGIN
    IF IsEmpty ( Tail (L) )
        THEN RETURN Head (L)
    ELSE
        RETURN Last(Tail (L))
    END (* if *)
END Last ;
```

(b)
```
PROCEDURE IsIn ( I : Infotype; L : List) : BOOLEAN ;
(* Postcondition: returns TRUE if item I is in list L *)

BEGIN
    IF IsEmpty (L) THEN
        RETURN FALSE
    ELSIF IsEqual (I, Head (L)) THEN
        RETURN TRUE (* see below *)
    ELSE
        RETURN IsIn (I, Tail (L))
    END (* if *)
END IsIn ;
```

2. Suppose that the type pole is declared as an enumerated type:

```
TYPE
    Pole = (Left, Middle, Right)
```

A neater iterative solution to the Towers of Hanoi problem would use a stack on which the number of disks (which is a cardinal) and variables of type `Pole` can all be pushed. How might we declare such a stack in Modula-2 ?

SUMMARY

The abstract data type *stack* is a linear sequence of an arbitrary number of items (all of the same type) together with a number of access procedures.

The type stack is isomorphic to the type list and may be used by block-structured languages to implement recursive procedures.

To convert an arbitrary recursive procedure to an iterative form the action of the run-time stack must be simulated.

A procedure is *tail recursive* if there is no code to be executed after the recursive call. Such recursion is particularly easy to convert to an iterative form.

To transform a tail recursive procedure into an iterative one the IF statement is changed to a WHILE loop and the procedure call is replaced by an assignment which explicitly evaluates the parameter list of the recursive procedure call.

The general solution for transforming recursion to iteration is to simulate the stack mechanism that a compiler uses and hence the recursion itself. The stack will hold:

(1) The current values of the parameters of the procedure;
(2) The current values of any local variables of the procedure.

A recursive solution to a problem is often more natural and requires less code than an iterative one. However, such a solution may require significantly more memory and run slower than the corresponding iterative solution.

In general, problems that are best solved recursively are those that can be stated in terms of a recurrence relation (for example, a relation which defines each member of a sequence in terms of the preceding members).

CHAPTER 5

The Abstract Data Type Set

INTRODUCTION

In this chapter we discuss the abstract data type *set*. The type set is provided by some programming languages (such as Modula-2 and Pascal) as a built-in type. We give the algebraic specification of the type set and then discuss the procedures which are provided by Modula-2 for set manipulation, showing, where possible, how these compare with the access procedures which were given in the specification. We then discuss the abstract data type *bag*, which differs from the type set in allowing multiple occurrences of an item to be present.

DEFINITION

The abstract data type *set* is a collection of an arbitrary number of distinct items (all of the same type) together with a number of access procedures.

Note the difference between this definition and that of the abstract data type list. The items in a list do not have to be distinct, and they have a linear ordering imposed on them which reflects the order in which the items were inserted into the list. Duplicate items are not allowed in a set, and the order in which items are placed in a set is not significant.

NOTATION

We will represent a set by listing its members in braces, and show the items in a set separated by commas:

{ 'a', 'e', 'i', 'o', 'u' } : a set of characters

We start by giving the algebraic specification of the abstract data type set.

ALGEBRAIC SPECIFICATION

As usual, we have two constructor functions, which are used to create an empty set and insert an item into a set. We have two predicate functions, one of which tests a set to see if it is empty and the other which tests it to see if it contains a named item. We have one selector function which returns a set without a named item and we have included some extra functions either because they are fundamental to our concept of the type set (Union, Intersection and Difference) or, in the case of the function Size, because of its usefulness.

Syntax of the access procedures

1. Constructor functions

```
PROCEDURE Empty ( ) : Set ;
(* Postcondition: returns an empty Set *)


PROCEDURE Insert ( I : InfoType ; S : Set ) : Set ;
(* Precondition: receives an item I and a Set S
   Postcondition:returns a new Set which consists
   all the items of S and I, if it was not already in S*)
```

2. Predicate functions

```
PROCEDURE IsEmpty ( S : Set ) : BOOLEAN ;
(* Precondition: receives a Set S
   Postcondition: returns TRUE if S is empty, otherwise
   FALSE. *)


PROCEDURE Contains ( I : InfoType ; S : Set ) : BOOLEAN ;
(* Precondition: receives an item I and a Set S
   Postcondition: returns TRUE if I is in S, otherwise
   FALSE. *)
```

3. Selector functions

```
PROCEDURE Remove ( I : InfoType ; S : Set ) : Set ;
(* Precondition: receives an item I and a set S
   Postcondition: returns a set which contains all the
   items of S but no item equal to I. *)
```

4. Auxiliary functions

```
PROCEDURE Union ( S1, S2 : Set ) : Set ;
(* Precondition: receives two Sets S1 and S2
   Postcondition: returns the set of all items which
   are either in S1 or in S2 or in both. *)


PROCEDURE Intersection ( S1, S2 : Set ) : Set ;
(* Precondition: receives two Sets S1 and S2
   Postcondition: returns the set of all items of S1
   which are also in S2. *)
```

```
PROCEDURE Difference ( S1, S2 : Set ) : Set ;
(* Precondition: receives two Sets S1 and S2
   Postcondition: returns the set of all items in S1 which
   are not in S2. *)

PROCEDURE Size ( S : Set ) : CARDINAL ;
(* Precondition: receives a Set S
   Postcondition: returns the cardinality of S *)
```

Semantics of the access procedures

The access procedures should satisfy the following axioms, where i and j are items and s and t are sets. The structure of the axioms is based on the fact that a set is either empty or has been constructed by inserting an item i into a set s, in which case it is of the form Insert (i, s). The first axiom specifies that an item i is not inserted into a set s if it is already in s. This ensures that a set will not contain duplicate items.

1. Insert (i, s) = *if* Contains (i, s) *then* s *else* Insert (i, s)

The next two axioms describe the behaviour of the predicate function IsEmpty, and they are identical to those which we have seen in earlier chapters.

2. IsEmpty (Empty ( )) = TRUE
3. IsEmpty (Insert (i, s)) = FALSE

The semantics for the procedure Contains describe how we can determine whether an item is in a set or not. The first axiom states that an item is not contained in the empty set:

4. Contains (i, Empty ( )) = FALSE

If the item which we are checking has just been inserted into the set then Contains must return True, otherwise we must determine whether the item was in the original set:

5. Contains (j,Insert (i, s)) = *if* i = j *then* TRUE *else* Contains (j, s)

Now consider the semantics for the procedure Remove. We will specify this procedure such that if the item to be removed is not in the set then the original set is returned. This gives us one axiom if the set is empty:

6. Remove (i, Empty ( )) = Empty ( )

If an item i which is about to be inserted into a set is equal to the item j being deleted, then all we need to do is to remove any other occurrence of j from the set. This follows because duplicates are not allowed (as stated by axiom 1), So we have:

Remove (j, Insert (i, s)) = if i = j then Remove (j, s)

Otherwise we still need to insert i into s, and we also need to remove the item j from the set:

else Insert (i, Remove (j, s))

Hence the second axiom describing the semantics for the procedure Remove is given by:

7. Remove (j, Insert (i, s)) = *if* i = j *then* Remove (j, s)
$\qquad\qquad\qquad\qquad\qquad\qquad$ *else* Insert (i, Remove (j, s))

Note that if the item *j* were not in the set *s* then eventually this would be rewritten to:

Remove (j, Empty ( ))

to which we could then apply axiom 6. For example, we can demonstrate the case of attempting the remove an item which is not contained in a set by rewriting the expression Remove (a, { f, c, e }). We will use a pair of curly brackets, { }, to represent the empty set.

Remove (a, { f, c, e }) → Remove (a, Insert (f, { c, e }))
$\qquad\qquad\qquad\quad$ → Insert (f, Remove (a, { c, e }))
$\qquad\qquad\qquad\quad$ → Insert (f, Insert (c, Remove (a, { e })))
$\qquad\qquad\qquad\quad$ → Insert (f, Insert (c, Insert (e, Remove (a, { }))))
$\qquad\qquad\qquad\quad$ → Insert (f, Insert (c, Insert (e, { })))
$\qquad\qquad\qquad\quad$ → { f, c, e }

Now let us demonstrate removing an item which is in the set by rewriting the call Remove (a, { f, a, e }):

Remove (a, { f, a, e }) → Remove (a, Insert (f, { a, e }))
$\qquad\qquad\qquad\quad$ → Insert (f, Remove (a, { a, e }))
$\qquad\qquad\qquad\quad$ → Insert (f, Remove (a, { e }))
$\qquad\qquad\qquad\quad$ → Insert (f, Insert (e, Remove (a, { })))
$\qquad\qquad\qquad\quad$ → Insert (f, Insert (e, { }))
$\qquad\qquad\qquad\quad$ → { f, e }

The procedure Union takes two sets and returns the set of all items which are either in one set or the other or in both. If one set is empty then we simply need to return the other set:

8. Union (s, Empty ( )) = s

If a set is not empty then it must be of the form Insert (i, t) where t is a set (and hence contains no duplicate items) and i is an item. In this case we simply need to return the result of inserting i into the union of the two sets:

9. Union (s, Insert (i, t)) = Insert (i, Union (s, t))

The procedure Intersection takes two sets and returns a set containing all the items which are in both sets. Obviously if one set is empty then the intersection will also be empty:

10. Intersection (s, Empty ( )) = Empty ( )

Otherwise we must ask whether an item which is about to be inserted into a set is contained in the other set, in which case it should be inserted into the intersection of the two sets:

Intersection (s, Insert (i, t)) = *if* Contains (i, s) *then* Insert (i, Intersection (s, t))

and if not then we simply ignore the item and look for the intersection of the sets:

else Intersection (s, t)

which gives us the axiom below:

11. Intersection (s, Insert (i, t)) = *if* Contains (i, s)
$\qquad\qquad$ *then* Insert (i, Intersection (s, t))
$\qquad\qquad$ *else* Intersection (s, t)

We wish to define the difference of two sets to be every item which is in the first set but not in the second. Thus if the second set is empty then we want the whole of the first set:

12. Difference (s, Empty ( )) = s

Otherwise we follow the axiom for Intersection except that we *remove* any item which occurs in the second set:

13. Difference (s, Insert (i, t)) = *if* Contains (i, s) *then*
$\qquad\qquad\qquad$ Remove (i, Difference (s, t))
$\qquad\qquad\qquad$ *else* Difference (s, t)

For example, suppose we rewrite the call Difference ({ a, f, c }, { a, e }):

Difference ({ a, f, c }, { a, e }) →Remove (a, Difference ({ a, f, c }, {e}))
$\qquad\qquad\qquad\qquad\qquad$ →Remove (a, Difference ({ a, f, c }, { }))
$\qquad\qquad\qquad\qquad\qquad$ →Remove (a, { a, f, c })
$\qquad\qquad\qquad\qquad\qquad$ →{ f, c }

The next two axioms give the semantics of the procedure Size. Note that it is not correct to give axiom 15 as:

Size (Insert (i, s)) = 1 + Size (s)

because the item i will not be inserted into the set s if it is already in it (as axiom 1 guarantees).

14. Size (Empty ( )) = 0
15. Size (Insert (i, s)) = 1 + Size (Remove (i, s))

The access procedures given in the specification were chosen because of the functions which they enable us to implement. With such a large number of axioms the question of showing that they are sufficiently complete, i.e. that we can determine the behaviour of every procedure in every possible case, is not trivial. Indeed, Guttag (1979) states that 'It can be shown that the problem of establishing whether or not a set of axioms is complete is undecidable'. Consistency (that is, determining whether or not any of the axioms contradict each other) is also unsolvable in theory, although the presence of contradictory axioms is relatively easy to observe in practice.

APPLICATIONS

From the specification it can be seen that the abstract data type set has no structure imposed on it, unlike the type list which has a linear structure. Consequently sets are more general, and have many applications. However, this generality means that sets are somewhat more complicated to manipulate. Sets are employed to represent attributes that some object may have. They are frequently used to test a value against a set of acceptable values. Another application is the implementation of the abstract data type *graph*, which will be discussed in Chapter 10.

   We will now compare the access procedures which we have specified above with those which are provided by Modula-2 to manipulate sets.

THE TYPE SET IN MODULA-2

Unlike the abstract data types discussed earlier in the book, the type set is provided by Modula-2 as a built-in structured type (it is also supplied by Pascal). There are five classes of access procedures provided to manipulate variables of this type in Modula-2, which are as follows:

(1)   A set constructor operator for creating a set from its member values. Given a type declaration of the form SET OF something, we can then construct a set by enclosing the values which we want to include in the set in braces and preceding them by this type. For example:

```
TYPE
    BaseType = [ 0..20 ] ;
    SomeIntegers = SET OF BaseType ;

VAR
    set1 : SomeIntegers ;

BEGIN
    set1 := SomeIntegers { 1, 4..6, 18 } ;
```

This statement constructs a set containing the integers 1, 4, 5, 6 and 18.

   If we were to implement sets using the access procedures we specified earlier the equivalent statement would be:

```
set1 := Insert ( 1, Insert ( 4, ( Insert ( 5, Insert
                        ( 6, Insert ( 18, Empty ( ) ))))))
```

Note: In Modula-2 the type identifier of the set must precede the braces. If it is omitted the set is assumed to be of type BITSET. This type is the only predefined set type, and is defined as:

```
BITSET = SET OF [ 0 .. W - 1 ]
```

where W is the number of bits in a word of the host machine (this is often 32). The numbers in a BITSET denote the bits of the word that are set to '1'. For example:

{ }	00000000000...000000000
{ 0 }	00000000000...000000001
{ 0 .. 5 }	00000000000...000111111
{ 4..6, 8, 9, 12..14 }	000...00111001101110000

assuming that the least significant bit is on the right.

The type BITSET is provided for low-level work such as manipulation of bits in a machine word.

The base type of the set must be ordinal, that is, BOOLEAN, CHAR, INTEGER, CARDINAL, enumerated or subrange type (note that this excludes the possibility of having sets of sets). However, sometimes the cardinality of sets is restricted by the implementation. For machines with 32-bit words, the number of items in a set is often limited to 32, although some compilers have implemented larger sets. Thus, for example, the type declaration below would produce error messages with many compilers:

```
TYPE
    AllIntegers = SET OF INTEGER ;
```

In Chapter 9 we discuss an implementation method, called *hashing*, which allows the restriction on cardinality to be circumvented. The specification of the abstract data type set did not impose any limit on the size of a set, and in theory, neither should the implementation.

(2) The syntax of Modula-2 also provides an intrinsic predicate procedure for set membership, denoted by IN. This corresponds to our predicate function Contains. For example:

```
TYPE
    Day = (Monday, Tuesday, Wednesday, Thursday, Friday,
           Saturday, Sunday) ;
    Days = SET OF Day ;

    VAR
        today : Day ;

    BEGIN
        today := Wednesday ;
        IF today IN Days { Monday, Tuesday } THEN ...
```

The last statement will be executed if today is either Monday or Tuesday.

If we were to use the function Contains the IF statement would be written:

```
IF Contains (today, Insert (Monday, Insert (Tuesday,
                                  Empty ()))) THEN...
```

(3) Binary operators to combine pairs of sets are also provided: union (+), intersection (*), difference (-) and symmetric difference (/). The semantics of the union, intersection and difference operators are exactly those of the corresponding access procedures which we gave earlier. We will look at each operator in turn using the customary Venn diagrams. The shaded area represents the set of values which is returned in each case.

(a) Figure 5.1 shows the union of two sets A and B, A + B:

A + B

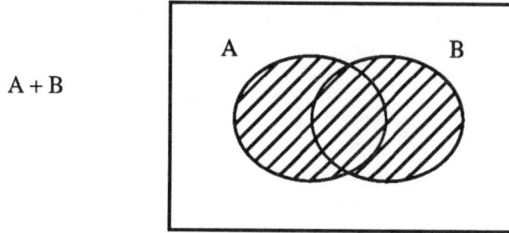

Figure 5.1

For example, if we had

```
set1 := SomeIntegers { 1, 4..6, 18 } ;
set2 := SomeIntegers { 2..5 } ;
```

as shown in the Venn diagram in figure 5.2

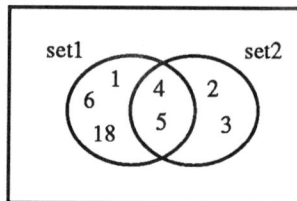

Figure 5.2

then the expression

```
set1 + set2
```

would return a set which contains the values { 1, 2..6, 18 }.

(b) Figure 5.3 shows the intersection of A and B, A * B:

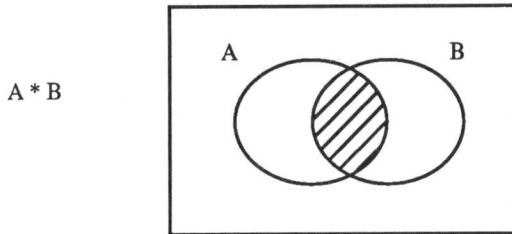

A * B

Figure 5.3

For example, using the values for set1 and set2 given above:

```
set1 * set2
```

returns the set { 4, 5 }

(c) The difference of the set A and B, A − B, is shown in figure 5.4.

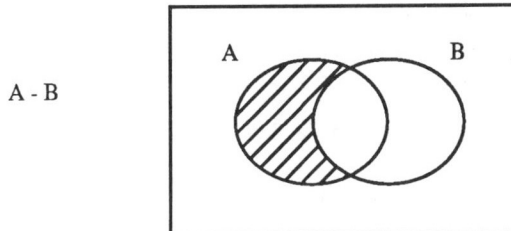

A - B

Figure 5.4

For example,

```
set1 - set2
```

returns the set { 1, 6, 18 }.

(d) Finally, symmetric difference, A / B, which returns all the values which are either in A or in B but not in both is shown in figure 5.5.

For example,

```
set1 / set2
```

returns the set { 1..3, 6, 18 }.

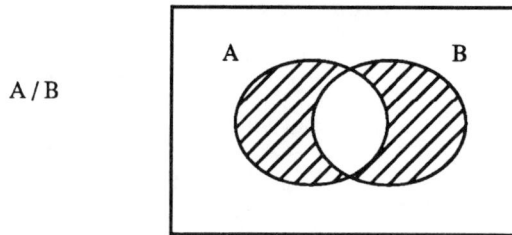

A / B

Figure 5.5

Although we did not supply an access procedure to find the symmetric difference between two sets, we can do this relatively easily by determining the union of the differences of the two sets, i.e.

```
Union ( Difference ( A , B), Difference ( B, A ))
```

(4) The relational operators, equality, '=', inequality, '<>', subset '<=' and superset '>=' are provided for set comparison. For example,

```
IF set1 = SomeIntegers{ } THEN ...
```

compares set1 with the empty set. For another example, suppose we declare the following types and variables:

```
TYPE
    BaseType = [ 0..20 ] ;
    SomeIntegers = SET OF BaseType ;
VAR
    set1, set2, set3 : SomeIntegers ;
```

then in Modula-2 we can write the following code:

```
BEGIN
    set1 := SomeIntegers { 1, 4..7, 18 } ;
    set2 := SomeIntegers { 1,1, 4..7, 18 } ;
    set3 := SomeIntegers { 5, 18, 1, 4, 7, 6 } ;
    IF set1 = set2 THEN ...
    IF set1 = set3 THEN ...
```

The first IF statement will be true because multiple occurrences of items in a set are ignored. The second statement will also be true because the order of items in sets is irrelevant.

The Venn diagram in figure 5.6 shows two sets A and B, where B is a subset of A (and A is a superset of B).

If the type set were not included in the language and we had implemented the abstract data type satisfying the algebraic specification given earlier, we could easily implement our own subset procedure by noting that a set S1 is a subset of a set S2 if all the items in S1 are contained in S2, i.e. the difference of the two sets is empty.

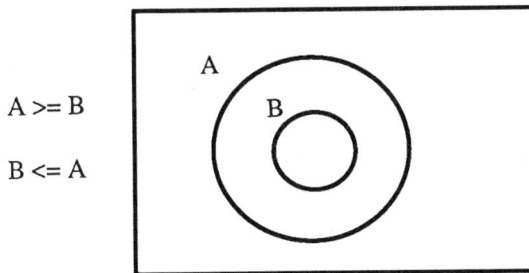

Such a subset procedure is given below:

```
PROCEDURE Subset ( S1, S2 : Set ) : BOOLEAN ;
(* Precondition: receives two sets S1 and S2
    Postcondition: returns TRUE if S1 is a subset of S2*)

BEGIN
    RETURN IsEmpty ( Difference ( S1, S2 )) ;
END Subset ;
```

Given this procedure we could also implement our own to determine whether two sets are equal or not by noting that if two sets are subsets of each other then they must be equal. The procedure is given below:

```
PROCEDURE AreEqual ( S1, S2 : Set ) : BOOLEAN;
(* Precondition: receives two sets S1 and S2
    Postcondition: returns TRUE if they contain the same
    items *)

BEGIN
  RETURN (Subset ( S1, S2) AND Subset ( S2, S1 ))
END AreEqual ;
```

(5) Modula-2 provides two standard generic procedures INCL and EXCL which can be used to include and exclude (respectively) an expression in a set. For example:

```
TYPE
    SomeChars = SET OF CHAR ;
    VAR
        ASet : SomeChars ;
        ch : CHAR ;

    BEGIN
        ASet := SomeChars { } ;
        ch := GetNextChar ( ) ;
        IF ch IN SomeChars { 'a', 'b', 'c' } THEN
            INCL ( ASet, ch ) ;
```

where GetNextChar is a function which returns a character from the input stream. If the character is either 'a', 'b' or 'c' then it is included in the set ASet. Note that INCL is not written in a functional style. It takes a variable parameter which is a set and an item and includes the item in the set by means of a side-effect.

Not only is the cardinality of sets restricted but also it is quite common for a programming language not to have the type set as a built-in type. When this is the case the abstract data type set would have to be implemented before it could be used, according to the specification given earlier. However, since Modula-2 does provide us with the built-in type, we will forego discussion of the implementation of the type set and instead turn our attention to the abstract data type *bag*. The only difference between a set and a bag is that a bag allows the multiple occurrence of items and so has a slightly different specification (some authors use the name *multiset* instead of bag).

THE ABSTRACT DATA TYPE BAG

Definition

The abstract data type *bag* is a collection of an arbitrary number of items (all of the same type) which are *not necessarily distinct* together with a number of access procedures.

The *multiplicity* of an item is the number of times it occurs in the bag. Since the Modula-2 type set does not allow the multiple occurrences of items we will have to implement the abstract data type bag ourselves.

The algebraic specification for the type bag is given below, where i and j are items, and b and c are bags. Note that the first axiom for the function Insert:

Insert (i, s) = *if* Contains (i, s) *then* s *else* Insert (i, s)

is no longer needed, as there are no longer any restrictions on insertion.

The first four axioms are identical to those for the type set:

1. IsEmpty (Empty ( )) = TRUE
2. IsEmpty (Insert (i, b)) = FALSE
3. Contains (i, Empty ( )) = FALSE
4. Contains (j, Insert (i, b)) = *if* i = j *then* TRUE *else* Contains (j, b)

The semantics for the procedure Remove must be changed to reflect the fact that multiple occurrences of items are allowed, and the function should only remove one instance of an item.

5. Remove (i, Empty ( )) = Empty ( )
6. Remove (j, Insert (i, b)) = *if* i = j *then* b
                                              else Insert (i, Remove (j, b))

When forming the union of two bags, we want the multiplicity of items in the resulting bag to be equal to their total multiplicity in both bags. For example,

Union ({ a, c, b }, { a, e, d, c, a }) = {a, c, b, a, e, d, c, a }

7. Union (b, Empty ( )) = b
8. Union (b, Insert (i, c)) = Insert (i, Union (b, c))

For intersection, we define the multiplicity of an item in the intersection of two bags to be equal to its least multiplicity in either. Thus, for example:

Intersection ({ a, c, b }, { a, e, d, c, a }) = {a, c }

9. Intersection (b, Empty ( )) = Empty ( )
10. Intersection (b, Insert (i, c)) = *if* Contains (i, b) *then*
                                   Insert (i, Intersection (Remove (b, i), c))
                                   else Intersection (b, c)

The axioms for Difference remain the same:

11. Difference (b, Empty ( )) = b
12. Difference (b, Insert (i, c)) = *if* Contains (i, b) *then*
                              Remove (i, Difference (b, c))
                              else Difference (b, c)

In fact we can simplify axiom 12 by using axiom 6, which states that an item is only removed from a bag if it is contained in the bag. So we can write axiom 12 as:

12. Difference (b, Insert (i, c)) = Remove (i, Difference (b, c))

and the second axiom for Size is slightly simpler:

13. Size (Empty ( )) = 0
14. Size (Insert (i, b)) = 1 + Size (b)

The comments accompanying the procedures Union, Intersection and so on must also be changed to show that for multiple occurrences of items are allowed. For example:

```
PROCEDURE Union ( S1, S2 : Set ) : Set ;
(* Precondition: receives two Sets S1 and S2
   Postcondition: returns their union including
   repetitions *)
```

As an example of a problem which uses the abstract data type bag, consider the following. Assume the existence of the access procedures which were specified earlier and suppose the items in the bag to be cardinal numbers (i.e. numbers ≥ 0). Given three cardinal numbers, find the bags of their prime factors, their highest common factor (the largest number which divides exactly into the three numbers) and their lowest common multiple or L.C.M. (the smallest number which is exactly divisible by all three). For example, suppose we have the numbers 30, 78 and 84. Let the bags of their prime factors be denoted by X, Y and Z respectively. Now (using '.' to represent multiplication)

$30 = 2.3.5$
$78 = 2.3.13$
$84 = 2.2.3.7$

$\therefore$ X = { 2, 3, 5 }, Y = { 2, 3, 13 } and Z = { 2, 2, 3, 7 }

The factors of the highest common factor are given by the intersection of the three bags. Now (using * for intersection):

$$X * Y * Z \ = \ \{2, 3, 5\} * \{2, 3, 13\} * \{2, 2, 3, 7\}$$
$$= \ \{2, 3\} * \{2, 2, 3, 7\}$$
$$= \ \{2, 3\}$$

∴   the highest common factor = 6

The factors of the lowest common multiple (L.C.M.) are given by the union of the symmetric difference of the three bags and their intersection. The symmetric difference of two bags A and B is given by:

$$(A + B) - (A * B),$$

(using '+' for union, and '-' for difference). The factors of the L.C.M. are given by:

$$(((X + Y) - (X * Y)) + Z) - (((X + Y) - (X * Y)) * Z)$$

Now

$$(((X + Y) - (X * Y)) + Z) \ = \ (\{2, 3, 5\} + \{2, 3, 13\} - \{2, 3\}) + \{2, 2, 3, 7\}$$
$$= \ (\{2, 2, 3, 3, 5, 13\} - \{2, 3\}) + \{2, 2, 3, 7\}$$
$$= \ \{2, 3, 5, 13\} + \{2, 2, 3, 7\}$$
$$= \ \{2, 2, 2, 3, 3, 5, 7, 13\}$$

and

$$(((X + Y) - (X * Y)) * Z) \ = \ (\{2, 3, 5\} + \{2, 3, 13\} - \{2, 3\}) * \{2, 2, 3, 7\}$$
$$= \ (\{2, 2, 3, 3, 5, 13\} - \{2, 3\}) * \{2, 2, 3, 7\}$$
$$= \ \{2, 3, 5, 13\} * \{2, 2, 3, 7\}$$
$$= \ \{2, 3\}$$

∴   the symmetric difference is $= \ \{2, 2, 2, 3, 3, 5, 7, 13\} - \{2, 3\}$
$$= \ \{2, 2, 3, 5, 7, 13\}$$

∴   the lowest common multiple $= 2 . 2 . 3 . 5 . 7 . 13 = 5460$

Exercises 5.1

1. Implement procedures to:
    (a) Find the prime factors of a number.
    (b) Find the highest common factor of three numbers.
    (c) Find the lowest common multiple of three numbers.

2. Use your procedures written in answer to (1) to find the highest common factor and lowest common multiple of 1024, 365, 432.

IMPLEMENTATION OF THE ABSTRACT DATA TYPE BAG

The abstract data type bag consists of a collection of items. We have already implemented the abstract data type list, which consists of a sequence of items: we could base our implementation of the type bag on that of the list. This will impose an ordering on the items in the bag, but one which the user need not be aware of: to the user, a bag is still an unordered collection of items. Therefore the access procedures which we will use for our implementation are:

```
PROCEDURE Empty ( ) : Bag ;
(* Postcondition: returns an empty Bag *)

PROCEDURE IsEmpty ( B : Bag ) : BOOLEAN ;
(* Postcondition: returns TRUE if B is empty, otherwise
    FALSE *)

PROCEDURE Head ( B : Bag ) : InfoType ;
(* Postcondition: returns the item which is the first in
    the bag *)

PROCEDURE Tail ( B : Bag ) : Bag ;
(* Postcondition: returns a bag which consists of the items
    in B other than the first *)
```

Since the order in which the member values of the bag are held is unimportant we can build the list simply by adding new members to the head of the list. So the function which will insert an item into a bag is actually identical to the function Cons which we used to insert an item into a list. We will rename the procedure Insert:

```
PROCEDURE Insert ( I : InfoType ; B : Bag ) : Bag ;
(* Postcondition: returns a bag containing the items in B
    and I *)

VAR
    Temp : Bag ;

BEGIN
    NEW ( Temp ) ;
    Temp^.Info := I ;
    Temp^.Next := B ;
    RETURN Temp
END Insert ;
```

Using these procedures we can now implement the access procedures: Contains, Remove, Union, Intersection, Difference, Size, and procedures which depend on the type of the items, such as a procedure to print the contents of a bag. We model each on the algebraic specification which was given earlier.

We start with the procedure Contains, the specification of which is given by:

3. Contains (i, Empty ( )) = FALSE
4. Contains (j, Insert (i, b)) = *if* i = j *then* TRUE *else* Contains (j, b)

Unfortunately we cannot use the procedure Insert when we are implementing Contains, because we do not know the names of the items which are in the bag and we have no means of extracting an arbitrary item from a bag. However, what we can do is to use the selector functions Head and Tail to select a particular item and the rest of the bag respectively. The specification then leads us to the procedure below:

```
PROCEDURE Contains( I : InfoType ; B : Bag ) : BOOLEAN ;
(* Precondition: receives an item I and a bag B
   Postcondition: returns TRUE if I is in B, otherwise
   FALSE *)

BEGIN
    IF IsEmpty( B ) THEN
        RETURN FALSE
    ELSIF I = Head ( B )THEN
        RETURN TRUE
    ELSE
        RETURN Contains( I, Tail ( B ) )
    END
END Contains ;
```

The procedure can be explained as follows: if the bag is empty the item is not in the bag. If the item is the first in the bag, then the procedure is TRUE, otherwise we must determine whether the item is contained in the rest of the bag.

The specification of the procedure Remove is given by:

5. Remove (i, Empty ( )) = Empty ( )
6. Remove (j, Insert (i, b)) = *if* i = j *then* b
                              else Insert (i, Remove (j, b))

Again, we can use the functions Head and Tail to implement this procedure as shown below. The correspondence between the specification and the procedure is straightforward and obvious.

```
PROCEDURE Remove( I : InfoType ; B : Bag ) : Bag ;
(* Precondition: receives an item I and a bag B
   Postcondition: returns a bag which contains all
   the items of B but with one less copy of I if I was
   present in B, otherwise return B *)

BEGIN
    IF IsEmpty( B ) THEN
        RETURN B
    ELSIF I = Head (B) THEN
        RETURN Tail (B )
    ELSE
        RETURN Insert( Head (B), Remove( I, Tail(B)) )
    END
END Remove ;
```

Now consider the procedure Union, the specification of which is given by:

7. Union (b, Empty ( )) = b
8. Union (b, Insert (i, c)) = Insert (i, Union (b, c))

Using Head and Tail we can immediately implement this as shown below:

```
PROCEDURE Union( B1, B2 : Bag ) : Bag ;
(* Precondition: receives two bags B1 and B2
Postcondition: returns their union including repetitions *)

BEGIN
    IF IsEmpty( B2 ) THEN
        RETURN B1
    ELSE
        RETURN Insert ( Head ( B2 ), Union ( B1, Tail (B2)))
    END
END Union ;

For the procedure Intersection, we have:
```

9. Intersection (b, Empty ( )) = Empty ( )
10. Intersection (b, Insert (i, c)) = if Contains (i, b) then
                                   Insert (i, Intersection (Remove (b, i), c))
                                   else Intersection (b, c)

which translates to the procedure below:

```
PROCEDURE Intersection( B1, B2 : Bag ) : Bag ;
(* Precondition: receives two bags B1 and B2
    Postcondition: returns the bag of all items of B1 which
    are also in B2. *)

BEGIN
    IF IsEmpty( B2 ) THEN
        RETURN Empty( )
    ELSE
        IF Contains( Head ( B2 ) , B1 ) THEN
            RETURN Insert (Head ( B2 ) ,
                Intersection ( Remove ( Head ( B2 ), B1 ),
                             Tail ( B2))
        ELSE
            RETURN Intersection ( B1, Tail ( B2 ))
        END ;
    END
END Intersection ;
```

The axioms for the procedure Difference are:

11. Difference (b, Empty ( )) = b
12. Difference (b, Insert (i, c)) = Remove (i, Difference (b, c))

which translates to:

```
PROCEDURE Difference ( B1, B2 : Bag ) : Bag ;
(* Precondition: receives two bags B1 and B2
   Postcondition: returns the bag of all items in B1 which
   are not in B2. *)

BEGIN
    IF IsEmpty( B2 ) THEN
        RETURN B1
    ELSE
        RETURN Difference (Remove( Head ( B2 ), B1 ), Tail
                         ( B2 )) ;
    END
END Difference ;
```

Finally, we have the procedure Size:

13. Size (Empty ( )) = 0
14. Size (Insert (i, b)) = 1 + Size (b)

which gives us the following:

```
PROCEDURE Size ( B: Bag) : CARDINAL ;
(* Precondition: receives a bag B
   Postcondition: returns the cardinality of B *)

BEGIN
    IF IsEmpty (B) THEN
        RETURN 0
    ELSE
        RETURN (1 + Size(Tail(B)))
    END
END Size ;
```

Note that these procedures would be very similar for the abstract data type set, the only differences being due to the fact that each item can only occur once in a set. The procedures Subset and AreEqual that we looked at earlier are also the same.

Dynamic implementation

The dynamic implementation may be identical to that of the abstract data type list given in Chapter 3. The declarations for the data structure would then be:

```
TYPE
    Bag = POINTER TO BagNode ;
    BagNode = RECORD
                    Element : InfoType ;
                    Next : Bag
              END ;
```

The implementation of the access procedures is also identical to those for the list. For example:

```
PROCEDURE Empty ( ) : Bag ;
(* Postcondition: returns an empty Bag *)

BEGIN
    RETURN NIL
END Empty ;

PROCEDURE IsEmpty ( B : Bag ) : BOOLEAN ;
(* Postcondition: returns TRUE if B contains items,
otherwise FALSE *)

BEGIN
    RETURN B = NIL
END IsEmpty ;
```

Characteristics of dynamic implementation

This implementation has the typical characteristics of all dynamic implementations:

(1) The amount of storage used is proportional to the actual number of components that exist in the data structure at any time.
(2) Storage of the pointers themselves imposes an overhead on the amount of storage used.
(3) Insertion of items is not restricted by the size of the data structure which has been declared.
(4) Due to the enforcement of linear search techniques, operations to remove an item or check an item for membership of a bag involve $O(n)$ comparisons, where n is the number of items in the bag.

Static implementation

The static implementation is also modelled on that of the list. The items will be held in an array:

```
CONST
    Max = 100 ; (* maximum number of items in bag *)

TYPE
    Bag = POINTER TO Node ;
    Node = RECORD
             Buffer: ARRAY [ 1..Max ] OF InfoType ;
             BagPtr : [ 1.. Max+1 ] ;
           END ;
```

As with static implementations discussed in earlier chapters, a pointer is used in the declaration of the type bag. This undermines the description of the implementation as static but is necessary so that the type bag can be declared as opaque and variables of type bag can be returned from functions.

Items could be inserted at the end of the existing bag (as in the static implementation of the list). However, storing the items of the bag in any arbitrary order means that once again we have to use a linear search through the members to implement the procedures to remove and check inclusion of an item. An alternative which is more efficient is to hold the members in ascending order of their values using a modified insert constructor function which performs its own search. Then we can use the *binary search* algorithm which is explained below to locate an item.

Binary search algorithm

The *binary search* algorithm is a particularly efficient search technique for data which are ordered. The algorithm uses a 'divide and conquer' approach which involves checking the value in the middle of the data sequence and then searching either to the left or the right of this value, depending on the value being searched for. We often use such a technique (in a modified form) when searching a telephone directory or dictionary: if the word at the top of a page precedes the one being sought we restrict subsequent searches to the later part of the dictionary, whereas if it succeeds it we only search the earlier part.

Often, the data to be searched are held in an array. For example, suppose we have an array of 8 integers, and we want to find the value '42' . We start by inspecting the middle element, that is, the (1+8) DIV 2 = 4th, and find it holds the value '7':

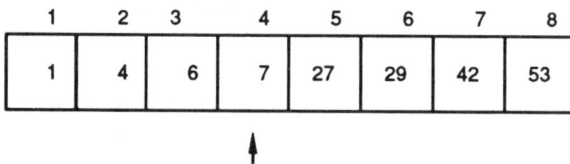

1	2	3	4	5	6	7	8
1	4	6	7	27	29	42	53

Since we know that 7 < 42, we now know to search the upper part of the array, and again we inspect the middle value of this part, i.e. the (5+8) DIV 2 = 6th value.

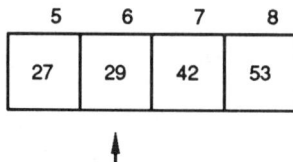

5	6	7	8
27	29	42	53

Now, since 29 < 42, we can again take the upper part of the remaining array and inspect the (7+8) DIV 2 = 7th value, this time with success:

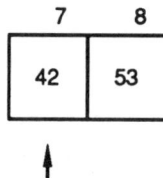

7	8
42	53

The binary search algorithm reduces the search time to $(O(\log_2(size))$, where size is the number of items in the bag. If the number of items is large this difference will be very significant. The following pseudocode implements this algorithm:

PROCEDURE BinarySearch (key, low, high : CARDINAL; A : ARRAY OF InfoType) :
CARDINAL ;

(* Precondition: 'key' is in the array 'A' of items stored in increasing order.
The bounds of A are 'low' and 'high'
Postcondition: returns the index of the position in A which contains 'key' *)

Check the value stored in the middle of the array
if this value = key *then*
   return the index of the middle
elsif key < middle value *then*
   Binary Search the lower half of the array
else Binary Search the upper half

Exercise 5.2

1. Write the procedure BinarySearch, the pseudocode for which is given above.

Characteristics of static implementation

1. The storage used is proportional to some predetermined maximum number of components, not the actual number that arises in any particular circumstance.
2. There is no storage overhead in storing individual member values.
3. Storing the components in order allows use of techniques such as binary search which improves the performance of operations such as removing an item or checking an item's presence.
4. Insertion and deletion may involve movement of existing items.

SUMMARY

The abstract data type *set* is a collection of an arbitrary number of distinct items (of the same type) together with a number of access procedures.

The type *set* exists in Modula-2 as a predefined (that is, built-in) type, and several access procedures are provided which support similar operations to the ones which we specified in the algebraic specification.

The cardinality of sets provided by Modula-2 may be restricted by the implementation. Some languages do not support the type set, in which case it must be implemented as an abstract data type by the programmer.

The type BITSET is provided by Modula-2 as a predefined set type.

The abstract data type bag is a collection of an arbitrary number of items (of the same type) which are *not necessarily distinct* together with a number of access procedures.

We used the type list to implement the type bag, partly because of the existence of the implementation for the type list and partly because it gave us the use of the selector functions Head and Tail, which we could use to extract an item from a set and return a depleted set respectively.

The *binary search* algorithm is a particularly efficient search technique for data which are ordered.

CHAPTER 6

The Abstract Data Type Tree: 1

INTRODUCTION

In the previous chapter it was stated that the type list has a linear ordering imposed on its items, in that each item in the list has at most one predecessor and one successor. Consequently the type list can be classed as *linear*. The abstract data type which we are going to discuss in this chapter, the type *binary tree* (which we will refer to simply as *tree*), is *non-linear* in that each item is allowed to have as many as two successors. Such abstract data types allow us to express more general relationships between the components of a compound structure.

We describe some of the properties of this type and introduce terminology which has come to be associated with it. The different methods of traversing a tree are also discussed together with examples of their applications. We show how to implement the higher-order functions Map and Reduce for the type tree, and finally we demonstrate how the type may be implemented. The definition of a binary tree is given below.

DEFINITION

The abstract data type *binary tree* is a finite set of nodes which is either empty or consists of a data item (called the *root*) and two disjoint binary trees (called the *left* and the *right subtrees* of the root), together with a number of access procedures.

An abstract data type which is more general than the type binary tree is an *n-ary* tree, in which an item may have more than two subtrees. This abstract data type will be discussed in Chapter 8. We will abbreviate the term 'binary tree' to 'tree' wherever this is not likely to lead to confusion. We start by giving the algebraic specification.

ALGEBRAIC SPECIFICATION

There are six access procedures for the abstract data type binary tree. Two of these are constructor functions which can be used to construct a tree; these are called EmptyTree and ConsTree. The predicate function which is used to test a tree to see if it is empty is called IsEmptyTree. There are three selector functions called Root, LeftTree and Right-Tree which select the value at the root, the left subtree and right subtree respectively.

117

Syntax of the access procedures

The procedure headings for the access procedures are contained in the definition module which is given below.

```
DEFINITION MODULE Trees;

FROM Items IMPORT InfoType ;

TYPE
    Tree ; (* an opaque type - see implementation module for
                                                        details *)

PROCEDURE EmptyTree ( ) : Tree ;
(* Postcondition: Returns an empty tree *)

PROCEDURE IsEmptyTree ( t : Tree ) : BOOLEAN ;
(* Postcondition: returns TRUE if tree t is empty,
    otherwise FALSE *)

PROCEDURE ConsTree ( i : InfoType; l, r : Tree ) : Tree ;
(* Precondition: takes an item i and two trees l and r
    Postcondition: returns a new tree which has item i at
    its root and l and r as its left and right subtrees
    respectively. *)

PROCEDURE Root ( t : Tree) : InfoType;
(* Postcondition : returns the data item at the root of the
    tree t *)

PROCEDURE LeftTree ( t : Tree) : Tree;
(* Postcondition : returns the left subtree of tree t*)

PROCEDURE RightTree ( t : Tree) : Tree;
(* Postcondition : returns the right subtree of tree t*)

END Trees.
```

Semantics of the access procedures

To derive the axioms for the access procedures we first note that a binary tree is either empty or of the form ConsTree (i, l, r), where i is an item and l and r are trees. The semantics of the access procedures are entirely analogous to those for the type list; for example, just as trying to find the head of an empty list results in an error, so does trying to find the root of an empty tree (axiom 3).

1. IsEmptyTree (EmptyTree ( )) = TRUE
2. IsEmptyTree (ConsTree (i, l, r)) = FALSE
3. Root (EmptyTree ( )) = error
4. Root (ConsTree (i, l, r)) = i
5. LeftTree (EmptyTree ( ))   = error
6. LeftTree (ConsTree (i, l, r)) = l
7. RightTree (EmptyTree ( )) = error
8. RightTree (ConsTree (i, l, r)) = r

APPLICATIONS

Non-linear data types are useful in simulating one-to-many relationships and can be used to implement the abstract data type set. Trees are often used during the syntax analysis stage of compilation to parse expressions, in which case they are referred to as *parse* trees.

Exercise

Using the access procedures, write a procedure which takes a tree as a parameter and returns the number of data items it contains.

Solution

The procedure heading is given below:

```
PROCEDURE NumberOfItems ( t : Tree ) : CARDINAL ;
(* Postcondition: returns the number of items in the tree
   t *)
```

We can specify the algorithm by considering the two forms a tree can take: a tree is either empty or of the form ConsTree (i, l, r), where i is a data item and l and r are trees. The first case is trivial:

NumberOfItems (EmptyTree()) = 0

In the second case we have

NumberOfItems (ConsTree (i, l, r)) = 1 + NumberOfItems(l) + NumberOfItems (r)

Translating this into Modula-2 we get:

```
PROCEDURE NumberOfItems ( t : Tree ) : CARDINAL ;
(* Postcondition: returns the number of items in the tree
   t *)

BEGIN
    IF IsEmptyTree ( t ) THEN
        RETURN 0
    ELSE
        RETURN ( 1 + NumberOfItems ( LeftTree ( t ) )
                        + NumberOfItems (RightTree ( t )))
    END
END NumberOfItems ;
```

NOTATION

There are several ways that we can represent a tree. The hierarchical representation that is used below clearly shows the data item at the root of the tree and the left and right subtrees (this

representation also gives the abstract data type its name). Note that the root is drawn at the top
of the tree.

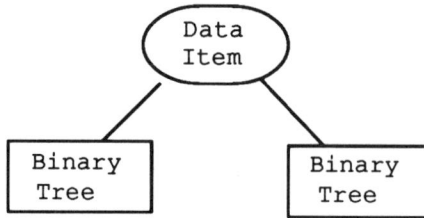

For example, a tree of characters is shown in figure 6.1, where the empty squares represent
empty trees (these are called *external* nodes, the other nodes being *internal*). By convention,
branches to empty trees are not usually shown. The nodes which do not have any successors
are called *leaves* or *terminal nodes*. For example, the leaves in the tree shown below contain
the characters 'K', 'F' and 'S'.

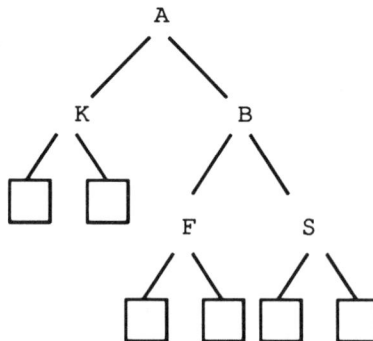

Figure 6.1

If we could 'flatten' the tree in figure 6.1 we could reduce the amount of space needed to
represent it. One way to do this is to represent a tree by a bracketed tuple with the root value
as first component, followed by left and right subtrees which also therefore appear in brackets.
Therefore the tree in figure 6.1 would be flattened to:

$(A, (K), (B, (F), (S)))$

As a second example, consider the expression

$x := y + z * 5$

This could be represented by figure 6.2 or by

$(:=, (x), (+, (y), (*, (z), (5))))$

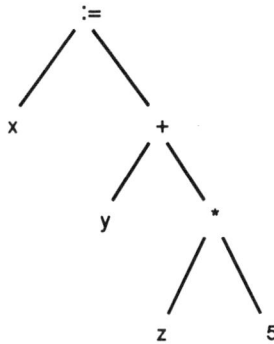

Figure 6.2

Definitions

A *path* of a tree is a sequence of root nodes of non-empty subtrees.

The *level* of a node in a tree is 1 if the node is the root of the tree, otherwise it is one more than the level of its parent.

For example, figure 6.3 shows the levels of all the nodes in a tree.

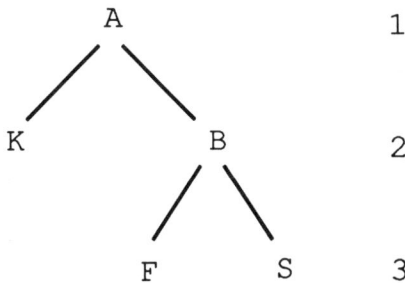

Figure 6.3

An important characteristic of a tree is its *height*. The *height* (or *depth*) of a tree is defined to be the maximum level of its nodes. An empty tree has height 0. More formally:

height (EmptyTree ( )) = 0
height (ConsTree (i, l, r)) = 1 + Max (height (l) , height (r))

where Max is a user-defined function which returns the maximum of two numbers. Thus, for example, the height of the tree in figure 6.3 is 3.

From this definition we can easily derive a function which takes a tree as parameter and returns its height:

```
PROCEDURE Height ( t : Tree ) : Tree ;
(* Postcondition: returns the height of the binary tree t *)
```

```
BEGIN
    IF IsEmptyTree ( t ) THEN
        RETURN 0
    ELSE
        RETURN ( 1 + Max ( Height ( LeftTree ( t )) ,
                           Height ( RightTree ( t ))))
    END
END Height ;
```

Similarly, the *shortest path* of a tree is defined as follows:

shortest path (EmptyTree ( )) = 0
shortest path (ConsTree (i, l, r)) = 1 + Min (shortest path (l) , shortest path (r))

where `Min` is a function which returns the minimum of two numbers.

Exercise 6.1

Write a function which takes a tree as parameter and returns its shortest path.

All the nodes shown in figure 6.3 are internal ones. The tree in figure 6.4 has been extended by replacing every empty subtree by an external node (shown by a rectangle). The *external path length* of an extended binary tree is the sum of the levels of all external nodes. For example, the external path length of the tree in figure 6.4 is 27.

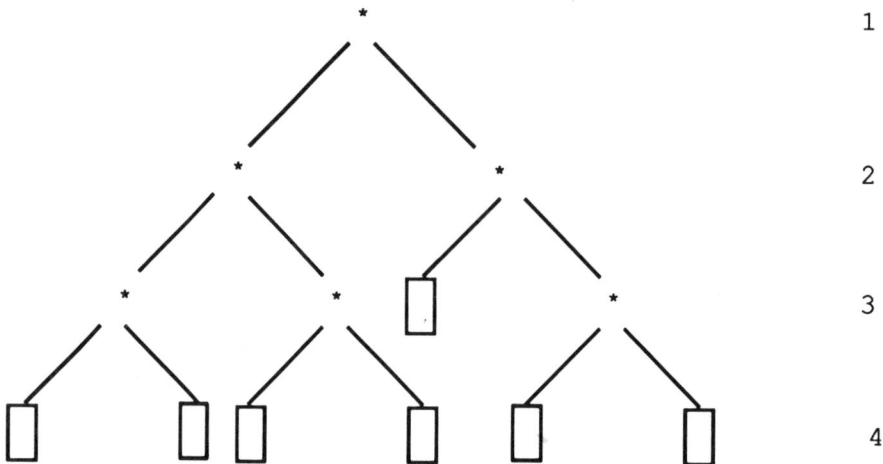

Figure 6.4 An extended binary tree

Similarly, the *internal path length* of a binary tree is the sum of levels of all the internal nodes. For example, the internal path length of the tree in figure 6.4 is 14.

Definition

A tree is said to be *perfectly balanced* (or *full*) if its height and its shortest path both have the same value.

Note that a *full* binary tree has the maximum possible number of nodes. That is, all its internal nodes have two children and so its leaves are all at the same level (figure 6.5).

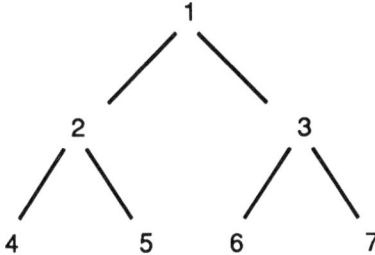

Figure 6.5 A full binary tree of height 3

The relationship between the number of nodes in a full binary tree and its height is given by the following theorem.

Theorem

The number of nodes in a perfectly balanced binary tree of height h ($h > 0$) is $2^h - 1$.

Proof

The proof is by induction on h. First we must prove the theorem for $h = 0$:

If $h = 0$ the tree is empty. An empty tree is perfectly balanced, and since $2^0 - 1 = 0$, the result holds for $h = 0$.

For the inductive hypothesis, we assume that for some $k > 0$ a full binary tree of height k has

$2^k - 1$ nodes

Now a perfectly balanced tree of height ($k + 1$) consists of a root and two subtrees which are both perfectly balanced trees of height k (by definition of a full tree). By the inductive hypothesis, the left subtree has $2^k - 1$ nodes and similarly for the right subtree. So the number of nodes in the tree is:

number of nodes in Left subtree + number of nodes in Right subtree + 1 (the root)

$$= 2^k - 1 + 2^k - 1 + 1 = 2 * (2^k - 1) + 1$$

$$= 2^{k+1} - 1$$

Therefore, by induction, the theorem is true for all h, that is, a full binary tree of height h has $2^h - 1$ nodes.

It follows that this is the maximum number of nodes that a binary tree of height h can have.

Corollary

A perfectly balanced tree with n nodes has a height of $h = \log_2(n+1)$.

Definitions

A tree is said to be *balanced* if the number of nodes in the left and right subtrees of every internal node do not differ by more than one.

A full tree is an example of a balanced tree. Note, however, that a balanced tree need not be full.

A *complete* tree of height h is a tree that is full down to level $h - 1$ with level h filled in from left to right. That is, a complete tree of height h has $2^h - 1$ nodes in the first $(h - 1)$ levels, and all non-empty leaves in level h are leftmost.

Thus complete trees are balanced. For example, the tree in figure 6.6(a) is a complete binary tree.

Note that, for a given number of nodes n, the tree which has the smallest height is a complete tree, and this has height h where

$$\log_2 (n + 1) - 1 < h \leq \log_2 (n + 1)$$

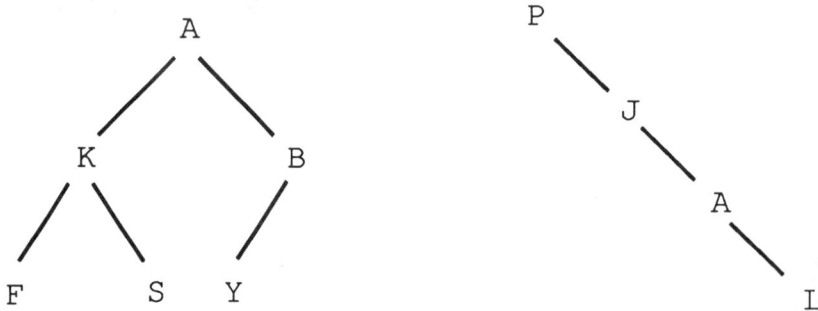

Figure 6.6 Two binary trees

Figure 6.6(b) shows an *imbalanced* tree (also called a *skewed, linear* or *degenerate* tree). It could be used to represent the abstract data type list, since it is a linear sequence in which each node has at most one subtree.

TREE TRAVERSAL

The process of visiting all the nodes in the abstract data type tree is called **tree traversal**. There are three methods which can be used to traverse a tree: *inorder, preorder* and *postorder*. For inorder, we visit the root *in between* visiting the subtrees. The left subtree is always visited first, then the root, and then the right subtree. For a preorder traversal the root is visited *before* visiting the left subtree and then the right subtree in preorder. Finally, postorder traversal means visiting the left subtree and then the right subtree in postorder and then *after* that, visiting the root.

Example

Visiting the nodes of the tree in figure 6.7 in each of these orders gives:

     1. Preorder (Root,Left,Right) 1 2 4 5 3 6 7
     2. Inorder   (Left,Root,Right) 4 2 5 1 6 3 7
     3. Postorder (Left,Right,Root) 4 5 2 6 7 3 1

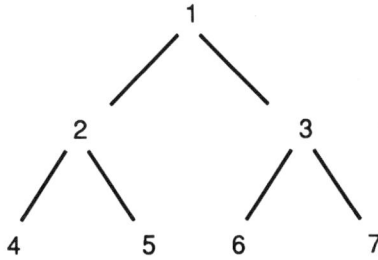

Figure 6.7

Using the description of inorder traversal given above, we can produce an algorithm. If the tree is empty then there is nothing to do. Otherwise, the tree has a left subtree, a root and a right subtree, which must be visited in that order. This gives us the procedure below:

```
PROCEDURE Inorder ( t : Tree ) ;
(* Postcondition: prints the items in the tree t in
     inorder *)

BEGIN
   IF NOT IsEmptyTree THEN
       Inorder ( LeftTree ( t )) ;
       WriteItem ( Root ( t ) )
       Inorder ( RightTree ( t ) )
   END
END Inorder ;
```

where WriteItem is a procedure which the implementor of the abstract data type has provided to output an item.

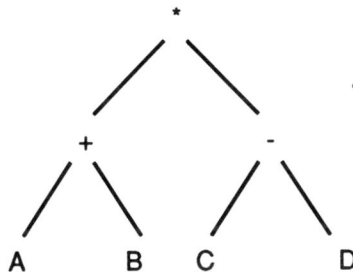

Figure 6.8

If the tree contains an arithmetic expression these methods of traversal correspond to prefix, infix and postfix notations. For example, consider the tree in figure 6.8.

Infix notation is the conventional way of writing expressions, with the operators in between the operands. The result of traversing the tree in figure 6.8 in inorder is:

$$(A + B) * (C - D) \tag{1}$$

However, infix notation requires parentheses to clarify expressions. If they were not used in the expression above, the multiplication might be assumed to apply to the operands B and C. Also, the order in which the operands and operators are written is not that in which the computer requires them, i.e. in which the operations are performed. With *postfix* notation each operator is written after the appropriate operands. For example, traversing the tree in figure 6.8 in postorder gives us:

$$A \ B + C \ D - \ *$$

This is equivalent to expression (1) above. Postfix is also known as *Reverse Polish*.

Similarly, *prefix* notation means writing the operator before the appropriate operands. Traversing the tree in figure 6.8 in preorder gives us the expression:

$$* + A \ B - \ C \ D$$

which is equivalent to both the expressions above. To transform it to infix notation, we start reading from right to left, and stop when an operator is found. The operator must be placed between the last two operands that were read. Using brackets to clarify the translation from prefix to infix, this would give:

$$* + A \ B \ (C - \ D)$$

and ... $$* (A + B) (C - \ D)$$

giving $$(A + B) * (C - \ D)$$

Exercises 6.2

1. Write the two procedures below:

```
PROCEDURE Preorder ( t : Tree ) ;
(* Postcondition: prints the items in the tree t in
    preorder *)


PROCEDURE Postorder ( t : Tree ) ;
(* Postcondition: prints the items in the tree t in
    postorder *)
```

2. Write down the result of traversing the tree below in inorder, preorder and postorder.

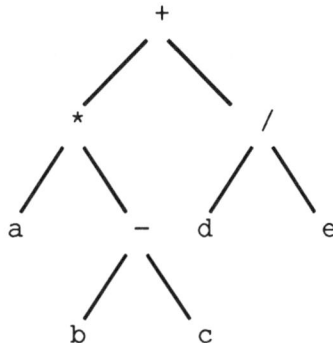

HIGHER-ORDER FUNCTIONS

In the same way that we developed higher-order functions for the abstract data type list, we can write them for the abstract data type tree. For example, suppose we wish to apply some function to every item in a tree; if the items are numbers, we may want to double every item, or triple it, or increment every item by one. We proceed as we did when when we discussed higher-order functions earlier, by declaring a procedure type which is a function of one argument:

```
TYPE
    Monadic = PROCEDURE ( InfoType ) : InfoType ;
```

Then we can write the higher-order function Map, which takes any monadic function and a tree and returns a tree in which the function has been applied to each item of the tree. A tree is either empty or it has a root and two subtrees (which may be empty). If the tree (T) is empty then there is nothing to do:

```
IF IsEmptyTree ( T ) THEN
    RETURN T
```

Otherwise, we must apply the function (called F below) to the root of the tree:

```
F ( Root ( t ))
```

and we must do this for the nodes in the left and right subtrees as well:

```
Map ( F, LeftTree ( t )), Map ( F, RightTree ( t ))
```

and then rebuild the tree using ConsTree:

```
RETURN ConsTree ( F ( Root ( t ) ), Map ( F, LeftTree
                    ( t )),Map ( F, RightTree ( t )))
```

This leads us to the function below:

```
PROCEDURE Map ( F : Monadic ; T : Tree ) : Tree ;
(* Precondition: takes a tree and a monadic function
   Postcondition: returns a tree in which the function has
   been applied to every item. *)

BEGIN
   IF IsEmptyTree ( T ) THEN
      RETURN T
   ELSE
      RETURN ConsTree ( F ( Root ( t ) ), Map ( F, LeftTree
                                                     ( t )),
                              Map ( F, RightTree ( t )))
   END
END Map ;
```

For example, suppose we have the tree of cardinal numbers below:

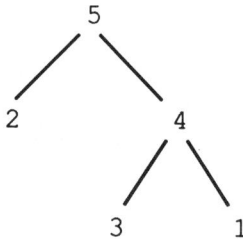

Following the notation introduced at the beginning of the chapter, we can represent this tree in the flattened form:

$$(5, (2), (4, (3), (1)))$$

If we wanted to increment every value in the tree then we would need a monadic function, which we have called Inc:

```
PROCEDURE Inc ( n: CARDINAL ) : CARDINAL ;
(* Postcondition: returns the increment of the argument n *)

BEGIN
     RETURN n + 1
END Inc;
```

(*Note*: We are not able to use the intrinsic function SUCC which is provided by the language because we are going to pass Inc as a parameter to the higher-order function Map, and built-in functions cannot be passed as parameters to higher-order functions.)

Now we can rewrite a call to increment every value in the tree:

Map (Inc, (5, (2) , (4, (3), (1))))
→ ConsTree (Inc (5), Map (Inc, (2)), Map (Inc, (4, (3), (1))))
→ ConsTree (6, ConsTree (Inc (2), Map (Inc, EmptyTree),
   Map (Inc, EmptyTree)), ConsTree (Inc (4), Map (Inc, (3), Map (Inc, (1))))
→ ConsTree (6, ConsTree (3, EmptyTree, EmptyTree),
                               ConsTree (5, Map (Inc, (3)), Map (Inc, (1))))
→ ConsTree (6, (3), ConsTree (5, ConsTree (Inc (3), EmptyTree, EmptyTree)),
                               ConsTree (Inc (1), EmptyTree, EmptyTree))
→ ConsTree (6, (3), ConsTree (5, (4), (2)))
→ (6, (3), (5, (4), (2)))

which is the flattened form of the tree below:

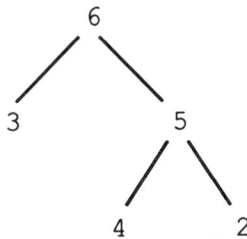

Similarly, we can write a higher-order function Reduce which takes all the values in a tree and reduces them to a single value. Suppose that we wish to reduce all the values to a single value of type CARDINAL. For this we need to declare a dyadic procedure type. This can be done as shown below:

```
TYPE
    Dyadic = PROCEDURE ( InfoType, CARDINAL ) : CARDINAL ;
```

This function will take an item of type InfoType and a cardinal number and return a cardinal. For example, the function below is of type Dyadic:

```
PROCEDURE DyadicInc ( i : InfoType; n: CARDINAL ) :
                                        CARDINAL ;
(* Postcondition: returns the increment of its second
   parameter *)

BEGIN
    RETURN n + 1
END DyadicInc;
```

If we apply this function to each node of a tree in turn, with an initial value for n of 0, then the final result will be the number of nodes in the tree.

There are several ways to write the function Reduce. A tail-recursive version is shown below. The function takes a dyadic function, F, a tree, T, and uses the parameter b to accumulate the result. The function can be derived by considering the two forms a tree can take: a tree is either empty or it consists of a root and two subtrees. If the tree is empty then we simply return the base case:

```
IF IsEmptyTree ( T ) THEN
    RETURN b
```

Now suppose that the tree is not empty. We must apply the function F to the value at the root of the tree and the value we have obtained by applying the function Reduce to (say) the right subtree.

```
F( Root ( T ), Reduce ( F, RightTree( T ), b))
```

Then we must also reduce the left subtree, using the value obtained by reducing the rest of the tree as the base case. (The order in which the subtrees are reduced is immaterial.) This gives us:

```
RETURN Reduce ( F, LeftTree ( T ), F( Root ( T ),
                          Reduce ( F, RightTree( T ), b)))
```

The right subtree is reduced first, then the root and finally the left subtree.

```
PROCEDURE Reduce ( F: Dyadic; T : Tree ; b: CARDINAL )
                                    :  CARDINAL ;
(* Precondition: takes a tree T, a dyadic function F and
    a base case b
    Postcondition: returns a tree in which the function F
    has been applied to the base case and every item. *)

BEGIN
    IF IsEmptyTree ( T ) THEN
        RETURN b
    ELSE
        RETURN Reduce ( F, LeftTree ( T ), F( Root ( T ),
                          Reduce  (  F, RightTree( T ), b)))
    END
END Reduce;
```

For example, suppose that F is the function DyadicInc which we had earlier and suppose we have the tree below, which can be written as (a, (b), (d)).

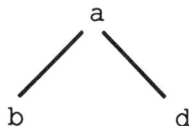

Let us rewrite a call to Reduce for this tree, the function DyadicInc and a base case of 0:

Reduce (DyadicInc, (a, (b), (d)), 0)
→ Reduce (DyadicInc, (b), DyadicInc ((a), Reduce (DyadicInc, (d), 0)))
→ Reduce (DyadicInc, (b), DyadicInc ((a), Reduce (DyadicInc, ( ),
  DyadicInc ((d), Reduce (DyadicInc, ( ), 0)))))
→ Reduce (DyadicInc, (b), DyadicInc ((a), Reduce (DyadicInc, ( ),
  DyadicInc ((d), 0))))
→ Reduce (DyadicInc, (b), DyadicInc ((a), Reduce (DyadicInc, ( ), 1)))
→ Reduce (DyadicInc, (b), DyadicInc ((a), 1))
→ Reduce (DyadicInc, (b), 2)
→ Reduce (DyadicInc, ( ), DyadicInc ((b), Reduce (DyadicInc, ( ), 2)))
→ Reduce (DyadicInc, ( ), DyadicInc ((b), 2))
→ Reduce (DyadicInc, ( ), 3)
→ 3

which is the number of items in the tree.

Another way to define Reduce is given below. This reduces the right subtree to a single value, then reduces the left subtree, using this value as the base case, and finally applies the dyadic function to the value at the root and the result of the reduction.

```
PROCEDURE Reduce ( F: Dyadic; T : Tree ; b: CARDINAL )
                                        : CARDINAL ;
(* Precondition: takes a tree T, a dyadic function F and
   a base case b
   Postcondition: returns a tree in which the function F
   has been applied to the base case and every item. *)

BEGIN
    IF IsEmptyTree ( T ) THEN
        RETURN b
    ELSE
        RETURN F( Root ( T ), Reduce ( F,
                    LeftTree ( T ), Reduce ( F, RightTree
                                ( T ), b )))
    END
END Reduce;
```

Exercises 6.3

1. Rewrite the call Reduce (DyadicInc, (a, (b), (d)), 0) using the second form of Reduce .
2. Assuming that the function f is triadic, write a symmetrical Reduce function by reducing both subtrees independently and then applying the reducing function to the results.

IMPLEMENTATION OF THE ABSTRACT DATA TYPE TREE

We will now look at possible implementations of the access procedures for the binary tree. As usual, there is a choice of implementation methods: dynamically, using pointer variables, or statically, using an array. We will concentrate on a dynamic implementation as this is simplest and, in general, more useful.

Dynamic implementation

Each node in a tree consists of a data item, a pointer to the left subtree and a pointer to the right one. This suggests the use of a record with three fields:

```
TYPE
   Tree = POINTER TO Node ;

   Node =  RECORD
              Value : InfoType ;
              Left, Right : Tree
           END ;
```

where InfoType has been imported from the module in which it is defined.

The implementation of two binary trees of characters using this data structure is shown in figure 6.9.

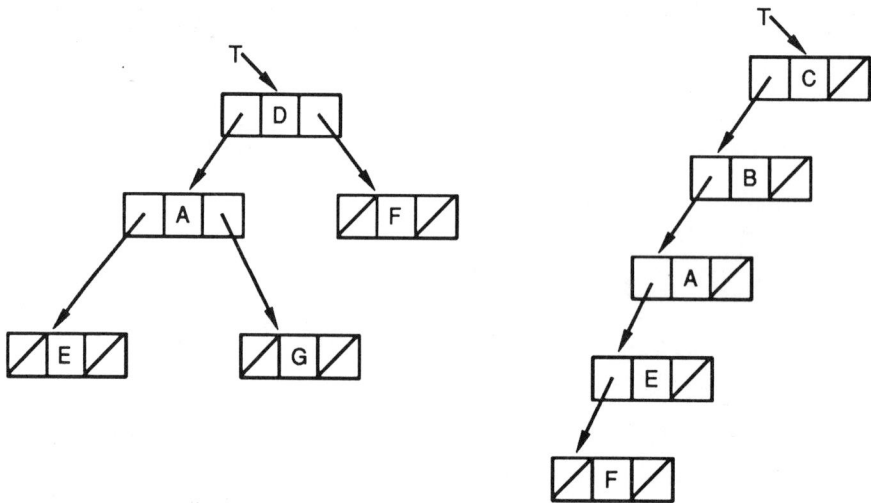

Figure 6.9 Two binary trees

We can now implement the access procedures, making sure that they satisfy the algebraic specification. The procedure EmptyTree simply needs to return a pointer which does not point to anything, that is, NIL.

```
PROCEDURE EmptyTree () : Tree ;
(* Postcondition: returns an empty tree *)

BEGIN
   RETURN NIL
END EmptyTree;
```

So the predicate procedure IsEmptyTree just needs to test whether a tree t is a null pointer:

```
PROCEDURE IsEmptyTree (t : Tree) : BOOLEAN;
(* Postcondition: returns TRUE if t is empty, otherwise
   FALSE *)

BEGIN
    RETURN (t = NIL)
END IsEmptyTree;
```

We can see that the boolean-valued expression IsEmptyTree (EmptyTree ( )) is true, whereas IsEmptyTree (ConsTree (i, l, r)) is false, verifying two of the axioms given in the specification.

The procedure ConsTree takes two trees and an item and produces a new tree by inserting the item at the root and using the two trees as its left and right subtrees. We only have to create one new node for the item by means of a call to NEW. We insert the new item in the Value field of this node and make the node's Left and Right fields point to the two trees which were passed in as parameters.

```
PROCEDURE ConsTree ( i : InfoType; l , r : Tree ) : Tree ;
(* Postcondition: returns a tree which has i at its root
       and l, r as its left and right subtree respectively *)

VAR Temp : Tree;

BEGIN
    NEW(Temp);
    WITH Temp^ DO
        Value := i;
        Left := l;
        Right := r
    END;
    RETURN Temp
END ConsTree;
```

Note that we have created a new tree with only one call to NEW. So the number of memory cells which have been allocated is only one more after a call to ConsTree than it was before.

The procedure Root returns the item at the root of the tree. For example, the root of the tree (A, (B), (C, (D), (E))) is the item 'A'.

The semantics specified that trying to find the root of a tree which is empty should be an error, and so we ensure that this is the case in the first part of the procedure by generating an error message and terminating the program. Otherwise we simply return the item which is in the Value field of the node pointed to by the tree t. To verify axiom 4, Root (ConsTree (i, l, r)) = i, we note that ConsTree assigns the item i to the Value field of the node at the root of the tree and Root returns the contents of the Value field of the tree which is passed to it.

```
PROCEDURE Root (t : Tree) : InfoType;
(* Postcondition: returns the data item at the root of the
       tree t *)
```

```
BEGIN
    IF IsEmptyTree(t) THEN
        WriteString("ERROR - can't find the Root of an empty
                                                     Tree");
        HALT
    ELSE
        RETURN t^.Value
    END
END Root;
```

The selector function LeftTree returns the left subtree of the tree which is passed to it. For example, the left subtree of the tree (A, (B), (C, (D), (E))) is the tree (B). The procedure leaves the original tree unchanged, as it is passed in as a value parameter. From the axioms for the procedure we know that trying to find the left subtree of an empty tree should result in an error, and, as usual, this is the first thing that we check. Otherwise all we have to do is to return a pointer to the Left field of the node.

```
PROCEDURE LeftTree (t : Tree) : Tree;
(* Postcondition: returns the left subtree of t *)

BEGIN
    IF IsEmptyTree(t) THEN
        WriteString("ERROR - can't take LeftTree of an empty
                                                     tree");
        HALT
    ELSE
        RETURN t^.Left
    END ;
END LeftTree;
```

By observation, we see that LeftTree returns the Left field of the node at the root of the tree, and so the result of LeftTree (ConsTree (i, l, r)) is the tree l, which verifies axiom 6.

The role of the procedure LeftTree is similar to that which Tail has in the implementation of the type List. The procedure Tail returns a pointer to the second node in a list, and the procedure LeftTree returns a pointer to the left subtree in the tree. No extra memory cells are needed by the procedure.

The procedure RightTree is identical except for returning the Right field of the node instead of the Left.

```
PROCEDURE RightTree (t : Tree) : Tree;
(* Postcondition: returns the right subtree of t *)

BEGIN
    IF IsEmptyTree(t) THEN
        WriteString("ERROR- can't take RightTree of an empty
                    tree");
        HALT
    ELSE
        RETURN t^.Right
    END ;
END RightTree;
```

Note that with this implementation the amount of space used is proportional to the number of ConsTree operations that we perform, since this is the only access procedure in which there is a call to NEW. ConsTree causes one new memory cell to be allocated for use.

One disadvantage of the dynamic implementation is that memory is allocated at run time and nodes must always be accessed indirectly (that is, each node is accessed via a pointer variable which gives the node's address in memory).

Static implementation of a binary tree

We will discuss two static implementations: first, using an array (in which the links or 'pointers' to the subtrees are implicit) and then using an array of records, in which integers are used to point to the subtrees.

An elegant implementation for the binary tree results from numbering the nodes sequentially, starting with the root as 1, and numbering from left to right at successive levels (figure 6.10).

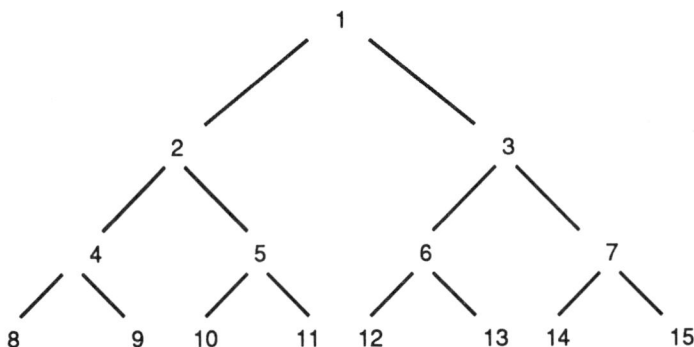

Figure 6.10 Full binary tree of depth 3 with sequential node numbers

We then use these numbers to index an array which will have 'gaps' in it if the tree is not full. The value in the root of the left child of Tree [i] is stored in Tree [2i], and of the right child in Tree [2i+1]. Also, the branches of the tree do not have to be stored at all. However, this can be a very wasteful implementation in terms of space if the tree is not complete. There is also the obvious disadvantage of a static implementation, that is, the constraint on the number of items that can be held in the tree (see figure 6.11).

The declaration for such a sequential implementation of a binary tree containing items of type InfoType is:

```
TYPE Tree = ARRAY [ 1 .. Max ] OF InfoType ;
```

Alternatively, we could use an array of records. Each record has three fields, which correspond to the value at a node and the positions in the array of its left and right subtrees. This implementation is similar to the cursor-based implementation which was discussed for the type list.

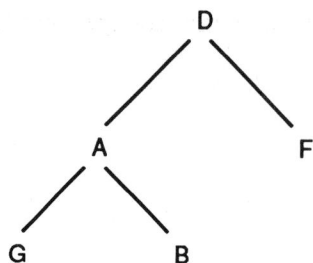

1	D
2	A
3	F
4	G
5	B

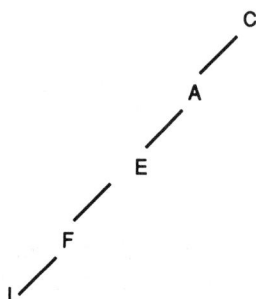

1	C
2	A
3	-
4	E
5	-
6	-
7	-
8	F
9	-
	-
16	L

Figure 6.11   Static implementations of a binary tree

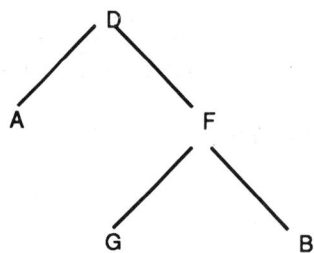

Tree

	Item	Left-Tree	Right-Tree
1	D	2	3
2	A	0	0
3	F	4	5
4	G	0	0
5	B	0	0
6			
⋮			

Implementation

Figure 6.12

Figure 6.12 assumes that the root is stored in the first array location and empty subtrees are indicated by the number 0.

The declarations that are needed are:

```
TYPE
    TreeSize = 100 ; (* this limits the size of the tree *)
    TreePtr = [ 0 .. TreeSize ] ;
    Node = RECORD
              Item : InfoType ;
              Left, Right : TreePtr ;
           END ;
    Tree = TreePtr ;
```

and we can declare an array of nodes ready for use:

```
VAR
    Nodes : ARRAY [ 1..TreeSize ] OF Node ;
```

The items can be stored in any order in the array (other than the root which is stored in the first location), since they will be explicitly referenced by their parent node. This implementation simulates the dynamic implementation in that each subtree can be located by looking for the node which is indicated by the parent node.

Static implementations have the disadvantage that the size allowed for the array may prove to be either too large (wasting storage) or too small (causing an overflow error). Also, each time a node is accessed the address of the array and the address of the node must be calculated, which may affect execution time. The implementation of the access procedures is left as an exercise for the reader.

SUMMARY

The abstract data type *binary tree* is a finite set of nodes which is either empty or consists of a data item (called the *root*) and two disjoint binary trees (called the *left* and the *right subtrees* of the root) together with a number of access procedures.

A *path* of a tree is a sequence of root nodes of non-empty subtrees.

The height of a tree is defined:

height (EmptyTree) = 0
height (Constree (i, l, r)) = 1 + Max (height (l) , height (r))

The *shortest path* of a tree is defined by:

shortest path (EmptyTree) = 0
shortest path (ConsTree (i, l, r)) = 1 + Min (shortest path (l) , shortest path (r))

A tree is *balanced* if the number of nodes in the left and right subtrees of every internal node do not differ by more than one.

A tree is said to be *perfectly balanced* if its height and its shortest path both have the same value.

The *level* of a node is 1 if the node is the root of the tree, otherwise it is defined to be one more than the level of its parent.

A *complete* tree of height h is a tree that is full down to level $h - 1$ with level h filled in from left to right.

There are three methods which can be used to traverse a tree: *inorder*, *preorder* and *postorder*.

Trees are important because they provide natural representations for many sorts of sets of data that occur both in life generally and arising from computing applications. Consequently they are useful for solving a wide variety of problems.

The type tree can be implemented either statically or dynamically. As with all abstract data types, since the implementation details are hidden from any module that imports the type Tree, the user will be unaware of the implementation and so is forced to use the access procedures to manipulate the tree. This guarantees the behaviour and integrity of the abstract data type.

CHAPTER 7

The Abstract Data Type Tree: 2

INTRODUCTION

This chapter deals with binary trees which have some sort of ordering imposed on the values they contain. The first of these abstract data types that we are going to study is a particularly useful form of tree called a *binary search tree*, or simply *search tree*. This binary tree has an ordering imposed on the data it contains, and so can be used to sort data. We also discuss the type *heap*, and another method of sorting which is very efficient called a *heap sort*. Finally, a more general method of maintaining the balance of binary trees is discussed.

The binary search tree gets its name from the algorithm discussed in Chapter 5, which used an array to hold the set of items to be searched. Unfortunately, the implementation given in Chapter 5 has all the usual disadvantages of static implementations: the number of values which can be stored is determined at compile time, and insertion and deletion of values is difficult. One alternative is to use a list implemented dynamically. However, this would mean initially traversing the list to determine the number of elements, then traversing it again to find the middle element, and so on, which is rather inefficient. Another alternative is to make use of a binary tree to hold the pre-sorted data. Such a data type is called a binary search tree, and will be discussed next: operations to store and retrieve data using this data type are particularly efficient.

DEFINITION

The abstract data type *binary search tree* is a binary tree in which the nodes are ordered, together with a number of access procedures. The ordering imposed on the nodes is such that for each node, all values in its left subtree are less than the value in that node and all values in its right subtree are greater than the value in that node.

The values in the nodes may be numbers, in which case the ordering will be numerical, or characters, where the ordering will be alphabetical. For example, figure 7.1 shows a binary search tree of integers.

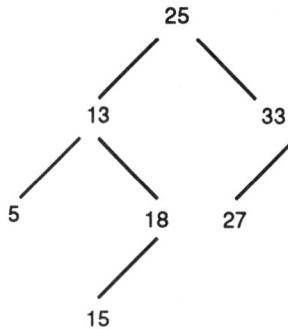

Figure 7.1 A binary search tree

Binary search trees are also called *ordered* trees. They are an important subclass of the abstract data type binary tree, since they enable us to search and sort data very efficiently. A value can be located by traversing the tree, taking either the left or right subtree, depending on whether the value being sought is less than or greater than that at the current root.

For example, to find the value '27' in the tree in figure 7.1 we first inspect the root and find that it holds '25'. Since 27 > 25, we now search the right subtree. The root of the right subtree holds the value '33', so we know to search its left subtree. Here we find the value we are looking for.

Theorem

In the worst case, the number of comparisons needed to find a particular value held in a binary search tree with n nodes is less than or equal to $\log_2 (n+1)$, if the tree is balanced.

This follows from the fact that the height of a balanced tree is less than or equal to $\log_2 (n+1)$, and since we always know which path to traverse, we never need to backtrack.

ALGEBRAIC SPECIFICATION

The algebraic specification of a binary search tree is very similar to that of a binary tree. The main difference is that the procedure ConsTree should no longer be visible to the user of the abstract data type since using it could create unordered trees. Instead we need:

```
PROCEDURE Insert ( i : InfoType ; t : Tree ) : Tree ;
(* Precondition: i is an item and t is a binary search tree
   Postcondition: returns a binary search tree with i
   inserted in the correct position *)
```

and we also need axioms to describe the semantics of this procedure:

Insert (i, EmptyTree ( )) = ConsTree (i, EmptyTree ( ), EmptyTree ( ))

Insert (i, ConsTree (j, l, r)) = *if* i = j *then* ConsTree (i, l ,r)
        elsif i < j *then* ConsTree (j, Insert (i, l), r)
        else ConsTree (j, l , Insert (i, r))

We can now go on to construct functions which use the access procedures.

Note that, due to the way that the items are ordered in a binary search tree, the smallest item in a non-empty tree is always the leftmost one. We can specify a procedure to locate the smallest item as below:

MinimumItem (ConsTree (i, l, r)) = *if* IsEmptyTree (l) *then* i
        else MinimumItem (l)

Similarly, we can easily specify a procedure to locate the largest item:

MaximumItem (ConsTree (i, l, r)) = *if* IsEmptyTree (r) *then* i
        else MaximumItem (r)

Exercise

Write a procedure which takes a binary search tree and an item and returns a binary search tree without the specified item.

Solution

If we find the item to be deleted at the root of the tree there are two simple cases. If the left subtree is empty we return the right subtree and, similarly, if the right subtree is empty we return the left. If neither subtree is empty, we must find some item to take the place of the item at the root. In doing so we must ensure that the tree remains a binary search tree. It can be seen by inspection that there are two items which are candidates for the replacement: the largest item in the left subtree and the smallest one in the right. The latter is referred to as the root's *inorder successor*, this being the item which succeeds the root when the tree is traversed in inorder. This is the item which we have (arbitrarily) decided to use. This leads us to the following specification for the algorithm:

```
PROCEDURE Remove ( i : InfoType ; t : Tree ) : Tree ;
(* Precondition: i is an item and t is a binary search
   tree
   Postcondition: returns a binary search tree without
   item i *)
```

If t is empty, then return an empty tree:

Remove (i, EmptyTree ( )) = EmptyTree ( )

If the item is at the root of the tree and the right subtree is empty (shown here by empty parentheses, ( )), then return the left subtree:

Remove (i, ConsTree (i, l, ( )) = l

Similarly, if the item is at the root of the tree and the left subtree is empty:

Remove (i, ConsTree (i, ( ), r) = r

If the item is at the root of the tree, then replace it by the minimum item in the right subtree (because this item is larger than all items in the left subtree and the smallest item in the right one) and remove this value from the right subtree:

Remove (i, ConsTree (i, l, r) = ConsTree (MinimumItem (r), l,
$\qquad\qquad\qquad\qquad$ Remove (MinimumItem (r), r)

If the item is not at the root, then remove it from whichever subtree contains it:

Remove (i, ConsTree (j, l, r) = if i < j *then* ConsTree (j, Remove (i, l), r)
$\qquad\qquad\qquad\qquad$ *else* ConsTree (j, l, Remove (i, r))

We can easily translate this into Modula-2:

```
PROCEDURE Remove ( i : InfoType ; t : Tree ) : Tree ;
(* Precondition: i is an item and t is a binary search tree
   Postcondition: returns a binary search tree without
   item i *)

BEGIN
    IF IsEmptyTree ( t ) THEN
        RETURN t
    ELSIF i = Root ( t ) THEN
        IF IsEmptyTree ( LeftTree ( t ) ) THEN
            RETURN RightTree ( t )
        ELSIF IsEmptyTree ( RightTree ( t ) ) THEN
            RETURN LeftTree ( t )
        ELSE
            RETURN ConsTree ( MinimumItem ( RightTree ( t )),
                                            LeftTree ( t ),
                Remove ( MinimumItem ( RightTree ( t )),
                                  RightTree ( t )))
        END
    ELSE
        IF i < Root ( t ) THEN
            RETURN ConsTree (Root ( t ), Remove (i, LeftTree
                                                    ( t )),
                                  RightTree ( t ))
        ELSE
            RETURN ConsTree ( Root ( t ), LeftTree,
                                  Remove ( i, RightTree ( t )))
        END
    END
END Remove ;
```

Exercise

Given the access procedures for the abstract data type binary tree, write an efficient program which returns a sorted sequence of items.

Solution

This problem can easily be solved by writing a procedure which returns a binary search tree from the given sequence and then flattening it into a list of items. The task of constructing a binary search tree is similar to that of sorting a list. We can use the procedure Insert to construct a binary search tree by starting with an empty tree and inserting items one at a time into the tree. Once the binary search tree has been constructed, the only task left is to print the nodes of the tree in the correct order. Note that the items in the left subtree precede the item at the root, whereas those in the right one succeed it. So to print the items in the tree we must use the inorder procedure which we looked at earlier.

Exercises 7.1

1. Write the procedure Insert, the heading and semantics of which were given earlier.

2. Write the procedure BuildTree, the heading for which is given below. (*Hint*: use the procedure Insert, and use t as an accumulating parameter.)

```
PROCEDURE BuildTree ( l : List ; t : Tree ) : Tree ;
(* Precondition: receives a list of items and a binary
      search tree
   Postcondition: returns a binary search tree *)
```

3. Prove that the answers to the first two exercises, together with the procedure Inorder, result in an ordered list of items. (*Hint*: use induction.)

4. Write the procedure below:

```
PROCEDURE Contains ( t : Tree ; key : InfoType ) : BOOLEAN ;
(* Precondition: takes a binary search tree and an item
   Postcondition: returns TRUE if key is in t, otherwise
      FALSE *)
```

5. Write a procedure which, given a binary search tree and an item of type InfoType, returns the subtree which has the item at its root or an empty subtree if the item is not present.

```
PROCEDURE FindTree ( t : Tree ; key : InfoType ) : Tree ;
(* Precondition: takes a binary search tree and an item
   Postcondition: returns the subtree which has the item
      at its root, or the empty tree if the item is not in
      the tree*)
```

6. Prove that the minimum height h of a tree with n nodes is:

$$\log_2 (n + 1) - 1 < h \leq \log_2 (n + 1)$$

Example

Write a program which accepts a list of words, some of which may be repeated, and returns the list sorted in alphabetical order, together with a count of the number of occurrences of each word. (This is called the *concordance* problem.)

Solution

As with the last exercise, one solution is to insert the words into a binary search tree as they are read, and then print the items in the tree using inorder. This time each item in the tree will consist of a word and a cardinal number which represents its frequency of occurrence. For example, figure 7.2, printed using inorder, gives:

(Arnold, 2) (Glinka, 1) (Haydn, 1) (Mozart, 1) (Schubert, 2)

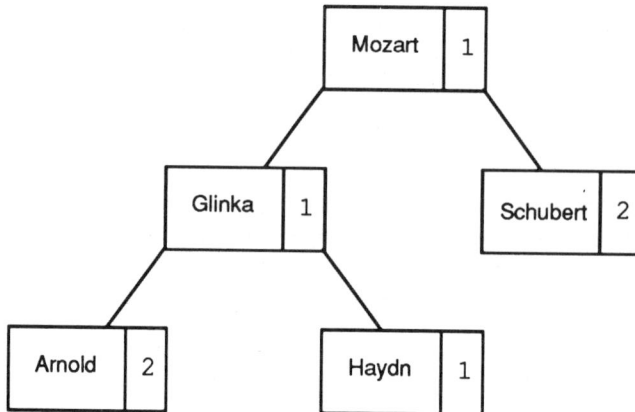

Figure 7.2

The declaration of `InfoType` must now allow each item to be a (word, number) tuple:

```
TYPE
    Word = ARRAY [ 1.. Max] OF CHAR ;

    InfoType = POINTER TO RECORD
                            Item : Word ;
                            Count : CARDINAL
                    END ;
```

Note: A pointer is used only to enable items of type `InfoType` to be returned from functions. `Max` is a user-defined constant which limits the maximum length allowed for a word.

When an item is first read its count field is initialized to one.

```
PROCEDURE ReadItem ( ) : InfoType ;
(* Postcondition: returns a node containing a word and a
    count of 1 *)
```

We will also need a procedure which will increment the count field of a node:

```
PROCEDURE IncCount ( i : InfoType ) : InfoType ;
(* Postcondition: increments the count associated with node
    i *)
```

We will need a boolean-valued procedure IsEqual which will take two nodes and return true if the words they contain are the same. The heading of the procedure is given below:

```
PROCEDURE IsEqual ( i, j : InfoType ) : BOOLEAN ;
(* Precondition: takes two nodes i and j
    Postcondition: returns TRUE if the items that they hold
    are equal *)
```

and the procedure Insert now has to deal with multiple occurrences of items:

```
PROCEDURE Insert ( i : InfoType ; t : Tree ) : Tree ;
(* Postcondition: returns a binary search tree which
    includes the node i if it was not previously in the
    tree, otherwise returns a tree with the count
    associated with i incremented *)
```

Exercise 7.2

Provide a solution to the concordance problem by implementing the procedures whose headings are given above.

We discussed the abstract data type queue earlier in the book, and one variation of it, the priority queue. This is a queue in which all items in the queue have an associated priority which is a cardinal number. For example:

$$((29, X), (25, Z), (24, Y))$$

where X, Y and Z stand for the items in the priority queue, 29, 24, and 25 for their respective priorities.

Items are removed from the front of the queue but must be inserted in such a way as to maintain the ordering of items in the queue. Consider the efficiency of inserting an item if a priority queue is implemented as a list. In the worst case the entire list may have to be traversed to find the correct position to insert the item. The efficiency of insertion is therefore O(N) (using the order notation introduced in Chapter 4), where N is the number of items in the queue. So a list implementation is not very efficient.

Alternatively, we could consider using a binary search tree to implement a priority queue. To insert an item we first have to search the tree to find where it should be placed. If the tree is balanced and there are N items in the tree this means inspecting, at most,

$$O (\log_2 N)$$

items, since this is the height of the tree. The delete operation is simpler, since we just delete the item which is furthest right in the tree, again involving O ($\log_2 N$) indirections (figure 7.3).

However, the efficiency of insertion depends on the height of the tree, and we cannot rely on a binary search tree remaining balanced. We will now discuss an abstract data type which is guaranteed to remain balanced, called a *heap*. The operations that we need to perform on a heap to keep it balanced are relatively simple compared with trying to maintain the balance of a binary search tree. We will then discuss two applications: an extremely efficient sorting algorithm called *heapsort* and the implementation of priority queues.

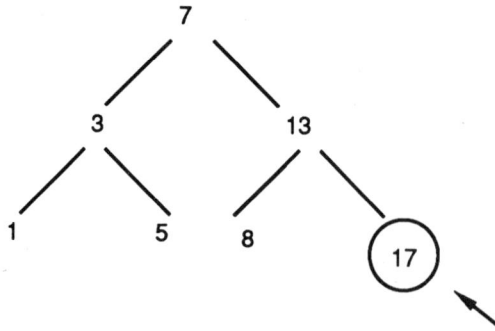

Figure 7.3 A binary search tree

THE ABSTRACT DATA TYPE HEAP

Definition

A *heap* is a complete binary tree which has an ordering imposed on its nodes such that the value at the root of the tree is greater than or equal to the values in both of its subtrees, and both subtrees are also heaps, together with a number of access procedures.

Algebraic specification

The algebraic specification of a heap is identical to that of a binary tree except that the procedure ConsTree should no longer be available to the user, but instead we need procedures which can be used to construct heaps.

Recall the definition of a *complete* binary tree: a complete binary tree of height h is a tree which is full down to level $h - 1$ with level h filled in from left to right. We can specify this more formally as below:

IsComplete (EmptyTree) = TRUE
IsComplete (ConsTree (i, l, r)) = *if* (Height (l) – Height (r)) <=1
                         and IsComplete (l) *and* IsComplete (r)
                         then TRUE
                         else FALSE

We can easily translate this into Modula-2:

```
PROCEDURE IsComplete ( t : Tree ) : BOOLEAN ;
(* Postcondition: returns TRUE if t is complete, otherwise
   FALSE *)

BEGIN
  IF IsEmptyTree ( t ) THEN
      RETURN TRUE
```

```
       ELSIF (Height ( LeftTree(t)) - Height ( RightTree(t))
                                           <=1 ) THEN
           RETURN (IsComplete(LeftTree(t)) AND IsComplete
                                      (RightTree(t)))
       ELSE
           RETURN FALSE ;
       END
   END IsComplete;
```

For example, the tree in figure 7.4 is complete. The numbers 1 to 6 indicate the order in which the items were inserted into the tree.

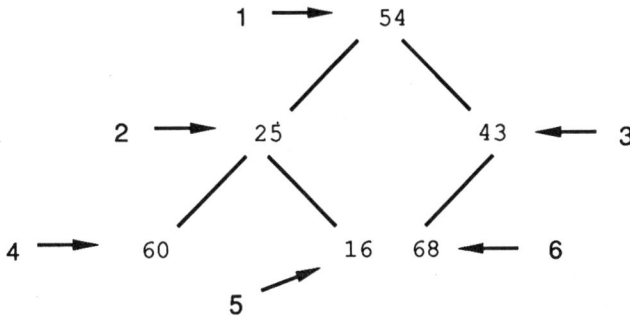

Figure 7.4

To construct a complete tree we create a tree which is full down to its last but one level, and filled from left to right in the lowest level. So we need a predicate function which returns true if a tree is full. A tree is full if it is empty or if the heights of its left and right subtrees are the same and they are both full. That is:

IsFull (EmptyTree) = TRUE
IsFull (ConsTree (i, l, r)) = *if* Height (l) = Height (r)
                                      and IsFull (l) *and* IsFull (r)
                                      then TRUE
                                      else FALSE

which, in Modula-2, is:

```
   PROCEDURE IsFull ( t : Tree ) : BOOLEAN ;
   (* Postcondition: returns TRUE if t is full, otherwise
      FALSE *)

   BEGIN
       IF IsEmptyTree ( t ) THEN
           RETURN TRUE
       ELSIF ( Height ( LeftTree(t)) = Height ( RightTree(t)))
           THEN
           RETURN (IsFull ( RightTree(t)) AND IsFull ( Left
                                              Tree(t)))
```

```
    ELSE
        RETURN FALSE ;
    END
END IsFull;
```

Of course, a heap can be empty (since an empty tree is complete). Figure 7.5 shows a heap of eight items.

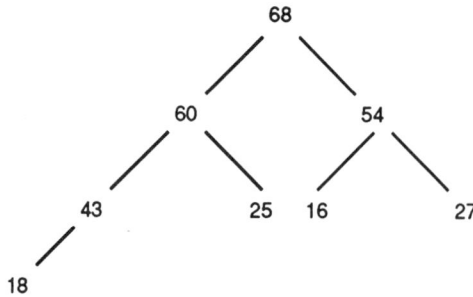

Figure 7.5 Heap of eight items

We must also provide a procedure which will insert an item into a complete binary tree in such a way that the resulting tree is complete. The procedure heading is given below:

```
PROCEDURE MakeComplete (i : InfoType ; t : Tree ) : Tree ;
(* Precondition: takes an item and a complete binary tree
   Postcondition: returns a complete binary tree *)
```

We can give the semantics for this procedure by considering the various forms the tree t may take. If t is empty, then we simply form a tree with i at the root and two empty subtrees:

MakeComplete (i, EmptyTree (t)) = ConsTree (i, EmptyTree( ), EmptyTree( ))

There are two situations in which we would insert an item into the right subtree: if the height of the left subtree is one greater than the height of the right and the left subtree is full, or if the two subtrees are of the same height and the right subtree is not full.

MakeComplete (i, ConsTree(j, l, r)) = *if* Height (l) = Height(r) +1 *and* IsFull(l)
                                     or Height (l) = Height(r) *and not* IsFull(r) *then*
                                     ConsTree (i, l, MakeComplete(i, r)))

Otherwise, we insert the item into the left subtree:

else ConsTree (j, MakeComplete (i, l), r)

Putting this together gives the procedure below:

```
PROCEDURE MakeComplete ( i : InfoType ; t : Tree ) : Tree ;
(* Precondition: takes an item and a complete binary tree
   Postcondition: returns a complete binary tree *)
```

```
BEGIN
   IF IsEmptyTree ( t ) THEN
      RETURN ConsTree (i, EmptyTree(), EmptyTree())
   ELSIF (( Height ( LeftTree(t)) = Height ( RightTree(t))
                                                        + 1)
      AND IsFull ( LeftTree(t))
      OR (( Height ( LeftTree(t)) = Height( RightTree(t)) )
      AND NOT IsFull ( RightTree(t)) THEN
      RETURN ConsTree(Root(t),LeftTree(t),
                              MakeComplete(i,RightTree (t)))
   ELSE
      RETURN ConsTree (Root(t), MakeComplete(i, LeftTree
                                                   (t)),
                                     RightTree(t))
   END
END MakeComplete ;
```

Given this procedure to return a complete binary tree, we will need a procedure which will take a complete tree and return a heap:

```
PROCEDURE BuildHeap ( t : Tree ) : Tree ;
(* Precondition: takes a complete binary tree
   Postcondition: returns a heap *)
```

Before we write this procedure, let us write one which takes an item and two trees which are heaps and returns a heap. The procedure's heading is given below:

```
PROCEDURE MakeHeap (i : InfoType ; l, r : Heap ) : Heap ;
(* Precondition: takes an item and two heaps which are such
   that height (l) - height (r) <=1
   Postcondition: returns a heap *)
```

The procedure BuildHeap, which will call this procedure, will check that the heights of the two trees satisfy the constraint given in the heading. The specification of the algorithm MakeHeap is explained below.

First, if l is empty, then r must be as well, because of the height constraint. So in this case we can simply return a tree with the item i at the root and two empty subtrees:

$$\text{MakeHeap} (i, (), ()) = \text{ConsTree} (i, l, r)$$

where the empty subtrees are denoted by open brackets, ( ).

Now if l is not empty but r is, then we must check i to find whether it is greater than the root of l, in which case we return the tree with i at its root. Otherwise we insert i into the left subtree of l, which must be empty because of the height constraint:

$$\text{MakeHeap} (i, l, ()) = \textit{if } i \geq \text{Root} (l) \textit{ then } \text{ConsTree} (i, l, r)$$
$$\textit{else } \text{ConsTree} (\text{Root} (l), \text{ConsTree} (i , (), ()), ())$$

If l and r are both non-empty, there are three possibilities: if i is greater than the items at the roots of both l and r then we return a tree formed with i at its root and l and r as its left and right subtrees:

MakeHeap (i, l, r) = *if* i > Root (l) *and* i > Root (r) *then* ConsTree (i, l, r)

Otherwise, if the item at the root of l is greater than that at the root of r, then form a tree with the root of l, the heap formed by calling MakeHeap with i and the two subtrees of l, and r:

elsif Root (l) ≥ Root (r) *then*
ConsTree (Root (l), MakeHeap (i, LeftTree (l), RightTree (l)), r)

Otherwise, do the same but with the root and subtrees of r:

else ConsTree (Root (r), l , MakeHeap (i, LeftTree (r), RightTree (r))

This gives us the following Modula-2 procedure:

```
PROCEDURE MakeHeap (i : InfoType ; l, r : Heap ) : Heap ;
(* Precondition: takes an item and two heaps which are such
   that height (l) - height (r) <= 1
   Postcondition: returns a heap *)

BEGIN
    IF IsEmptyTree (l) THEN      (* r must also be empty *)
       RETURN ConsTree ( i, l, r )
    ELSIF IsEmptyTree (r) THEN
       IF i >= Root ( l) THEN
          RETURN ConsTree ( i, l, r )
       ELSE
                             (* the subtrees of l must be
                                empty *)
          RETURN ConsTree ( Root   (l), ConsTree(i,
                                                  EmptyTree(),
                                                  EmptyTree()),r)
       END ;
    ELSIF (( i >= Root (l)) AND (i >= Root ( r ))) THEN
       RETURN ConsTree ( i, l, r )
    ELSIF Root ( l ) >= Root (r) THEN
       RETURN ConsTree ( Root(l), MakeHeap (i, LeftTree(l),
          RightTree(l)), r)
    ELSE
       RETURN ConsTree ( Root(r), l, MakeHeap (i,
                                                LeftTree(r),
          RightTree(r)))
    END
END MakeHeap ;
```

Now we can easily implement the procedure BuildHeap. We first have to ensure that the tree's subtrees are both heaps, and then we can call MakeHeap with the root of the tree and the two heaps as parameters. There is also a check to ascertain that the difference between the height of the left and right subtrees is no greater than one.

```
PROCEDURE BuildHeap ( t : Tree ) : Tree ;
(* Precondition: takes a complete binary tree
   Postcondition: returns a heap *)
```

```
BEGIN
   IF IsEmptyTree ( t) THEN
      RETURN t
   ELSIF (Height(LeftTree(t)) - Height ( RightTree (t))
                                              <= 1) THEN
      RETURN (MakeHeap ( Root(t), BuildHeap (LeftTree(t)),
                                  BuildHeap(RightTree(t))));
   END
END BuildHeap;
```

Example

As an example of how these access procedures work, suppose the items are numbers and consider forming a complete tree from the list: (54, 25, 43, 60, 16, 68) The procedure to insert a list of items into an empty tree is as follows:

```
PROCEDURE InsertItems ( l : List ; t : Tree ) : Tree ;
      (* Postcondition: returns a complete tree containing the
         items in the list l *)

BEGIN
   IF IsEmpty ( l ) THEN
      RETURN EmptyTree ( )
   ELSE
      RETURN InsertItems ( Tail (l), MakeComplete ( Head
                                              (l), t ))
   END
END InsertItems ;
```

We will rewrite a call to InsertItems with the list of numbers given above:

InsertItems ((54, 25, 43, 60, 16, 68), ( )) →
                    InsertItems ((25, 43, 60, 16, 68), MakeComplete (54, ( ))

Now, MakeComplete (54, ( )) → ConsTree (54, EmptyTree ( ), EmptyTree ( ))
                    → (54)

Therefore,
InsertItems ((25, 43, 60, 16, 68), MakeComplete (54, ( ))
                    → InsertItems ((25, 43, 60, 16, 68), (54))

Now, InsertItems ((25, 43, 60, 16, 68), (54))
                    → InsertItems ((43, 60, 16, 68), MakeComplete (25, (54))

And, MakeComplete (25, (54)) → ConsTree (54, MakeComplete (25, ( )), ( ))
                    →(54, (25), ( ))

Therefore,
InsertItems ((43, 60, 16, 68), MakeComplete (25, (54))
                    → InsertItems ((43, 60, 16, 68), (54, (25), ( ))

and so on:

InsertItems ((43, 60, 16, 68), (54, (25), ( ))
          → InsertItems (60, 16, 68), MakeComplete (43, (54, (25), ( ))
          → InsertItems (60, 16, 68), ((54, (25), (43))
          → InsertItems (16, 68), MakeComplete (60, (54, (25), (43))
          → InsertItems (16, 68), ((54, (25 , (60), ( )), (43))
          → InsertItems (68), MakeComplete (16, ((54, (25 , (60), ( )), (43))
          → InsertItems (68), ((54, (25 , (60), (16)), (43))
          → InsertItems ( ), MakeComplete (68, ((54, (25 , (60), (16)), (43))
          → InsertItems ( ), ((54, (25 , (60), (16)), (43, (68), ( )))
          → ((54, (25 , (60), (16)), (43, (68), ( )))

The reader may find it instructive to work through this example, drawing the tree at each stage
of the operation.
The complete tree which is the result of this process is shown in figure 7.6. To create a heap
from this tree, we can simply use the access procedure BuildHeap that we discussed earlier.

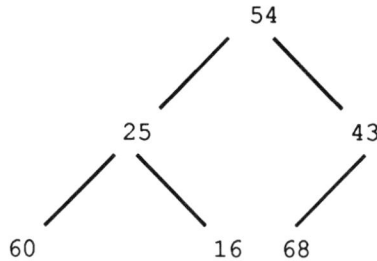

Figure 7.6

Buildheap (54, (25, (60), (16)), (43, (68), ( )))
        → MakeHeap (54, BuildHeap (25, (60), (16)), Buildheap (43, (68), ( )))
BuildHeap (25, (60), (16)) → MakeHeap (25, Buildheap (60), BuildHeap (16))
BuildHeap (60) → MakeHeap (60, ( ), ( ))
         → (60)
BuildHeap (16) → (16)
MakeHeap (25, Buildheap (60), BuildHeap (16)) → MakeHeap (25, (60), (16))
                     → Constree (60, MakeHeap (25, ( ), ( )), (16))
                     → Constree (60, (25), (16))
                     → (60, (25), (16))
which is the heap shown below:

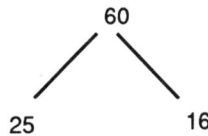

and,

Buildheap (43, (68), ( )) → MakeHeap (43, Buildheap (68), ( ))
                          → MakeHeap (43, (68), ( ))
                          → Constree (68, (43), ( ))
                          → (68, (43), ( ))

So the second heap is:

```
            68
           /
         43
```

MakeHeap (54, (60, (25), (16)), (68, (43), ( )))
→ ConsTree (68, (60, (25), (16)), MakeHeap (54, (43), ( )))
→ ConsTree (68, (60, (25), (16)), (54, (43), ( )))
→ (68, (60, (25), (16)), (54, (43), ( )))

The final heap is shown in figure 7.7.

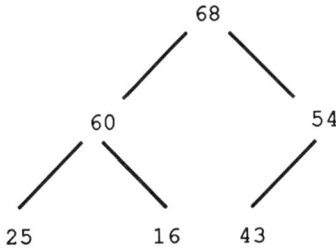

```
              68
            /    \
          60      54
         /  \    /
        25  16  43
```

Figure 7.7

We will now consider two applications of the type heap, first in a sorting algorithm and then as an implementation for priority queues.

HEAPSORT

An efficient sorting algorithm can be implemented by using a heap. The algorithm called *heapsort* (Williams 1964) has two stages:

1. Convert the data to be sorted into a heap.
2. Successively output the root and restructure the remaining tree into a heap.

Example

Suppose we wish to sort the list of numbers which we had earlier:

(54, 25, 43, 60, 16, 68)

Using the access procedures we insert these numbers into a complete tree and then restructure the resulting tree into a heap as shown above, resulting in the heap shown in figure 7.7.

To produce a sorted list, we output the root of the tree, leaving us with two trees which are both heaps. To reform the heap, we take an item from one of the heaps and use this item and the two heaps (one of which has just had an item removed) as the parameters for the procedure MakeHeap. The item which is easiest to remove is contained in the last node of the tree, i.e. the rightmost node on the lowest level. Removing this node leaves a tree which is still complete. For example, after removing the root from the heap in figure 7.7, we are left with the two heaps shown in figure 7.8.

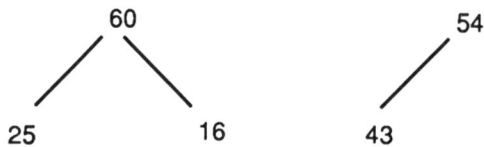

Figure 7.8

The last node of the tree in figure 7.7 contains '43', so this is the value that we use to reform the heap by calling MakeHeap:

MakeHeap (43, (60, (25), (16)), (54))
$\quad\quad\quad\quad\quad\quad\quad\quad$ → ConsTree (60, Makeheap (43, (25), (16)), (54))
$\quad\quad\quad\quad\quad\quad\quad\quad$ → ConsTree (60, ConsTree (43, (25), (16)), (54))
$\quad\quad\quad\quad\quad\quad\quad\quad$ → (60, (43, (25), (16)), (54))

This heap is shown in Figure 7.9.

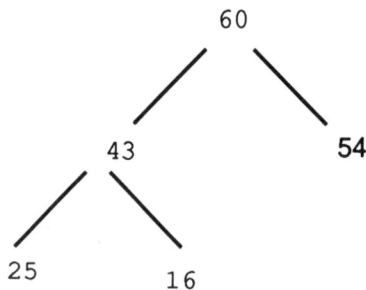

Figure 7.9

Exercises 7.3

1. Write the procedure FindLast, the heading for which is given below:

```
PROCEDURE FindLast ( t : Tree ) : InfoType ;
(* Precondition: takes a complete tree
   Postcondition: returns the rightmost item in the lowest
   level of the tree *)
```

2. Write the procedure `Remove`, which has the following heading:

```
PROCEDURE Remove (i: InfoType; t : Tree ) : Tree ;
(* Precondition: takes an item and a complete tree
   Postcondition: returns t without the item, or t if the
   item is not in t *)
```

3. Write the procedure `HeapSort`:

```
PROCEDURE HeapSort ( l : List, t : Tree ) : List ;
(* Precondition: takes an empty list and a heap
   Postcondition: returns an ordered list containing the
   items in the heap *)
```

How efficient is the heapsort algorithm?

A complete binary tree with n nodes has a height of O ($\log_2 n$). To create the heap in the first place, we have to call `MakeHeap` for every node. So the maximum number of comparisons and swaps for this stage is O ($n \log_2 n$). Each time a value is removed from the heap, again there will be O($\log_2 n$) comparisons, and this happens n times. So overall the efficiency of heapsort is O ($n \log_2 n$).

As this is the worst-case analysis, heapsort compares well with algorithms such as quicksort, which has O ($n \log_2 n$) performance on average, but O (n^2) performance in the worst case.

Priority queues

We can consider a heap as an implementation for a priority queue, where the ordering on the items is that of their priorities. For example, consider the heap in figure 7.10 in which the numbers represent priorities.

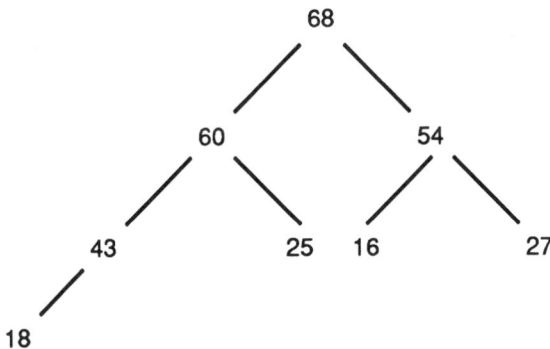

Figure 7.10

Removing an item from the front of the priority queue means removing the item with highest priority, i.e. that at the root of the tree. This will leave two disjoint heaps which will then have to be transformed back into a single one. As we discussed for the heapsort algorithm, the node which is easiest to remove is the last node of the tree (the node which contains the value '18' in figure 7.10). We can then use the access procedure `MakeHeap` which takes an item and two heaps and returns a heap.

Consider the efficiency of this algorithm. In the worst case the number of comparisons we will have to do is equal to the height of the tree. As was shown in the last chapter, the height of a complete binary tree is $\leq \log_2 (n + 1)$, where n is the number of nodes in the tree.

The fact that a heap is always balanced means that it is a very efficient implementation of a priority queue, although deletion is still faster with a binary search tree.

Implementation of heaps

As was mentioned earlier, the access procedures for the heap are based on those for the type tree, with additional constructor, selector and predicate functions already discussed. It should not matter how the type tree is implemented as long as the semantics of the access procedures meet their specification.

BALANCED SEARCH TREES

When discussing the use of trees for data management we have already seen how the efficiency of all the operations is of the order of the height of the tree. Consequently it is extremely important to try to ensure that the tree remains *balanced*. The kind of search tree that we are going to study next remains balanced in all situations and so can always be searched efficiently. A complete binary tree is balanced, but we wish to relax the restriction that states that the nodes must be filled in from left to right on the lowest level.

AVL trees: height-balanced trees

AVL trees, or *height-balanced trees*, are named after their inventors, Adelson-Velskii and Landis. In 1962 they gave the definition of height balance for binary search trees which is given below. They also described algorithms for inserting and deleting nodes without disturbing the balance of the tree. In nearly all cases the average path length of an AVL tree approximates that of a completely balanced binary search tree. Because the tree is height balanced, operations to retrieve, insert and delete are all proportional to $O(\log_2 N)$ time, where N is the number of nodes. The tree is still height balanced after the operation.

Definition

A tree is *height balanced* or *AVL* if it is empty or if both its left and right subtrees are height balanced and the difference in the heights of its left and right subtrees is less than or equal to one, i.e.

| height (left subtree) - height (right subtree) | ≤ 1

Definition

Horowitz and Sahni (1976) define the *balance factor* of a node in a binary tree to be:

height (left subtree) - height (right subtree)

So for an AVL tree, the balance factor of a node is either 1, 0, or -1. AVL trees can be used to implement a binary search tree, so that items in the left subtree of a node are less than the value at that node, and all values in the right subtree are greater. Figure 7.11 shows two such trees.

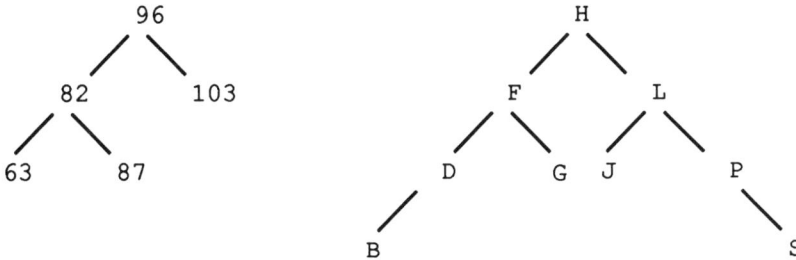

Figure 7.11 AVL trees

If we use an AVL tree to implement a binary search tree then we also inherit the algebraic specification of the binary search tree, given earlier in the chapter, which is actually the same as that of a binary tree except for the procedure Insert. However, we will need a procedure which, given an item and an AVL tree, will return an AVL tree with the item inserted. How such a procedure may be written is discussed next.

Inserting an item

Inserting an item into a tree may result in a tree which is still balanced, or it may cause the balance factor of a subtree to become 2 or -2, which means that rebalancing is required. The rebalancing must be such that:

1. The inorder traversal of the new tree is the same as that of the original tree.
2. The transformed tree must be height balanced.

The rebalancing is done by means of rotations, several of which are performed on the tree, until it becomes balanced. There are two kinds of rotations: right and left. In a right rotation, the root of the tree moves down and to the right, its position being taken by its left subtree, the right subtree of which becomes the (old) root's left subtree (see figure 7.12).

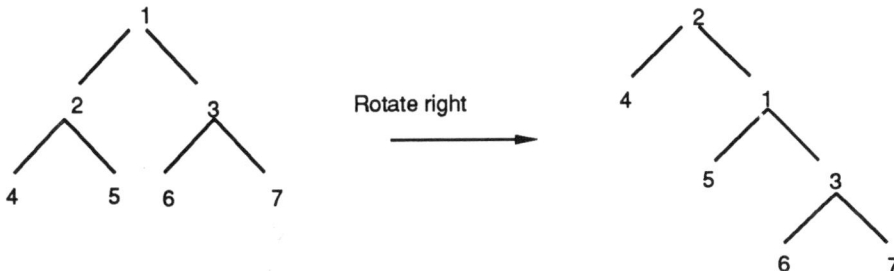

Rotate right

Figure 7.12

Note that the inorder traversal of the tree on the left, 4 2 5 1 6 3 7, is the same as that of the tree on the right.

The specification of the `RotateRight` algorithm is given below:

RotateRight (EmptyTree ( )) = ( )
RotateRight (ConsTree (i, l, r)) = ConsTree (Root (l), LeftTree (l),
                                                            ConsTree (i, RightTree (l), r))

In a left rotation the root of the tree moves down and to the left, its position being taken by its right subtree, the right subtree of which becomes the (old) root's right subtree (see figure 7.13).

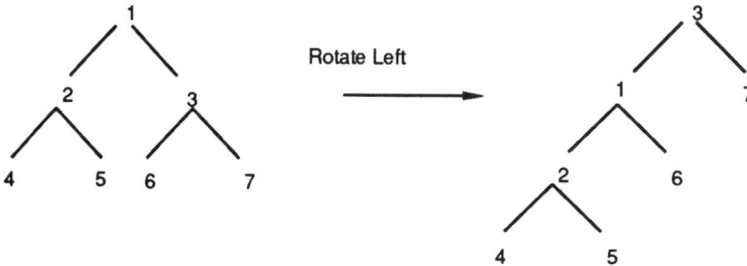

Figure 7.13

The specification of this `RotateLeft` algorithm is the mirror image of the one given for right rotation:

RotateLeft (EmptyTree ( )) = ( )
RotateLeft (ConsTree (i, l, r)) = ConsTree (Root (r),
                                                ConsTree (i, l, LeftTree (r)), RightTree (r))

Again the inorder traversal of the two trees is the same.

Example

Suppose we have just inserted an item which has priority '15' into the binary search tree below using the insert procedure discussed on page 140:

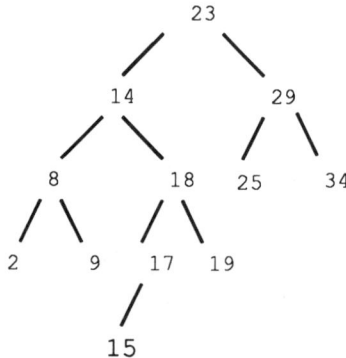

The balance factor of the root of the tree is now 2, so the tree is no longed height balanced.

To transform the tree back in to an AVL tree we must use two rotations, first a left rotation about the node containing the value 14, then a right rotation about the node containing the value 23:

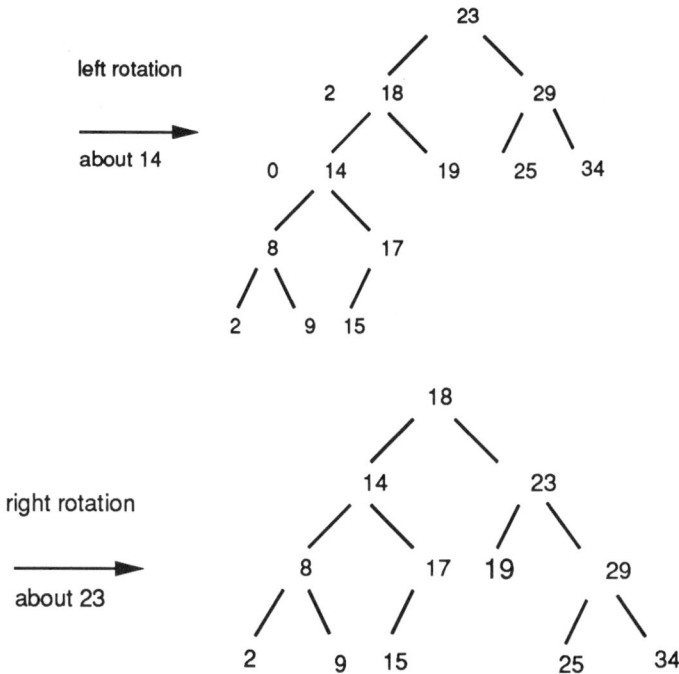

Note that the inorder traversal of this tree (2, 8, 9, 14, 15, 17, 18, 19, 23, 25, 29, 34) is the same as that of the tree we started with.

SUMMARY

Binary trees can be used to write efficient sorting and searching routines.

A *binary search tree* is a binary tree which has an ordering imposed on the nodes such that, for each node:

(1) All values in its left subtree are less than the value in that node; and
(2) All values in its right subtree are greater than the value in that node.

A *heap* is a complete binary tree which has an ordering imposed on its nodes such that the value at the root of the tree is greater than or equal to the values in both of its subtrees, and both subtrees are heaps, together with a number of access procedures.

An efficient sorting algorithm can be implemented by using a heap. The algorithm called *heapsort* has two stages:

(1) Convert the data to be sorted into a heap;
(2) Successively output the root and restructure the remaining tree into a heap.

A heap can be used as an implementation for a priority queue.

A tree is *height balanced* if it is empty or if both its left and right subtrees are height balanced and the difference in the heights of its left and right subtrees is less than or equal to one.

Height-balanced trees are also called AVL trees after their inventors, Adelson-Velskii and Landis.

CHAPTER 8

The Abstract Data Type n-ary Tree

INTRODUCTION

The definition of the abstract data type binary tree given in Chapter 6 stated that each node has two disjoint subtrees. In this chapter we discuss a more general abstract data type in which each node can have more than two subtrees. Such a tree is called an *n-ary* or *multiway* tree. We then go on to discuss 2-3 trees, which are those in which the number of items in a node may vary between one and two and the number of subtrees of a node can vary between two and three. We start by defining an *n*-ary tree.

DEFINITION

The abstract data type *n-ary tree* is a finite set of nodes which is either empty or consists of a data item (called the *root*) and a number ($\leq n$) of disjoint *n*-ary trees, called *subtrees*, together with a number of access procedures.

The type *n*-ary tree is useful for modelling one-to-many relationships between items. For example, the relationship between a student and the books that he or she owns is one-to-many. The relationship between a mother and her children is also one-to-many (see Figure 8.1).In the

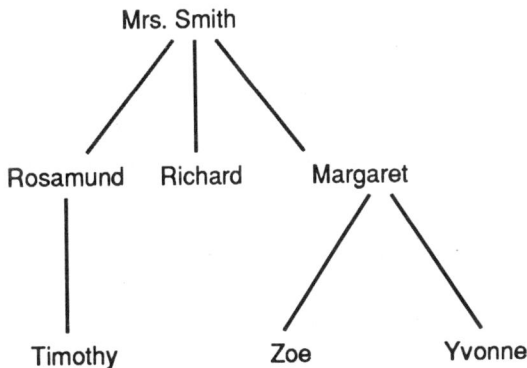

Mrs. Smith

Rosamund   Richard   Margaret

Timothy   Zoe   Yvonne

Figure 8.1

161

figure, the node containing 'Mrs. Smith' is the root of the tree and the leaf nodes are the nodes 'Richard', 'Yvonne', 'Zoe' and 'Timothy'.

ALGEBRAIC SPECIFICATION

The algebraic specification for an *n*-ary tree is a straightforward extension to that of a binary tree. For example, the specification for a 3-ary or *ternary* tree would have the function EmptyTree, which would return a ternary tree, the predicate function IsEmptyTree which would take a ternary tree as its parameter, and ConsTree, which would take an item and three trees and return a ternary tree with the item at its root. We also need an extra selector function MiddleTree, which together with Root, LeftTree and RightTree gives a total of four selector functions to return the various parts of the tree. We will demonstrate later in the chapter that all *n*-ary trees can be converted to binary trees, with the correspondingly simpler specification.

Definitions

A node which is not a leaf node is called a *non-terminal* or *interior* node.

The *degree* of a *node* is the number of subtrees it has.

The *degree* of a *tree* is the maximum degree of the nodes in the tree.

For example, the degree of the root node of the tree in figure 8.1 is 3, the degree of the node containing 'Rosamund' is 1, the degree of the node containing 'Margaret' is 2 and the degree of the tree is 3.

From the definition of an *n*-ary tree it follows that the degree of an *n*-ary tree is at most *n*. The terms *m*-ary and *t*-ary are also used occasionally.

An analogy can be drawn with the well-known diagrams of family trees. The node containing 'Mrs. Smith' is said to be the *parent* of the nodes 'Rosamund', 'Richard' and 'Margaret'. These nodes are said to be the *children* of the root, and are also *siblings*, with 'Rosamund' as the eldest sibling.

As mentioned earlier, it is possible to represent a tree of any degree as a binary tree. The rules for conversion are:

(1) Apart from the leftmost child, the links from all children to their parent are removed .
(2) All siblings are then linked together.
(3) Any links that have become horizontal are rotated clockwise about the left-hand end through 45 degrees.

For example, the tree of Figure 8.1 can be converted to a binary tree in figure 8.2.

(1) Remove links to parent:

Mr. Smith, Mrs. Smith

Rosamund   Richard   Margaret

Timothy   Zoe   Yvonne

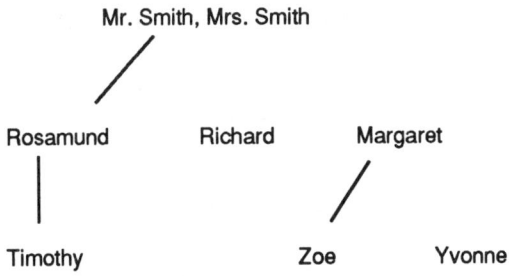

(2) Link siblings together:

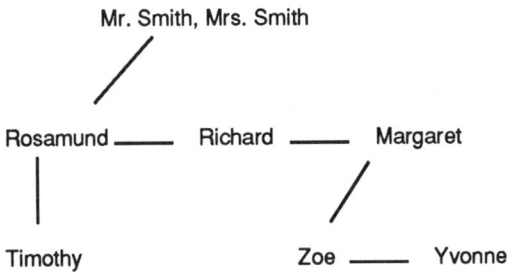

Mr. Smith, Mrs. Smith

Rosamund ——— Richard ——— Margaret

Timothy   Zoe ——— Yvonne

(3) Rotate horizontal links through 45 degrees:

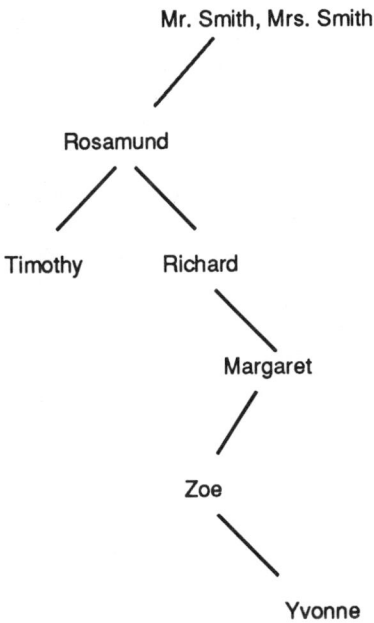

Mr. Smith, Mrs. Smith

Rosamund

Timothy   Richard

Margaret

Zoe

Yvonne

Figure 8.2

The structure of the family tree is not as apparent as it was in the *n*-ary tree: in fact the right spine of the left subtree of each node now holds the node's children.

Note: The right *spine* of a tree consists of the root node and all other nodes which are found by taking successive right branches from the root node.

THE ABSTRACT DATA TYPE 2-3 TREE

We have already seen how the efficiency with which a binary search tree can be used to store and retrieve sorted data depends on whether the tree is balanced. A *2-3 tree* is similar to an AVL tree in that it remains balanced in all situations. The difference is that in a 2-3 tree a node can contain either one or two items. Whenever the tree becomes unbalanced because of an insertion or a deletion it is immediately rebalanced so that the heights of all the subtrees are the same. It is easier to maintain the shape of a 2-3 tree on insertion of an item than it is to maintain that of a binary tree, because the number of items in a node can vary. A 2-3 tree will only 'grow' (that is, its height will increase) if all the nodes in the tree contain two items. We will examine the insertion algorithm later in detail.

Definition

The abstract data type *2-3 tree* is a finite set of nodes which is either empty or consists of a root containing one item and two disjoint subtrees, or of a root containing two items and three disjoint subtrees (called left, middle and right), where the subtrees are 2-3 trees of the same height, together with a number of access procedures.

For example, figure 8.3 shows a 2-3 tree in which the values in the nodes have an ordering imposed on them (the reader may recognize this ordering as being similar to that imposed on nodes in binary search trees). All the values in the left subtree of a node are less than the value (or values) at the node, all values in the right subtree are greater than the values (or values) at the node, and all those in a middle subtree (where one exists) are such that they lie between the two values in the node. In fact this tree is an example of a 2-3 *search* tree, which is an extension of a binary search tree, and which will be defined formally later.

Note that if a node has two subtrees then it must contain only one item, whereas if it has three subtrees then it must contain two items.

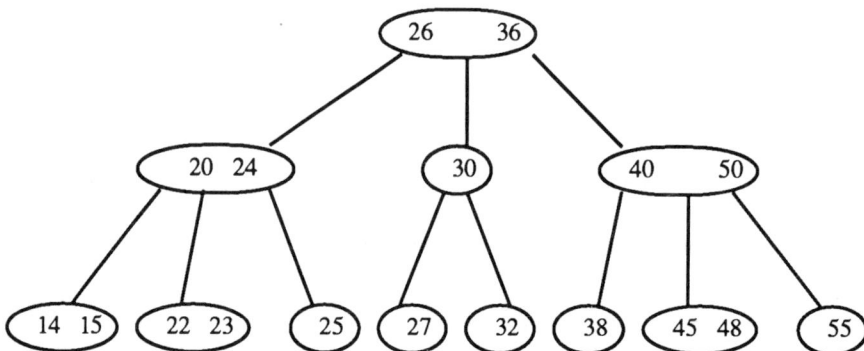

Figure 8.3 A 2-3 tree

From the fact that the subtrees have the same height, it follows that a 2-3 tree of height h always has at least as many nodes as a full binary tree of height h; that is, it always has $\geq 2^h - 1$ nodes.

Algebraic specification

When specifying a 2-3 tree algebraically we can use the specification of a binary tree as a basis and add extra procedures to deal with the middle subtree and the fact that the root may contain either one or two items. The entire specification is given below.

Syntax of the access procedures

The first four access procedures are identical to four of those given for the abstract data type binary tree.

```
PROCEDURE EmptyTree ( ) : Tree ;
(* Postcondition: returns an empty tree *)

PROCEDURE IsEmptyTree ( t : Tree) : BOOLEAN;
(* Postcondition: returns TRUE if t is
   empty, otherwise FALSE *)

PROCEDURE LeftTree ( t : Tree) : Tree;
(* Postcondition: returns the left subtree of tree t *)

PROCEDURE RightTree ( t : Tree) : Tree;
(* Postcondition: returns the right subtree of tree t *)
```

and in addition we will need:

```
PROCEDURE MiddleTree ( t : Tree) : Tree;
(* Postcondition: returns the middle subtree of tree t *)
```

The selector function Root is restricted to trees which have only one item at their root:

```
PROCEDURE Root ( t : Tree) : InfoType;
(* Precondition: takes a tree which has one item at its root
   Postcondition: returns the data item at the root of
   tree t *)
```

and we need new selector functions to deal with trees which have two items at their root:

```
PROCEDURE FirstVal ( t : Tree) : InfoType;
(* Precondition: takes a tree which has two items at its
   root
   Postcondition: returns the first item in the root of
   tree t *)

PROCEDURE SecondVal ( t : Tree) : InfoType;
(* Precondition: takes a tree which has two items at its
   root
```

```
Postcondition: returns the second item in the root of
tree t *)
```

Similarly, ConsTree is restricted to constructing trees which have only one item at their root:

```
PROCEDURE ConsTree ( i : InfoType; l, r : Tree ) : Tree ;
(* Precondition: takes an item and two trees
    Postcondition: returns a tree which has item i at its
    root and l and r as its left and right subtrees
    respectively *)
```

and we need a new constructor function to construct trees with two items at the root:

```
PROCEDURE Cons3Tree ( i,j : InfoType; l, m, r : Tree ) :
                                                    Tree ;
(* Precondition: takes two items and three trees
    Postcondition: returns a tree which has items i,j at its
    root and  l, m, r as its left, middle and right subtrees
    respectively *)
```

Finally, we need a function which returns the number of items at the root of a tree:

```
PROCEDURE NumberOfValues ( t: Tree) : Number;
(* Postcondition: returns either 1 or 2, i.e. the number
    of items at the root of t *)
```

Semantics of the access procedures

The axioms describing the semantics of the access procedures are very similar to those for the binary tree, the only difference being that a 2-3 tree can have one of three forms: EmptyTree, ConsTree (i, l, r) or Cons3Tree (i, j, l, m, r) where i and j are items and l, m, and r are trees. We now have to specify the action of the access procedures for each of these cases.

1. IsEmptyTree (EmptyTree ( )) = TRUE
2. IsEmptyTree (ConsTree (i, l, r)) = FALSE
3. IsEmptyTree (Cons3Tree (i, j, l, m, r)) = FALSE
4. Root (EmptyTree ( )) = error
5. Root (ConsTree (i, l, r)) = i
6. Root (Cons3Tree (i, j, l, m, r)) = error
7. FirstVal (EmptyTree ( )) = error
8. FirstVal (ConsTree (i, l, r)) = error
9. FirstVal (Cons3Tree (i, j, l, m, r)) = i
10. SecondVal (EmptyTree ( )) = error
11. SecondVal (ConsTree (i, l, r)) = error
12. SecondVal (Cons3Tree (i, j, l, m, r)) = j
13. LeftTree (EmptyTree ( )) = error
14. LeftTree (ConsTree (i, l, r)) = l
15. LeftTree (Cons3Tree (i, j, l, m, r)) = l

16. RightTree (EmptyTree ( )) = error
17. RightTree (ConsTree (i, l, r)) = r
18. RightTree (Cons3Tree (i, j, l, m, r)) = r
19. MiddleTree (EmptyTree ( )) = error
20. MiddleTree (ConsTree (i, l, r)) = error
21. MiddleTree (Cons3Tree (i, j, l, m, r)) = m

We will now go on to discuss the 2-3 search tree which was mentioned briefly in the last section.

THE ABSTRACT DATA TYPE 2-3 SEARCH TREE

Definition

The abstract data type *2-3 search tree* is a 2-3 tree which has an ordering imposed on the nodes such that, if there is one item at the root, all values in its left subtree are less than the value at the root, and all values in its right subtree are greater than the value at the root, and both subtrees are also 2-3 search trees. Otherwise, if there are two items at the root of the tree, the smaller value of the two must be greater than all values in the left subtree and less than all values in the middle one, and the larger of the two must be greater than all values in the middle subtree and less than all values in the right. Again, all the subtrees must be 2-3 search trees.

Notice that a 2-3 search tree is entirely analogous to a binary search tree.

Algebraic specification

The algebraic specification of the 2-3 search tree is a straightforward extension of the specification of the 2-3 tree. However, instead of allowing the user access to the procedures ConsTree and Cons3Tree, we must provide a procedure for insertion of an item which will ensure that values in the tree remain ordered. The procedure heading is given below:

```
PROCEDURE Insert ( i : InfoType ; t : Tree ) : Tree ;
(* Precondition: i is an item and t is a 2-3 search tree.
   Postcondition: returns a 2-3 search tree with i inserted
   in the correct position *)
```

Before we examine the semantics of Insert, let us consider other auxiliary functions that we will need. It will be necessary to find the smallest and largest values in a node which contains two values. Then we need procedures MinVal and MaxVal which return the smallest and largest values, respectively, in the node at the root of a tree.

```
PROCEDURE MinVal (t : Tree) : InfoType;
(* Precondition: t is a 2-3 tree which has a node
   containing 2 values at its root
   Postcondition: returns the smallest of the two values *)
```

We can specify the procedure as follows:

MinVal (Cons3Tree (i, j, L, M, R)) = Min (i, j)

where i and j are items, L, M, R are 2-3 trees, and Min is a procedure which we have provided which returns the smallest of two items. This translates into the Modula-2 code below:

```
PROCEDURE MinVal (t : Tree) : InfoType;
(* Precondition: t is a 2-3 tree which has a node
    containing 2 values at its root
    Postcondition: returns the smallest of the two values *)

BEGIN
   RETURN Min ( FirstVal(t), SecondVal(t))
END MinVal ;
```

The procedure MaxVal can be specified and implemented in the same way, by replacing the function Min with a user-defined function Max which returns the largest of two items. We will also need a procedure which returns the middle value of three items. Using the functions Min and Max we can easily implement this:

```
PROCEDURE Mid ( a, b, c : InfoType ) : InfoType ;
(* Postcondition: returns the middle value of three items *)

BEGIN
  IF ((a < Max ( b, c )) AND (a > Min ( b, c ))) THEN
     RETURN a
  ELSIF ((b < Max ( a, c )) AND (b > Min ( a, c ))) THEN
     RETURN b
  ELSE
     RETURN c
  END
END Mid ;
```

Now we can return to our insert procedure. The easiest case to specify occurs when the tree is empty. Using parenthesis, ( ), to denote an empty tree we can specify this as:

Insert (i, ( )) = ConsTree (i, ( ), ( ))

If the tree consists of one value then we can simply insert the new item in the root of the tree and return a 2-3 tree with 2 items at the root:

Insert (i, ConsTree (j, ( ), ( ))) = Cons3Tree (i, j, ( ), ( ), ( ))

If the tree, t, only consists of two values, then we return a binary tree with one value in each node. We use our auxiliary procedures Min, Max, Mid, MinVal and MaxVal which we discussed earlier to ensure that the resulting tree is ordered:

Insert (i, Cons3Tree (j, k, ( ), ( ), ( ))) = ConsTree (Mid (i, j, k),
                                ConsTree (Min (MinVal (t), i), ( ), ( )),
                                ConsTree (Max (i, MaxVal (t)), ( ), ( )))

Now we must consider the cases which may arise if the subtrees are not empty. Finding the correct position to insert the item is simple: we just compare the item with the value or values at the root and call Insert recursively in the way which we did with the binary search tree insertion procedure. However, we must also ensure that the resulting tree is a 2-3 tree. This may mean reshaping the tree to ensure that all the subtrees of the root are of the same height. We will assume that we have a procedure called Reshape which will perform any necessary alterations and return a 2-3 search tree:

```
PROCEDURE Reshape ( t : Tree ) : Tree ;
(* Postcondition: returns a 2-3 search tree *)
```

Using this procedure we can continue to specify the 'Insert' procedure:

First suppose that there is only one value at the root:

Insert (i, ConsTree (j, L, R)) = if i < j $then$ Reshape (ConsTree (j, Insert (i, L), R)
$$else$$
Reshape (ConsTree (j, L, Insert (i, R))

The case of insertion into a tree with two values at the root is simply an extension of this:

Insert (i, Cons3Tree (j, k, L M, R)) = if i < j $then$
Reshape (Cons3Tree (j, k, Insert (i, L), M, R))
$elsif$ i < j $then$
Reshape (Cons3Tree (j, k, L, Insert (i,M), R))
$else$
Reshape (Cons3Tree (j, k, L, M, Insert (i,R)))

The complete insertion procedure is given below in Modula-2:

```
PROCEDURE Insert (i : InfoType; t : Tree ) : Tree ;
(* Precondition: i is an item, t is a 2-3 search tree.
   Postcondition: returns a 2-3 search tree with the item i
   inserted in the correct position *)

BEGIN
  IF IsEmptyTree(t) THEN
    RETURN ConsTree(i,EmptyTree(), EmptyTree())
  ELSIF (NumberOfValues (t) = one) THEN
    IF (IsEmptyTree(LeftTree(t)) AND
          IsEmptyTree ( RightTree(t))) THEN
      RETURN Cons3Tree(i, Root(t), LeftTree(t),
                                        EmptyTree(),
                                        RightTree(t))
    ELSIF ( i < Root (t)) THEN
        RETURN Reshape (ConsTree(Root(t), Insert
                                (i,LeftTree(t)),
                          RightTree(t)))
    ELSE
        RETURN Reshape(ConsTree(Root(t), LeftTree(t),
                                Insert(i, RightTree(t))))
    END ;
  ELSE
    IF (IsEmptyTree ( LeftTree (t)) AND
          IsEmptyTree ( RightTree (t))) THEN
```

```
        RETURN  ConsTree  ( Mid ( i, MinVal(t), MaxVal(t)),
             ConsTree(Min (MinVal(t), i), EmptyTree(),
                                          EmptyTree()),
            ConsTree  (Max (MaxVal(t),i),EmptyTree(),
                                         EmptyTree()))
     ELSIF i < MinVal(t) THEN
        RETURN  Reshape(Cons3Tree ( FirstVal(t),
                                          Second Val(t),
         Insert ( i, LeftTree(t)), MiddleTree(t),
                              RightTree(t)))
     ELSIF ( i > MinVal (t)) AND (i < MaxVal(t)) THEN
        RETURN     Reshape(Cons3Tree  ( FirstVal(t),
                              SecondVal(t),
          LeftTree(t), Insert (i,  MiddleTree(t)),
                                   RightTree(t)))
     ELSE
        RETURN  Reshape(Cons3Tree   (  FirstVal(t),
                                  Second Val(t),
          LeftTree(t), MiddleTree(t), Insert (i,
                                   RightTree(t))))
     END ;
   END ;
 END Insert ;
```

This procedure assumes that the relational operators '<', '>' can be used on items of type `InfoType`. For generality a boolean procedure `IsLess` which would take two items of any type should be provided.

The search for the correct place to insert an item always ends at a leaf. Note that a tree only grows in height if we are inserting an item into a node which already contains two items. When this happens, the new subtree contains one value at its root and has two subtrees. Since the tree is reshaped after each insertion it will never grow by more than one level before it is rebalanced.

Exercises

1. Rewrite the expression `Insert ( n, ( g, ( a ), (j, m )))`.

Solution

The tree `( g, ( a ), ( j, m ))` is shown in figure 8.4. The item 'n' is to be inserted into this tree. The rewrite of the expression proceeds as follows:

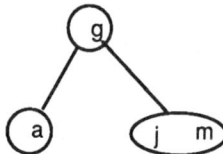

Figure 8.4

Insert (n, (g, (a), (j, m))) → Reshape (ConsTree (g, (a), Insert (n, (j, m))))

Now,

Insert (n, (j, m)) → ConsTree (Mid (n, j, m), ConsTree (Min (j, n), ( ), ( )),
                                                   ConsTree (Max (m, n), ( ) , ( )))

$\rightarrow$ ConsTree (m, (j), (n))
$\rightarrow$ (m, (j), (n))

∴ Reshape (ConsTree (g, (a), Insert (n, (j, m))))
$\rightarrow$ Reshape (ConsTree (g, (a), (m, (j), (n))))
$\rightarrow$ Reshape ((g, (a), (m, (j),(n))))

The tree with the item n inserted is shown in figure 8.5. Note that all the items are in the correct positions according to alphabetical ordering. The reshaping algorithm will be explained after the next example, and we will then show how to reform this tree into a 2-3 one.

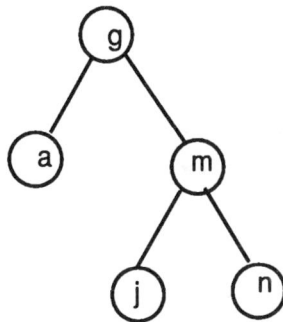

Figure 8.5

2. Rewrite the expression `Insert ( k, ( g, m, ( a, c), ( h, j ), (n, p ) )))`.

Solution

The tree into which the item 'k' is to be inserted is shown in Figure 8.6.

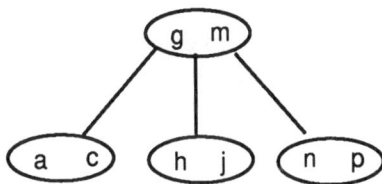

Figure 8.6

Insert (k, (g, m, (a , c), (h, j), (n, p))))
$\rightarrow$ Reshape (Cons3Tree (g, m, (a , c), Insert (k, (h, j)), (n, p))

Now,
Insert (k, (h, j)) $\rightarrow$ ConsTree (Mid (k, h, j), ConsTree (Min (h, k), ( ), ( )),
ConsTree (Max (k, j), ( ) , ( )))

$\rightarrow$ ConsTree (j, (h, ( ), ( )), (k, (), ( )))
$\rightarrow$ (j, (h), (k))

∴ Reshape (Cons3Tree (g, m, (a , c), Insert (k, (h, j)), (n, p)))
                 → Reshape (Cons3Tree (g, m, (a, c), (j, (h), (k)), (n, p)))
                 → Reshape ((g, m, (a , c), (j, (h), (k)), (n, p)))

The tree with 'k' inserted is shown in Figure 8.7. Although the tree is no longer a 2-3 tree search tree (because the middle subtree has grown in height) all the items are in their correct positions according to alphabetical ordering.

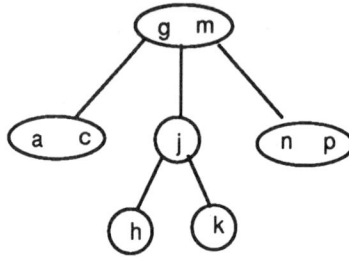

Figure 8.7

We now turn our attention to the algorithm Reshape. There is no need to reshape an empty tree:

Reshape (EmptyTree) = EmptyTree

Suppose that there is only one item in the node at the root of the tree. If the height of the two subtrees is the same after the insertion of an item then there is no need to reshape the tree:

Reshape (ConsTree (i, L, R)) = if height (L) = height (R) then
                             ConsTree (i, L, R)

Otherwise if the height of the left subtree is greater than the height of the right, then we must find a way of rebalancing the left subtree. We do this by taking the root of the left subtree and inserting it into the root of the tree. We use the subtrees of the left subtree to form the left and middle subtrees of the new tree. The right subtree is the same as it was in the original tree. So the specification is:

     if height (L) > height (R) *then*
            Cons3Tree (Root (L), i, LeftTree (L), RightTree (L), R)

This has the effect of reducing the height of the left subtree while maintaining the ordering imposed on the nodes. All the values in the new left subtree will be less then the smallest value in the root, because that value was the root of the left subtree. Similarly, all values in the middle subtree are greater than the smallest value in the root and less than the largest value. The right subtree remains unchanged and so all the items in the right subtree are greater than both values in the root of the tree.

If the height of the right subtree is greater than that of the left then the algorithm for rebalancing is the mirror image of the one above. The specification of the entire algorithm for a root which only contains one item is given below:

Reshape (ConsTree (i, L, R)) = *if* height (L) = height (R) *then* ConsTree (i, L, R)

      elsif height (L) > height (R) *then*

      Cons3Tree (Root (L), i, LeftTree(L), RightTree (L), R)

      else

      Cons3Tree (i, Root (R), L, LeftTree(R), RightTree (R))

Now suppose that the root contains two items and has three subtrees. The method for reshaping the tree is similar to the case explained above. If the heights of the three subtrees are all the same after the insertion then the tree does not need reshaping:

Reshape (Cons3Tree (i, j, L, M, R)) = *if* height (L) = height (M) = height (R)

        then (Cons3Tree (i, j, L, M, R))

If the left subtree has grown due to the insertion of an item, then we rebalance the tree by forming a tree with only one value at the root and only two subtrees. Because the unbalancing occurred due to the growth of the left subtree, we choose the smallest value in the root to be the item in the new root. The left subtree is formed from the root of the left subtree and its left and right subtrees. The right subtree is formed from the larger of the two items in the root and the middle and right subtrees of the original tree. The specification is given below. We assume that 'i' is the smaller of the two items in the root.

 if height (L) > height (M) *then*

   ConsTree (i, ConsTree (Root (L), LeftTree (L), RightTree (L)),

     ConsTree (j, M, R))

If the middle subtree has increased in height due to the insertion of an item, then the algorithm for reshaping is analogous to the one above. This time, though, the item at the new root of the tree must be that which was at the root of the middle subtree. The left subtree is formed from the smaller of the two values in the root, the left subtree of the tree and the left subtree of what was the middle subtree. The right subtree is formed from the larger of the two values in the root, the right subtree of what was the middle subtree and the right subtree of the original tree:

 if height (M) > height (L) *then*

   ConsTree (Root (M), ConsTree (i, L, LeftTree (M)),

     ConsTree (j, RightTree (M), R))

The final case to consider occurs when the right subtree has grown. Here we take the larger of the two values at the root to be the new root, and construct the left subtree from the smaller of the two values and the left and middle subtrees of the original tree. The right subtree is formed from the root of what was the right subtree and its two subtrees:

 else

   ConsTree (j, ConsTree (i, L, M),

     ConsTree (Root (R), LeftTree (R), RightTree (R)))

The procedure is given below in Modula-2.

```
PROCEDURE Reshape ( t : Tree ) : Tree ;
(* Postcondition : returns a 2-3 search tree *)

BEGIN
  IF IsEmptyTree (t ) THEN
    RETURN t
  ELSIF (NumberOfValues (t) = one) THEN
    IF (Height (LeftTree(t)) = Height(RightTree(t)))
                                                              THEN
        RETURN t
    ELSIF ( Height (LeftTree(t)) > Height(RightTree(t)))
                                                              THEN
        RETURN Cons3Tree ( Root(LeftTree(t)), Root(t),
           LeftTree(LeftTree(t)), RightTree(LeftTree(t)),
                                        RightTree(t))
    ELSE
        RETURN Cons3Tree ( Root(t), Root(RightTree(t)),
           LeftTree(t), LeftTree(RightTree(t)), RightTree
                                        (RightTree(t)))
    END ;
  ELSE
    IF (Height (LeftTree(t)) = Height(RightTree(t))) AND
       (Height (LeftTree(t)) = Height ( MiddleTree(t)))
                                                              THEN
        RETURN t
    ELSIF ( Height (LeftTree(t)) > Height(RightTree(t)))
                                                              THEN
        RETURN ConsTree (MinVal(t),
           ConsTree(Root(LeftTree(t)),LeftTree(LeftTree(t)),
                                RightTree(LeftTree(t))),
           ConsTree(MaxVal(t), MiddleTree(t),RightTree(t)))
    ELSIF ( Height (MiddleTree(t)) > Height(RightTree(t)))
                                                              THEN
        RETURN ConsTree ( Root(MiddleTree(t)),
           ConsTree( MinVal(t), LeftTree(t), LeftTree
                                        (MiddleTree(t))),
           ConsTree(MaxVal(t), RightTree(MiddleTree(t)),
                                        RightTree(t)))
    ELSE
        RETURN ConsTree( MaxVal(t),
           ConsTree(MinVal(t), LeftTree(t), MiddleTree(t)),
           ConsTree(Root(RightTree(t)), LeftTree
                                        (RightTree(t)),
                        RightTree(RightTree(t)))))
    END ;
  END;
END Reshape;
```

Examples

1. Rewrite the expression: Insert (n, (g, (a),(j, m))).

Solution

Earlier in this chapter we showed that the expression can be rewritten to the following form:

Reshape ((g, (a), (m, (j), (n))))

From the Reshape algorithm, we have:

Reshape ((g, (a), (m, (j), (n)))) -> Cons3Tree (g, m, (a), (j), (n))

The resulting 2-3 tree is shown in figure 8.8.

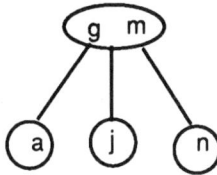

Figure 8.8

2. Rewrite the expression: Insert (k, (g, m, (a, c), (h, j), (n, p)))).

Solution

We saw earlier that:

Insert (k, (g, m, (a ,c), (h, j), (n, p))))
$\rightarrow$ Reshape ((g, m, (a, c), (j, (h), (k)), (n, p)))

Now from the Reshape algorithm, we have:

Reshape ((g, m, (a ,c), (j, (h), (k)), (n, p)))
$\rightarrow$ ConsTree (j, ConsTree (g, (a, c), (h)), ConsTree (m, (k), (n, p)))
$\rightarrow$ ConsTree (j, (g, (a, c), (h)), (m, (k), (n, p)))
$\rightarrow$ (j, (g, (a, c), (h)), (m, (k), (n, p)))

The final tree is shown in figure 8.9.

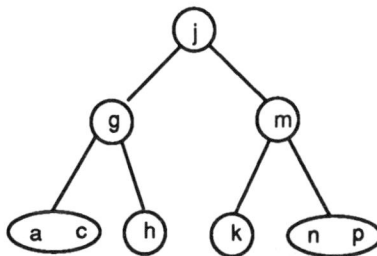

Figure 8.9

Note that a 2-3 search tree only grows in height during insertion if all the nodes on the path from the root to the leaf into which the new item will be inserted contain two items. When it does grow, the tree is reshaped so that all the subtrees of the root have the same height.

HIGHER-LEVEL PROCEDURES

Example 1

Write a procedure to search a 2-3 search tree for a particular item.

Solution

Retrieving an item from a 2-3 tree is similar to retrieval from a binary search tree. The items held in the tree may well consist of a number (or key) together with some information. Given a number, we wish to retrieve the associated information. For example, a search tree may hold information about students, in which case a number may be used to identify a student, and the associated information could be a name and other personal details such as age, address, examination results, etc.

To find a particular item, we first inspect the root of the tree. If the item is in the root, then we have finished. Otherwise, there are two cases to consider: the root has either one or two items. In the first case we search either the left subtree or the right, depending on whether the item we are looking for is less than or greater than the item in the root respectively. If there are two items in the root, the procedure is very similar, except that we have the possibility that the desired item may be in the middle subtree. The procedure heading and specification are given below.

```
PROCEDURE Find ( i : InfoType ; t : Tree ) :InfoType ;
    (* Precondition: takes an item i and a 2-3 search tree
        Postcondition: returns the information associated
        with i  if i is in the tree, otherwise indicate
        that i is not present *)
```

Find (EmptyTree) = error
Find (i, ConsTree (i, L, R)) = i
Find (i, ConsTree (j, L, R)) = *if* i < j *then* Find (i, L)
$\qquad\qquad\qquad\qquad\qquad$ *else* Find (i, R)
Find (i, Cons3Tree (i, j, L, M, R)) = i
Find (i, Cons3Tree (j, k, L, M, R)) = *if* i < MinVal (t) *then* Find (i, L)
$\qquad\qquad\qquad\qquad\qquad$ *elsif* i > MinVal (t) *and* i < MaxVal (t) *then*
$\qquad\qquad\qquad\qquad\qquad$ Find (i, M)
$\qquad\qquad\qquad\qquad\qquad$ *else* Find (i, R)

Example 2

Suppose that we wished to 'flatten' a 2-3 search tree into a list of items. The procedure heading is given below:

```
PROCEDURE Flatten ( t : Tree ) : List ;
 (* Precondition: takes a 2-3 search tree
     Postcondition: returns a list containing the items
     which are in the tree *)
```

Solution

An empty tree can easily be flattened by returning an empty list:

Flatten (EmptyTree) = Empty

If there is one value in the root of the tree, than we can flatten the tree by inserting this value at the head of a list using the procedure Cons. The list which this value is inserted into is formed by first flattening the left subtree, then the right, and then joining the resulting lists together. The procedure that we use to join two lists together was discussed in Chapter 2, and is called Append. The specification is thus:

Flatten (ConsTree (i, L, R)) = Cons (i, Append (Flatten (L), Flatten (R)))

Now if there are two values in the root of the tree, then we follow the same principle, except that we now have two values to insert into the list, and we must also flatten the middle subtree. This gives us:

Flatten (Cons3Tree (i, j, L, M, R)) = Cons (i, Cons (j, Append (
                    Append (Flatten (L), Flatten (M)), Flatten (R))))

The final procedure is given in Modula-2 below:

```
PROCEDURE Flatten ( t : Tree ) : List ;
(* Precondition: takes a 2-3 search tree
   Postcondition: returns a list containing the items which
   are in the tree *)
BEGIN
    IF IsEmptyTree ( t ) THEN
        RETURN Empty ()
    ELSIF (NumberOfValues(t) = one ) THEN
        RETURN Cons (Root(t), Append (Flatten (LeftTree (t)),
                                Flatten (RightTree (t))))
    ELSE
        RETURN Cons (FirstVal(t), Cons (SecondVal(t),Append
            (Append (Flatten (LeftTree (t)), Flatten
                                ( MiddleTree (t))),
                                Flatten (RightTree
                                    (t)))))
    END
END Flatten ;
```

Example 3

Now suppose that we wished to delete an item from a 2-3 search tree, and return a tree which is still a 2-3 search tree.

Solution

Removing an item may mean restructuring the tree entirely. For example, suppose that there were two items at the root of the tree and we wished to remove one of them. Then the root could no longer have three subtrees, as it would only contain one value. In fact there is a simple solution to this problem. We can flatten the tree into a list using the procedure Flatten, and then insert all the items (except for the one we wished to delete) into a 2-3 search tree, using the procedure Insert.

The first step is to write a procedure `TakeFromList` which removes a specified item from a list and inserts the other items into a 2-3 search tree We will use an accumulating parameter to return the tree:

```
PROCEDURE TakeFromList (i : InfoType ; l : List ; t :
Tree ) : Tree ;
(* Precondition: takes an item, a list and a tree
    Postcondition: returns a 2-3 search tree containing the
    items in l except for i *)
```

If the list is empty, then we return the accumulating parameter which will be an empty tree initially:

$$\text{TakeFromList} \, (\, i, \text{Empty}, t \,) = t$$

If the item at the head of the list is not to be deleted, then we return the result of inserting this item into the accumulating parameter, and also calling the `TakeFromList` function recursively with the tail of the list:

$$\text{TakeFromList} \, (\, i, l, t \,) = \text{if Head} \, (\, l \,) <> i \; then$$
$$\text{TakeFromList} \, (\, i, \text{Tail} \, (\, l \,), \text{Insert} \, (\, i, t \,))$$

Otherwise the item is to be deleted and so we simply ignore it:

$$\text{else TakeFromList} \, (\, i, \text{Tail} \, (\, l \,), t \,)$$

This gives us the following procedure:

```
PROCEDURE TakeFromList (i : InfoType ; l : List ; t : Tree
.) : Tree ;
(* Precondition: takes an item, a list and a tree
    Postcondition: returns a 2-3 search tree containing the
    items in l except for i *)
BEGIN
    IF IsEmpty ( l ) THEN
        RETURN t
    ELSE
        IF Head ( l ) = i THEN
            RETURN TakeFromList ( i, Tail (l), t )
        ELSE
            RETURN TakeFromList ( i, Tail(l), Insert (Head(l),
                                                        t))
        END
    END
END TakeFromList ;
```

Now we can easily write a procedure to delete an item from a 2-3 search tree by flattening the tree and using the `TakeFromList` procedure:

```
PROCEDURE Delete ( i : InfoType ; t : Tree ) : Tree ;
(* Precondition: takes an item and a 2-3 search tree
```

```
          Postcondition: returns a 2-3 search tree *)

   BEGIN
      RETURN TakeFromList ( i, Flatten (t), EmptyTree())
   END Delete ;
```

IMPLEMENTING THE TYPE 2-3 TREE

Each node of the tree can contain either one or two items, as well as pointers to the left, right and (possibly) middle subtrees. This suggests use of a variant record as the data structure to implement a 2-3 tree. For example, the declarations for a dynamic implementation could be:

```
TYPE
  Number = ( one, two ) ;
  Tree = POINTER TO NODE;
  NODE =   RECORD
                CASE Num : Number OF
                  one : Value : InfoType |
                  two : FirstValue : InfoType ;
                        SecondValue : InfoType ;
                        Middle : Tree ;
                END ;
                Left, Right : Tree
          END;
```

The access procedures are given below:

```
  PROCEDURE EmptyTree ( ) : Tree ;
  (* Postcondition: returns an empty tree *)

    BEGIN
       RETURN NIL
    END EmptyTree;

  PROCEDURE ConsTree ( i : InfoType; l , r : Tree ) : Tree ;
  (* Precondition: takes an item and two trees
     Postcondition: returns a tree which has item i at its
     root  and l and r as its left and right subtrees
     respectively *)

  VAR
      Temp : Tree;

    BEGIN
      NEW(Temp);
      Temp^.Num := one ;
      WITH Temp^ DO
        Value := i;
        Left := l;
        Right := r
      END;
      RETURN Temp
    END ConsTree;
```

```
PROCEDURE Cons3Tree (i,j : InfoType; l ,m, r : Tree ) :
Tree ;
(* Precondition: takes two items and three trees
   Postcondition: returns a tree which has items i and j
   at  its root and l, m and r as its left, middle and
   right   subtrees respectively *)

    VAR
      Temp : Tree;

    BEGIN
       NEW(Temp);
       Temp^.Num := two ;
       WITH Temp^ DO
         FirstValue := i;
         SecondValue := j;
         Left := l;
         Middle := m ;
         Right := r
       END;
       RETURN Temp
     END Cons3Tree;

PROCEDURE Root (t : Tree) : InfoType;
(* Precondition: takes a tree which has one item at its
   root
   Postcondition: returns the data item at the root of
   tree t *)

 BEGIN
    IF IsEmptyTree(t) THEN
       WriteString("ERROR - can't take the Root of an
                                      empty Tree");
       HALT
    ELSIF (NumberOfValues ( t ) = two ) THEN
       WriteString("ERROR - can't take the Root of this
                                      Tree");
       HALT
    ELSE
       RETURN t^.Value
    END
 END Root;

 PROCEDURE FirstVal (t : Tree) : InfoType;
(* Precondition: takes a tree which has two items at its
   root
   Postcondition: returns the first item in the root of
   tree t *)

 BEGIN
    IF IsEmptyTree(t) THEN
       WriteString("ERROR  - can't find FirstVal of an
                                      empty Tree");
       HALT
    ELSIF (NumberOfValues ( t ) = one ) THEN
       WriteString("ERROR - can't find FirstVal of this
                                      Tree");
```

```
          HALT
       ELSE
          RETURN t^.FirstValue
       END
  END FirstVal;

    PROCEDURE SecondVal (t : Tree) : InfoType;
   (* Precondition: takes a tree which has two items at its
       root
       Postcondition: returns the second item in the root of
       tree  t *)

    BEGIN
       IF IsEmptyTree(t) THEN
          WriteString("ERROR -can't find SecondVal of an
                                          empty Tree");

          HALT
       ELSIF (NumberOfValues ( t ) = one ) THEN
          WriteString("ERROR - can't find SecondVal of this
                                              Tree");

          HALT
       ELSE
          RETURN t^.SecondValue
       END
    END SecondVal;

  PROCEDURE LeftTree (t : Tree) : Tree;
  (* Postcondition: returns the left subtree of tree t *)

    BEGIN
        IF IsEmptyTree(t) THEN
           WriteString("ERROR - can't take LeftTree of empty
                                              Tree");

           HALT
        ELSE
           RETURN t^.Left
        END ;
   END LeftTree;

    PROCEDURE RightTree (t : Tree) : Tree;
    (* Postcondition: returns the right subtree of tree t *)

   BEGIN
       IF IsEmptyTree(t) THEN
          WriteString("ERROR - can't take RightTree of empty
                                              Tree");

          HALT
       ELSE
          RETURN t^.Right
       END ;
   END RightTree;

    PROCEDURE MiddleTree (t : Tree) : Tree;
    (* Precondition: takes a tree with three subtrees *)
    (* Postcondition: returns the middle subtree of tree t *)
```

```
BEGIN
    IF IsEmptyTree(t) THEN
        WriteString("ERROR - can't take MiddleTree of
                                        empty Tree");
        HALT
    ELSIF (NumberOfValues ( t ) = one ) THEN
        WriteString("ERROR - can't take MiddleTree of
                                        this Tree");
        HALT
    ELSE
        RETURN t^.Middle
    END ;
END MiddleTree;

PROCEDURE IsEmptyTree (t : Tree) : BOOLEAN;
(* Postcondition: returns TRUE if t is empty, otherwise
                                        FALSE *)

BEGIN
    RETURN (t = NIL)
END IsEmptyTree;

PROCEDURE NumberOfValues (t: Tree) : Number;
(* Postcondition: returns either one or two, depending on
    the number of values at the root *)

BEGIN
    RETURN t^.Num
END NumberOfValues;

END access.
```

There are several reasons for our interest in 2-3 trees. One is that they generalize to a structure which can be used to implement a table stored in external memory (such as a disk). This structure is called a *B-tree* (named after Bayer 1972). Such a structure can have any number of items in each node. If the number of items held in each node is, at most, two then each node has a maximum of three subtrees: in this case the B-tree, which is said to be of *order* three, is identical to a 2-3 tree.

Also, due to the fact that 2-3 search trees remain perfectly balanced at all times, they can be searched very efficiently ($O(\log_2 n$), where n is the number of items in the tree). Consequently, they can be used as an efficient implementation of the abstract data type *table*, which we are going to discuss in the next chapter.

Exercises 8.1

1. Using the access procedures for the abstract data type 2-3 search tree, write a procedure to traverse such a tree, printing out each key in increasing order.

2. By rewriting, determine the trees which result from inserting each of the following items in succession into the 2-3 search tree (g, m, (c), (j), (n)), using the procedure Insert which was given earlier for 2-3 search trees:

(i)   a
(ii) p
(iii) h
(iv) k
(v)   b

3. Implement the procedure F i n d, the heading of which is given below:

```
PROCEDURE Find ( i : InfoType ; t : Tree ) : InfoType ;
(* Precondition: takes an item i and a 2-3 search tree
    Postcondition: returns the information associated with
    i if i is in the tree, otherwise indicate that i is not
    present *)
```

4. Write a procedure which flattens a 2-3 search tree in inorder, so that the resulting list of items is in ascending order (for example, a 2-3 search tree of characters would be flattened to a list which was in alphabetical order). The procedure heading is given below:

```
PROCEDURE OrderFlatten ( t : Tree ) : List ;
(* Precondition: takes a 2-3 search tree
    Postcondition: returns a list (in ascending order) of
    the items which are in the tree *)
```

5. Rewrite the following expressions:

(i)   Delete (g, (g, m, (a), (j), (n))

(ii)   Delete (m, (g, m, (a), (j), (n))

(iii) Delete (n, (g, m, (a), (j), (n))

(iv)   Delete (a, (g, m, (a), (j), (n))

(v)   Delete (j, (g, m, (a), (j), (n))

(vi)   Delete (j, (j, (e, (c, (a), (d)), (g, (f), (h))), (p, (n, (k, l), (o)), (r, (q), (u)))
       ))

SUMMARY

The abstract data type *n-ary tree* is a finite set of nodes which is either empty or consists of a data item (called the *root*) and a number ($\leq n$) of disjoint *n*-ary trees, called *subtrees*, together with a number of access procedures.

A node which is not a leaf node is called a *non-terminal* or *interior* node.

The *degree* of a node is the number of subtrees it has.

The *degree* of a *tree* is the maximum degree of the nodes in the tree.

The algebraic specification for an *n*-ary tree is a straightforward extension to that of a binary tree.

The abstract data type *2-3 tree* is a finite set of nodes which is either empty, or consists of a root containing one item and two disjoint subtrees, or of a root containing two items and three disjoint subtrees, (called left, middle and right), where the subtrees are 2-3 trees of the same height, together with a number of access procedures.

When specifying a 2-3 tree algebraically we can use the specification of a binary tree as a basis and add extra procedures to deal with the middle subtree and the fact that the root may contain either one or two items.

The abstract data type *2-3 search tree* is a 2-3 tree which has an ordering imposed on the nodes such that, if there is one item at the root, all values in its left subtree are less than the value at the root, and all values in its right one are greater than the value at the root, and both subtrees are also 2-3 search trees. Otherwise, if there are two items at the root of the tree the smaller value of the two must be greater than all values in the left subtree and less than all values in the middle one, and the larger of the two must be greater than all values in the middle subtree and less than all values in the right. Again all the subtrees must be 2-3 search trees.

A 2-3 search tree is always perfectly balanced, and the insertion algorithm ensures that if it does grow, it will remain balanced. Consequently, searching such a tree is very efficient ($O(\log_2 n)$, where n is the number of items in the tree).

CHAPTER 9

The Abstract Data Type Table

INTRODUCTION

In this chapter we discuss the abstract data type *table*. Information which is to be sorted and searched is often stored in tabular form. The items in the table consist of several different parts, one of which is chosen to be the *key*, that is, it is used to identify the item. Often the key will be numerical. Various implementation methods will be discussed, one of which, the *hash table*, provides us with an operation to retrieve items which is very efficient. Consequently this is the implementation that we will concentrate on.

DEFINITION

The abstract data type *table* is a collection of an arbitrary number of distinct items (all of the same type), each of which is identified by a distinct key, together with a number of access procedures.

ALGEBRAIC SPECIFICATION

The algebraic specification of the abstract data type table consists of constructor functions (Empty and Insert), predicate functions (IsEmpty and IsIn) and a selector function (Retrieve).

Syntax of the access procedures

```
PROCEDURE Empty ( ) : Table ;
(* Postcondition: returns an empty table *)


PROCEDURE IsEmpty ( T : Table ) : BOOLEAN ;
(* Postcondition: returns TRUE if T is empty, else FALSE *)


PROCEDURE Insert ( T : Table ; k : CARDINAL ; i : InfoType
                                          ) : Table;
```

```
(* Postcondition: returns a table with key k and data i
    inserted, if they were not already in T, otherwise
    return T *)

PROCEDURE Retrieve ( T : Table ; k : CARDINAL ) : InfoType ;
(* Postcondition: returns the data associated with k *)

PROCEDURE IsIn ( T : Table ; k : CARDINAL ) : BOOLEAN ;
(* Postcondition:returns TRUE if key k is in table
    T, else FALSE *)
```

Semantics of the access procedures

The axioms are given below: T is a table, k and j are cardinal numbers, and i is the data associated with k.

1. IsEmpty (Empty ( )) = TRUE
2. IsEmpty (Insert (T, k, i)) = FALSE
3. Retrieve (Insert (T, k, i), j) = if j = k $then$ i $else$ Retrieve (T, j)
4. Retrieve (Empty ( ), i) = error
5. IsIn (Empty ( ), j) = FALSE
6. IsIn (Insert (T, k, i), j) = if j = k $then$ TRUE $else$ IsIn (T, j)

APPLICATIONS

Search tables are used in a multitude of areas of computer science. Examples of applications include the basic kernels of many database systems and the symbol table of some compilers. We will consider the latter of these applications in more detail.

A symbol table for a compiler for a block-structured language holds all the identifiers used by a program and information concerning them. For example, if we have a procedure:

```
PROCEDURE Cons ( i : InfoType ; l : List ) : List ;
```

then the symbol table must record that Cons is a procedure and must maintain a list of its parameters.

In block-structured languages (such as Modula-2 and Pascal) the identifiers which are currently in scope must be held in the symbol table. On exit from a block all the identifiers declared within that block are no longer accessible and must be removed from the symbol table which returns to its state before entry to the block.

The algebraic specification for the type symbol table is exactly the same as that given for the abstract data type table given above. (We need to create an empty symbol table, insert an item into it, retrieve an item from it, and ask whether the table is empty or whether a specific item is in the table.) So we can use the type table to implement a symbol table. However, every time we enter a new block we will need a new symbol table because variables are only in scope during the lifetime of the block in which they are declared. When a new symbol table is created we need an abstract data type to hold the previous symbol table so that it can be retrieved on exit from the block. The obvious choice for this is the type *stack*, since if a variable is not declared in the current symbol table we can pop a symbol table off the stack and search that instead.

Alternatively, instead of creating a new symbol table on entry to each block we could simply add to the current symbol table (while simultaneously putting a copy of it on the stack), overwriting any entries which are already present. On exit from the block the old symbol table is popped off the stack.

IMPLEMENTATIONS OF THE ABSTRACT DATA TYPE TABLE

There are several ways to implement the abstract data type table, some of which involve the use of abstract data types discussed earlier in the text. Since a table is essentially a list of the values we could use our implementation of the abstract data type list. The implementation of the list can be either dynamic or static. Figure 9.1 shows a possible dynamic implementation.

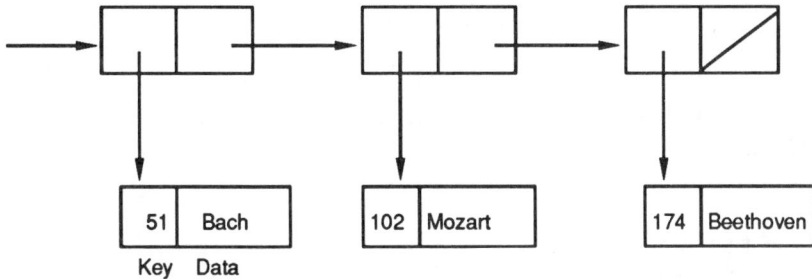

| 51 | Bach | | 102 | Mozart | | 174 | Beethoven |
| Key | Data |

Figure 9.1

Note that `InfoType` will be a structured type consisting of two values. One of these is a key (a cardinal number) and the other is the data which are associated with that key. The items are held in increasing order of their key values to aid searching. In fact this structure is the same as that used to implement a priority queue.

```
TYPE
   InfoType = POINTER TO RECORD
                          key  : CARDINAL ;
                          data : Datatype
                 END ;
```

With a dynamic implementation we have the advantage of dynamic memory allocation and also efficient sequential processing. However, the efficiency of retrieval by key (for example, in answer to the question 'What information is associated with key 531? ') is $O(n)$.

The static implementation uses an array of records. Figure 9.2 shows the static implementation corresponding to figure 9.1.

A static implementation gives us efficient sequential processing as well as reasonably efficient random access, because the binary search algorithm can be used to locate items if these are held in order of their key values. However, this would mean that insertion would require $O(\log_2 n)$ comparisons and $O(n)$ item shifts, where n is the number of items in the table. Also, as with all static implementations, we are restricted by the size of the data structure which must be declared at compile time. If we use the abstract data type binary search tree we have

	Key	Data
1	51	Bach
2	102	Mozart
3	174	Beethoven

Figure 9.2

the advantage of a dynamic implementation which we can still look up using a binary search. Thus we might declare:

```
TYPE
 Table = POINTER TO Node ;
 Node =   RECORD
            data : Infotype ;
            left, right : Table
          END ;
```

The efficiency of the algorithms to search, insert and delete items in a binary search tree obviously depends on the shape of the tree. These algorithms all compare a specified value with the values in the nodes along a path in the tree. The path always starts at the root and takes the left or right branch, until the value is found. The number of comparisons is equal to the number of nodes in the path. As was shown earlier, the height of a binary tree is O ($\log_2 n$), where n is the number of nodes in the tree. So the maximum number of comparisons is also O ($\log_2 n$) if the tree is balanced. Consequently, a 2-3 search tree, which remains balanced and only grows on insertion of an item in certain circumstances, is also a good implementation for the type table. However, locating an item with all of the techniques discussed above involves searching. The implementation we are about to discuss allows us to locate an item in nearly constant time.

If sequential processing of items is not required a *hash table* is a suitable implementation for the type table. This is a static implementation which uses an array:

```
TYPE Table = ARRAY [ 0 .. N - 1 ] OF InfoType ;
```

However, instead of inserting the items sequentially into the array, a *hash function* is used to organize the insertions. A hash function is a mapping from the key values to cardinals in the range 0 to N - 1. For example, suppose N to be 101. The hash function:

$h(x) = x \text{ MOD } 101$

maps key values to cardinals in the range 0 to 100. So, for example, the entry with key 174 is mapped to the array location

174 MOD 101 = 73

The aim of the hash function is to scatter the keys randomly throughout the array.

Figure 9.3 is the hash table representation of the example in figure 9.2 using the hash function $h(x)$. With this technique random access is very efficient, but sequential processing is not because items are distributed randomly in the table. Consequently hash tables are frequently used to implement randomly accessed tables (for example, symbol tables used by compilers, tables of files used by operating systems, databases, etc.) Hash tables are also often used to store *sparse* sets of data: that is, sets of data which are potentially very large but which in fact only contain a small number of *significant* values (values which differ from some default value). A set of integers, for example, is potentially infinite, and so it is not possible to declare such a type in many imperative languages (including Modula-2). Databases are often sparse: when they are first created they might have very few members, but they must be able to hold all potential members that may be added over a number of years. Only the significant values are stored in the hash table.

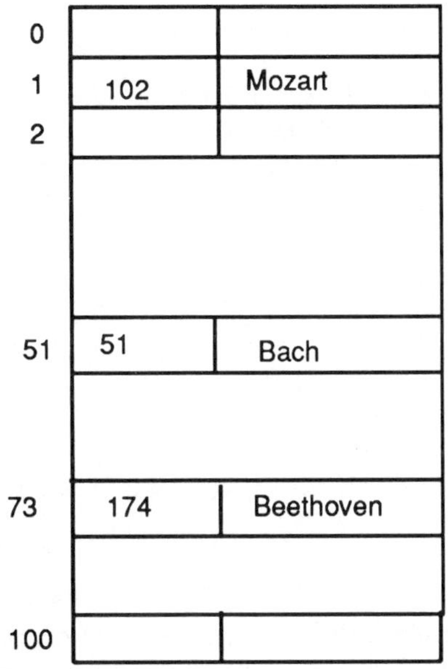

Figure 9.3

A hash function maps key values to a restricted range of numbers. Because of this, a hash function is necessarily a many-to-one function, and this introduces the possibility of *collisions*. Consider, for example, finding the positions of items with keys 233 and 536 using the hash function $h(x)$:

h (233) = 233 MOD 101 = 31.
h (536) = 536 MOD 101 = 31.

A collision has occurred because the hash function is a many-to-one mapping. There are many values which are mapped to position 31 by the hash function given above (figure 9.4). Keys which collide are said to be *synonyms* with respect to h.

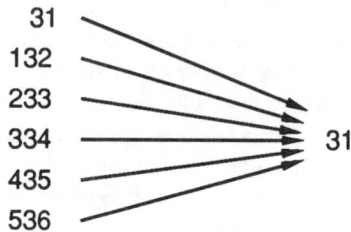

Figure 9.4

The probability that there will not be any collisions is extremely small. This is known as the 'birthday paradox': if there are 23 people together in a room, the probability that at least two people have a common birthday is greater than 0.5 (Feller 1950). Thus hash functions with no collisions are so rare that it is worth looking for them in only special circumstances (for example, if speed is critical).

The position which a key hashes to is known as its *home address*. When a collision does occur it must be resolved in some way. This involves calculating second, third, etc. choice positions $p2$, $p3$, ... for a key and trying each in turn until a vacant position is found. This process is known as *rehashing* and the sequence $p1$, $p2$, ... for any key is known as its *probe sequence*.

The simple *linear rehash* function tries successive positions in turn. If the table is full and the item cannot be inserted then the final rehashed position will be equal to the initial one. For example, for a table with 101 spaces we would have the statement

$$p (x) := (p (x) + 1) \text{ MOD } 101$$

where initially $p (x) = h (x)$. So the first rehashed position for the key 536 would be:

$$p (536) = 32 \text{ MOD } 101 = 32$$

Later in the chapter we will look at more hash functions and alternative methods of resolving collisions. First, though, we turn to the implementation of the access procedures. We will assume the following declarations:

```
TYPE
   Item = RECORD
            key : CARDINAL ;
            info : InfoType ;
          END ;

   Table = ARRAY [0..TableTop] OF Item ;
```

where `TableTop` is a constant which limits the size of the table. Since many Modula-2 compilers do not allow arrays to be returned from functions, a pointer to an array may have to be used instead to allow a functional style. However, in the following pseudocode we take the liberty of assuming that an object which is an array can be returned from a function. The form of the access procedures will be sketched: the reader is invited to implement them fully as an exercise.

First, consider the procedure `Empty`, which has the heading:

```
PROCEDURE Empty ( )  : Table ;
(* Postcondition: returns an empty table *)
```

We will use a constant of type `InfoType` called `null` to indicate that the information field of a slot in the table is empty. The procedure `Empty` can then be implemented by returning a table in which the information field of every slot is empty, i.e. for some variable `T` of type `Table` and a cardinal number `i` we have:

```
FOR i := 0 TO TableTop DO
    T[i].info := null ;
END ;
RETURN T
```

Since we need to be able to determine when a slot of the table is empty, we will implement a function called `IsEmptySlot`, as shown below:

```
PROCEDURE IsEmptySlot ( T: Table ; i : CARDINAL) : BOOLEAN ;
(* Postcondition: returns true if slot i of table T is
    empty, otherwise returns false *)

BEGIN
  RETURN T[ i ].info = null
END IsEmptySlot ;
```

Now we can easily implement IsEmpty:

```
PROCEDURE IsEmpty ( T : Table ) : BOOLEAN ;
(* Postcondition: returns TRUE if T is empty, else FALSE *)

VAR i : CARDINAL ;

BEGIN
  FOR i := 0 TO TableTop DO
    IF NOT IsEmptySlot ( T, i ) THEN
      RETURN FALSE ;
    END ;
  END ;
  RETURN TRUE ;
END IsEmpty ;
```

Now consider the procedure `Insert`. We first determine whether the slot in the table indexed by the home address is empty, and if it is, we insert the key and its associated information. If it is not empty then we must determine whether the slot indexed by the *rehash* function is empty. If it is, then the values can be inserted; if not, the process must be repeated until an empty slot is found or all the slots have been checked and found to be full. With a linear rehash, this occurs when the slot found by the rehash function is the same as the home address. This gives us the following pseudocode:

PROCEDURE Insert (T : Table ; k : CARDINAL ; i : InfoType) : Table;
(* Postcondition: returns a table with key k and data i inserted, if they were not already
   in T, otherwise return T *)

if IsEmptySlot (T, Hash (k)) *then*
    insert k and i
else
    while rehash (k) <> hash (k) *and not* IsEmptySlot (T, rehash (k)) *do*
        calculate rehash (k)
    end
    if IsEmptySlot (T, rehash (k)) *then*
        insert k and i
    else
        indicate that the table is full
    end
end

The pseudocode for the procedure Retrieve is given below:

PROCEDURE Retrieve (T : Table ; k : CARDINAL) : InfoType ;
(* Postcondition: returns the data associated with k *)

if the key field of T indexed by hash (k) = k, *then* *return* the corresponding info field
else
    while rehash (k) <> hash (k) and the key field of rehash (k) <> k *do*
        calculate rehash (k)
    end
    if the key field of rehash (k) = k *then*
        return the corresponding info field
    else
        indicate that k is not in T
    end
end

Finally, here is the pseudocode for the procedure IsIn:

PROCEDURE IsIn (T : Table ; k : CARDINAL) : BOOLEAN ;
(* Postcondition:returns TRUE if key k is in table T, else FALSE *)

if the key field of T indexed by hash (k) = k *then*
    return true
else
    while rehash(k)<> hash (k) and the key field of rehash (k) <> k *do*
        calculate rehash (k)
    end

if the key field of rehash (k) = k *then*
   return true
else
   return false
  end
end

Before discussing several different hash functions we consider how we can produce a number from a key which consists of characters. In such a case a number must be derived from the key so that the number can then be hashed. There are several ways to do this, most of which are based on using the ordinal number of each character in the key. For example, we could sum the ordinal values of each character. The procedure `Hash` below takes a key which consists of characters and adds their ordinal values before returning this sum modulo the table size.

```
CONST
   TableSize = 40;
TYPE
   Index = 0..TableSize - 1;
   Length = [ 0 .. 20 ] ; (* maximum word size = 20
                                        characters *)

PROCEDURE Hash ( AKey : ARRAY OF CHAR ) : Index ;
(* Postcondition: returns the home address of 'AKey' *)

VAR
   Count : Length ;
   Temp : CARDINAL ;

BEGIN
   Temp := 0 ;
   FOR Count := 0 TO HIGH ( AKey ) DO
     Temp := Temp + ORD ( AKey [ Count ] )
   END ;
   RETURN Temp MOD TableSize
END Hash ;
```

Note

(1) The array `AKey` is a *conformant* or *open* array, which means that we can pass it as a parameter as shown in the procedure `Hash` above, without specifying any bounds on its size.
(2) `HIGH` is a function which takes a one-dimensional array and returns the upper bound of the array.

For example, if we execute the procedure with the key ML we have

$$\text{Temp} = \text{ORD ('M')} + \text{ORD ('L')}$$
$$= 77 + 76 = 153$$

So ML would be mapped onto the value 33.

Alternatively, we could consider each ordinal number as a 7-bit binary string, and then concatenate them to produce the result:

ORD ('M') = 77 = 1001101
ORD ('L') = 76 = 1001100

So the key ML would map to:

$$1001101 \mid 1001100 = 128 * 77 + 76$$
$$= 9932$$

If the hash function is given by $h(x) = x$ MOD Tablesize, and Tablesize = 40, then ML would be mapped to 9932 MOD 40 = 12.

Hash functions

Two desirable properties of a good hash function are:

(1) The function must be quick and easy to compute. The most frequently used hash functions require only a single multiplication or division.
(2) It should scatter values randomly throughout the array so that the probability of collisions is minimal.

Another way of stating the second property is to say that a hash function should be *uniform*. A hash function is uniform if a particular key is equally likely to hash to any of the available locations.

i.e. the probability that $h(x) = i$ is $\dfrac{1}{\text{Number of available locations}}$

for all locations i. We will consider techniques which provide this uniformity.

1. Division

This is a simple and effective hash function which we have seen in previous examples:

h (key) = key MOD n

where n is the size of the hash table. The effectiveness of the function depends on the choice of n. For example, if n is divisible by 2 then odd keys are mapped to odd locations and even keys are mapped to even ones, in which case the use of the hash table would be biased. Knuth (1973) has shown that a good choice of n (and hence the size of the table) is a large prime number. This is a safeguard against many subtle kinds of patterns of data (for example keys whose digits are likely to be permutations of one another).

2. Multiplication

This is also called the *mid-square* method. This hash function is computed by first squaring the key and then extracting the middle digits of the number:

h (key) = middle digits of (key * key)

Thus for the key ML, using the character to integer mapping described earlier and a four-digit index :

h (ML) = middle digits of (9932 * 9932)
       = middle digits of (98,644,624)
       = 6446

The advantages of this method are that it is easy to calculate and that the middle digits of the square will usually depend on all the characters in the key, so the probability of collisions occurring should be minimal.

3. Digit selection

Extracting a number of digits from the key gives a random distribution of values if the key was chosen from a random population. For example, suppose the keys to be hashed are nine-digit numbers. The hash function

h (key) = key MOD 1000

will return the last three digits of the key. So

h (612 308 572) = 572

As a second example, consider the hash function:

h ($d1$ $d2$ $d3$ $d4$ $d5$ $d6$ $d7$ $d8$ $d9$) = $d1$ $d2$

It may be necessary to determine whether the chosen digits will produce a uniform distribution of values. For example, if the numbers to be hashed are telephone numbers, including their dialling codes, then all numbers which have the same dialling code will collide (for example, all London numbers will hash to 01). To prevent this, a technique called *digit analysis* (Lum *et al* 1971) can be used. In this method the values of each digit are analysed and the digit is removed from the key if its distribution is found to be skewed. However, this technique is not very practical in the majority of situations.

4. Folding

There are several variations of this method. The simplest version just adds the individual digits of the key:

$$h (d_1 \ldots d_n) = \sum_{i=1}^{n} d_i$$

For example, suppose the key has five digits. Then

$$h\,(\,d1\ d2\ d3\ d4\ d5\,) = d1 + d2 + d3 + d4 + d5$$

The result will be an integer in the range 0 to 45. For example,

$$\begin{aligned}h\,(\,38219\,) &= 3 + 8 + 2 + 1 + 9 \\ &= 23\end{aligned}$$

If a larger range of possible values is needed, the digits may be considered in pairs. In this case, the hash function is given by:

$$h\,(dsub1\ ...\ d_n) = \sum_{i=1}^{n\,DIV\,2} d_{2i-1}\ d_{2i} \qquad \text{if } n \text{ is even}$$

$$h\,(dsub1\ ...\ d_n) = \sum_{i=1}^{n\,DIV\,2} d_{2i-1}\ d_{2i} + d_n \quad \text{if } n \text{ is odd}$$

where the juxtaposition of the digits denotes exactly that, and not multiplication. For example,

$$h\,(\,d1\ d2\ d3\ d4\ d5\,) = d1d2 + d3d4 + d5$$

Therefore
$$\begin{aligned}h\,(\,38219\,) &= 38 + 21 + 9 \\ &= 68\end{aligned}$$

The method could obviously be extended to considering the digits in threes, and so on.

Of course, any variation of these methods can be used. For example, we could fold a key by considering the digits in groups of four:

$$\begin{aligned}key &= 01\ 598\ 5111 \\ Fold\,(\,key) &= 0159 + 8511 + 1 \\ &= 8671\end{aligned}$$

and then take this number modulo 101 to produce the home address:

$$\begin{aligned}h\,(key) &= Fold\,(\,key\,)\ MOD\ 101 \\ &= 8671\ MOD\ 101 \\ &= 86\end{aligned}$$

COLLISIONS

The techniques for resolving collisions which we are going to discuss fall into two categories: *open-address methods* (of which linear rehashing is an example) and *external chaining*.

Open-address methods

Keys which hash to a position which is already full are rehashed to some other position in the table that is unoccupied or 'open'. We will consider four open-address rehashing techniques: linear, double, random and quadratic.

Linear rehashing

Linear rehashing, which was discussed earlier in this chapter, is a simple open-address method. To insert a key the home address is first calculated. If a collision occurs the table is then searched sequentially from this address until an open position is found or the table is exhausted.

Example

> Hash function $h(x)$ $= x$ MOD 7
> rehash function $r(x) = (h(x) + i)$ MOD 7

where $i = 1, 2$, etc.

Suppose the key values are (listed in the order of insertion) 48, 85, 351, 563, 108 and 92. The keys 48 and 85 can be inserted immediately. The home address of the key value 351 is 1, but this collides with the value which has already been inserted and so is rehashed:

$$r(351) = (h(351) + 1) \text{ MOD } 7 = 2$$

The key 563 can be inserted at its home address (3). The next key, 108, also hashes to slot 3 and so must be rehashed to slot 4. Finally, 92 hashes to slot 1. Since this slot is full, 92 is rehashed to slot 2. However, again, the slot is full and so we have to rehash once more. Eventually, on the fourth attempt, we find an empty slot in which the key can be inserted. The resulting hash table is shown in figure 9.5 (the data associated with each key value have not been included).

Now consider what happens when an item is deleted from the table. For example, suppose that the item in position 4 (108) is deleted. If the position is only marked as empty, then a search for an item which has been rehashed from this position might terminate at this slot without finding the item that was in the table. One solution to this problem is to mark locations from which items have been deleted with a special value. However, searches for keys that have been rehashed will then take longer than necessary because of the extra checking for this special value. To solve this, the table could be rearranged from time to time.

There are two problems with linear rehashing:

(1) Any key that collides with another will have to collide with all other keys that have already been rehashed (due to collisions with the same key) before an empty position is found. This is called *primary clustering*.

(2) Rehash address sequences eventually start to overlap. This is called *secondary clustering*. In the example above, the search for a rehash from position 1 merges with the search for a rehash from position 3.

Random rehashing

If the hash function is to distribute the keys randomly in the table each rehash should be a random jump to a new location. Because we need to be able to locate all the items we should actually use a different hash function to determine each random jump. In fact we could use a pseudo-random number generator, using the key as the seed. Alternately, we could store the random number with the address which is being hashed from. This has the advantage of speed but uses more space.

Table Address	Key Value
0	
1	85
2	351
3	563
4	108
5	92
6	48

Figure 9.5

Random rehashing has the advantage of eliminating primary and secondary clustering, but is more difficult to implement.

Double hashing

With this method the increment for successive probes is calculated by using a second hash function. This saves the work needed with random rehashing, such as having a large number of hash functions or storing the random number.

Example

Suppose that the hash function $h(x) = x$ MOD 7 produces the table in figure 9.6 for a given set of keys. Also, suppose that the second function is

$$f(x) = x \text{ MOD (tablesize} - 2) + 1$$

and we want to store the value 64. This will clash with 85, so the second function is calculated:

$$f(x) = (64 \text{ MOD } 5) + 1 = 5$$

and the table is probed at:

$$(h(x) + 5) \text{ MOD } 7 = 6 \text{ (collision again)}$$
$$(h(x) + 5 + 5) \text{ MOD } 7 = 4 \text{ (empty)}$$

The performance of double hashing in terms of the expected number of probes is close to that of random rehashing.

Table
Address   Table Contents

Table Address	Table Contents
0	empty
1	85
2	empty
3	563
4	empty
5	40
6	48

Figure 9.6

Quadratic hashing

Collisions are resolved by using a quadratic function of i, (where i takes the values 1, 2, etc.) to calculate possible locations for a key which is a synonym. So the rehash function is of the form:

$$(\text{ home address} + i^2) \text{ MOD tablesize}$$

For further details see Radke (1970).

Open-address methods have the disadvantage of causing clustering. Also, because the implementation is static the table may become full. The collision-resolution method we look at next is a dynamic implementation which resolves some of these problems.

External chaining

An alternative to the static open address methods is to consider each table address as referring to a list (implemented dynamically) of key values.

For example, using the key values of figure 9.5 and the hash function $h(x) = x$ MOD 7, we obtain the structure shown in figure 9.7.

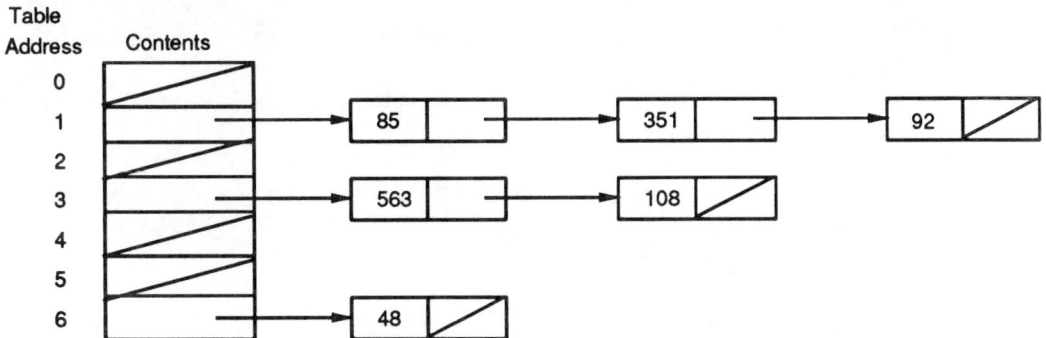

Figure 9.7

One of the advantages of external chaining is that the implementation is straightforward. There are no problems with deletion and clustering does not occur (although obviously each list grows in proportion to the number of collisions there are). There is also the advantage that storage for items is allocated dynamically and so depends on the number of items which are actually present in the table at any time. We will see later that the efficiency with which an item can be retrieved compares well with that of open-address methods.

HOW EFFICIENT IS HASHING?

The number of comparisons needed to find an item which is in a hash table depends on the number of collisions which occurred during its insertion. If no collisions occurred, there will only be one comparison to locate an item which is in the table. An indication of the probability of collisions occurring is given by the *loading factor*, alpha, which is defined as:

$$\text{alpha} = \frac{\text{Number of locations occupied}}{\text{Table size}}$$

As alpha increases, so does the probability of collisions occurring (assuming that all locations in the table are equally likely to be hashed to). We can obviously decrease the value of alpha (and so improve the efficiency of hashing) by increasing the size of the hash table.

The method used to resolve collisions also affects the number of comparisons which will be needed to find an item. With open-address methods the number of comparisons needed to locate an item increases significantly as alpha tends to one. See Knuth, (1973) for more details. However, for external chaining the number of comparisons needed to find an item increases in direct proportion to the number of collisions which occur, as the size of the list to be searched increases.

Exercises 9.1

1. What is a *sparse* set of data?
2. What are the qualities that are essential for a good hashing function?
3. What is meant by a *collision*?
4. Explain what is meant by an *open-address* method for resolving collisions, and demonstrate the method by giving two examples.
5. Explain the concept of *external chaining* and state the advantages of using this technique. Are there any disadvantages and if so, what?
6. Use the hash function Hash given earlier in this chapter to generate hash indices in the range 0...39 for the names of the following programming languages:

```
BASIC COBOL FORTRAN COMAL PASCAL MODULA APL ALGOL60 ALGOL68
MODULA2 HOPE ML MIRANDA ADA PL1 FORTH PROLOG SIMULA CORAL
LISP FP FL
```

7. Draw a diagram of the hash table that results from question (7), assuming that the table is of size 40 and a linear rehash is used to resolve collisions.
8. Calculate the average number of comparisons required to locate a *valid* language name in a

hash table of size 40 which uses the hash function Hash, again assuming a linear rehash to resolve collisions.

9. Calculate the average number of comparisons required to determine that a language name is *invalid* using such a scheme.

10. Use the hash function given below with a table size of 29 to generate hash indices for the names of the programming languages in the list below. Assume that if there are any digits in the name their value is added to the value of the key.

h (key) = (sum of positions of letters of key in alphabet) MOD tablesize

```
BASIC COBOL FORTRAN COMAL PASCAL MODULA APL ALGOL60 ALGOL68
MODULA2 HOPE ML MIRANDA ADA PL1 FORTH PROLOG SIMULA CORAL
LISP FP FL
```

11. Successively insert the keys of question (11) in a hash table of size 29, using external chaining to resolve collisions.

12. Write and test the implementation of the data type table which was described earlier.

SUMMARY

The abstract data type *table* is a collection of an arbitrary number of distinct items (all of the same type), each of which is identified by a distinct key, together with a number of access procedures.

Search tables are used in a multitude of areas of computer science. Examples of applications include the basic kernels of many database systems and the symbol table of some compilers.

There are several ways to implement the abstract data type table. The one which we concentrated on in this chapter was hashing. This is a static implementation which uses an array and a hash function to organize the insertions. A hash function is a mapping from the key values to cardinal numbers which represent the indices of the array.

Hashing is also a possible implementation technique for sparse sets of data, i.e. sets of data which are potentially very large but which actually only have a few items which differ from some default value.

Hash functions must be chosen carefully so as to be quick to calculate, and must attempt to minimize the probability of collisions by scattering data as randomly as possible.

We discussed two categories of rehashing methods: *open-address methods* and *external chaining*.

The number of comparisons which must be made to locate an item which is in a hash table depends on:

1. The loading factor, alpha $= \dfrac{\text{Number of locations occupied}}{\text{Table size}}$

and

2. The method used to resolve collisions

Hash tables should be used if sequential access in a particular order is *not* required but efficient *random* access is.

CHAPTER 10

The Abstract Data Type Graph

INTRODUCTION

The abstract data type tree is non-linear, i.e. each item may have multiple successors, although no more than one predecessor. The abstract data type *graph* is also a non-linear type, and is more general in that each item may have zero or more successors and predecessors. In this chapter we introduce some terminology associated with the type graph and give an algebraic specification. We discuss two possible implementations, the adjacency matrix and the adjacency list. Finally, as an example of an application, we describe the use of graphs in the evaluation of expressions written in functional languages.

DEFINITION

The abstract data type *graph* consists of a finite set of *nodes* and a set of *edges*, where an edge is a connection between two nodes, together with a number of access procedures.

The word *vertex* is sometimes used instead of node and *arc* may be used instead of edge.

REPRESENTATION

Diagrammatically, an edge is shown as a line joining the associated nodes. If the graph consists of two or more disjoint sets of nodes then it is said to be *disconnected*, and otherwise it is *connected*. For example, figure 10.1 shows two graphs, (a) which is connected and (b) which is not.

(a)   (b)

Figure 10. 1

The abstract data type graph is an extension of the type tree, which in turn is a extension of the type list. Because of its generality the type graph has many applications, such as the representation of chip circuit diagrams, departments in a university, courses within a department, finding shortest routes and evaluation of expressions in functional languages, to name but a few.

Example

In figure 10.2, the nodes are cities and the edges are train lines between them. The edges may be labelled with information such as the length of time for the journey. Such transport maps are often used on public transport systems to convey information to passengers.

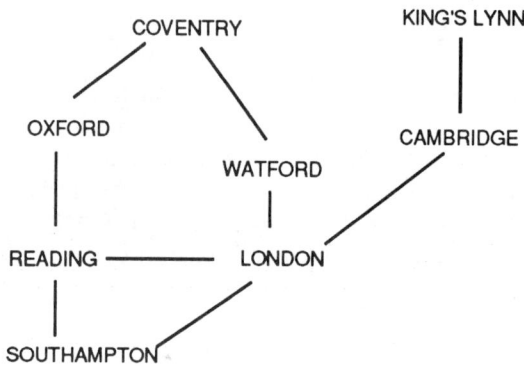

Figure 10. 2

Before we give the algebraic specification of the type graph we will introduce some terminology.

TERMINOLOGY

Two nodes are said to be *adjacent*, or *neighbours*, if there is an edge connecting them. Nodes which are adjacent may be represented by a tuple (a,b) where a and b are the values of the nodes. Examples of some of the adjacent nodes in figure 10.2 include London and Watford, London and Southampton, Oxford and Coventry.

A *path* is a sequence of nodes $n_1, n_2, ..., n_m$ such that for all i from 1 to $(m-1)$, each pair of nodes (n_i, n_{i+1}) are adjacent.

For example, in figure 10.2 there is a path from London to Oxford via Reading. There is also one from London to Oxford via Watford and Coventry and one via Southampton and Reading.

A path is *simple* if each of its nodes occurs only once in the sequence. All the examples of paths given so far have been simple. A *cycle* is a path that is simple except that the first and last nodes are the same. For example, in figure 10.2 there is a cycle which contains the nodes London, Southampton, Reading and London. If a path from a node to itself does not contain any other nodes then it is said to be a *degenerate cycle*.

A graph which does not have any cycles is said to be *acyclic*.

ALGEBRAIC SPECIFICATION

The specification must comprise constructor functions to create an empty graph, add a node and add an edge; selector functions which will return a graph without a particular node or without a particular edge; and predicate functions which test whether a graph is empty and whether two nodes are adjacent. The following specification allows for graphs which may be disconnected.

Syntax of the access procedures

1. Constructor function

```
PROCEDURE Empty ( )  : Graph ;
(* Postcondition: returns an empty graph *)

PROCEDURE AddNode ( g : Graph ; n : Node ) : Graph ;
(* Postcondition: returns a graph which consists of
    all the nodes and edges in g and the unconnected
    node n, if it was not in g, otherwise return g *)

PROCEDURE AddEdge ( g : Graph ; n, m : Node ) : Graph ;
(* Postcondition: returns a graph which consists of
    the same nodes and edges as the graph g and an edge
    between n and m if it did not previously exist in G *)
```

2. Predicate functions

```
PROCEDURE IsEmpty ( g : graph ) : BOOLEAN ;
(* Postcondition: returns TRUE if g is an empty
    graph, otherwise FALSE *)

PROCEDURE Contains ( g : Graph ; n : Node ) : BOOLEAN ;
(* Postcondition: returns TRUE if n exists in g,
    otherwise FALSE *)

PROCEDURE IsAdjacent ( g : Graph ; n, m : Node ) : BOOLEAN ;
(* Postcondition: returns TRUE if n is adjacent to m,
    otherwise FALSE *)
```

3. Selector functions

```
PROCEDURE DeleteNode ( g : Graph ; n : Node ) : Graph ;
(* Postcondition: returns a graph which consists of
    all the nodes in g except the node n *)

PROCEDURE DeleteEdge ( g : Graph ; n, m : Node ) : Graph ;
(* Postcondition: returns the graph which results
    from removing the edge between n and m from g *)
```

Semantics of the access procedures

The access procedures must satisfy the following axioms, where g is a graph and m, n, p and q are nodes. Note that a graph can exist in one of three forms: it is either empty, or has been constructed using the constructor function AddNode, or has been constructed using the function AddEdge.

The first axiom just states that we cannot add a node to a graph if it is already in the graph:

1. AddNode (g, n) = *if* Contains (g, n) *then* g *else* AddNode (g, n)

and similarly for an edge:

2. AddEdge (g, n, m) = *if* IsAdjacent (g, n, m) *then* g *else* AddEdge (g, n, m)

The next three axioms describe the behaviour of the function Contains for each of the three forms of graph:

3. Contains (Empty, n) = FALSE
4. Contains (AddNode (g, m), n) = *if* n = m *then* TRUE *else* Contains (g, n)
5. Contains (AddEdge (g, p, q), n) = *if* n = p or n = q *then* TRUE
                                        else Contains (g, n)

The next three give the behaviour of IsAdjacent. The first says that two nodes cannot be adjacent in an empty graph:

6. IsAdjacent (Empty, n, m) = FALSE

If a graph has been formed by the addition of a node, then we ignore this node (since it is not connected to any others) and ask whether the two nodes were adjacent in the graph that existed prior to the addition:

7. IsAdjacent (AddNode (g, p), n, m) = IsAdjacent (g, n, m)

If a graph has been formed by the addition of an edge, then we check to see whether the edge consists of the two nodes we are interested in and return true if it does. Otherwise we ask whether the two nodes were adjacent in the graph which existed before the new edge was added:

8. IsAdjacent (AddEdge (g, p, q), n, m) = *if* (n = p and m = q) or (n = q and m = p)
                                        then TRUE *else* IsAdjacent (g, n, m)

The following three axioms give the semantics of IsEmpty:

9. IsEmpty (Empty) = TRUE
10. IsEmpty (AddNode (g, n)) = FALSE
11. IsEmpty (AddEdge (g, n, m)) = FALSE

The next three describe the behaviour of DeleteNode. First, a node cannot be deleted from an empty graph:

12. DeleteNode (Empty, n) = Empty

If a node, *m*, which is about to be added is equal to the node, *n* say, that we want to delete, then the addition is not performed. However, the node may already have existed in the original graph and so we must use the DeleteNode procedure to check this. Otherwise we delete the node *n* from the original graph and the add the node *m*.

13. DeleteNode (AddNode (g, m), n) = *if* n = m *then* DeleteNode (g, n) *else*
$$AddNode (DeleteNode (g, n), m)$$

If an edge were about to be added and one of the nodes is equal to the one to be deleted, then we cannot add the edge. We must also check the node did not exist in the graph prior to the addition of the node:

Delete (AddEdge (g, p, q), n) = *if* n = p or n = q *then* DeleteNode (g, n)

If neither of the nodes in the edge to be added are equal to the node to be deleted, then the edge can be added to the graph which results from deleting the node from the original graph:

$$else \text{ AddEdge (DeleteNode (g, n), p, q)}$$

This gives us axiom 14:

14. DeleteNode (AddEdge (g, p, q), n) = *if* n = p or n = q *then* DeleteNode (g, n)
$$else \text{ AddEdge (DeleteNode (g, n), p, q)}$$

The last three axioms describe the behaviour of DeleteEdge. We cannot delete an edge from an empty graph:

15. DeleteEdge (Empty, n, m) = Empty

If a node were about to be added to the graph, then we add the node to the graph which results from deleting the edge from the original graph:

16. DeleteEdge (AddNode (g, p), n, m) = AddNode (DeleteEdge (g, n, m), p)

If an edge which is equal to the edge to be deleted were about to be added to a graph g, then the addition does not take place. We still need to delete the edge if it existed in the graph g:

DeleteEdge (AddEdge (g, p, q), n, m) = *if* (n = p and m = q) or (n = q and m = p) *then*
$$DeleteEdge (g, n, m)$$

Otherwise the addition can take place, and the edge must still be deleted from the graph g:

$$else \text{ AddEdge (DeleteEdge (g, n, m), p, q)}$$

This gives us axiom 17:

17. DeleteEdge (AddEdge (g, p, q), n, m) = *if* (n = p and m = q) *or* (n = q and m = p) *then*
DeleteEdge (g, n, m)
else AddEdge (DeleteEdge (g, n, m), p, q)

From the specification of the abstract data type graph we can see that multiple edges and multiple nodes are not allowed in the graph.

The access procedures were chosen because of the operations which they enable us to perform. We have constructor functions which allow us to create an empty graph and insert nodes and edges into a graph. The selector functions enable us to select parts of a graph and the predicate functions give us the ability to answer certain questions about one.

DIRECTED GRAPHS

A *directed graph*, or *digraph*, is defined to be one in which the edges are *directed*. For each edge, one node is said to be the *source* node and the other the *destination* node. This is denoted by drawing an arrow from the source node to the destination node:

Source → Destination

The source node is said to *precede* the destination node and the destination node *succeeds* the source node. If the edges are labelled then the graph is said to be *weighted*.

For a directed graph, instead of IsAdjacent, we will need two extra access procedures:

```
PROCEDURE IsPredecessor ( g : Graph ; n, m : Node ) :
                                             BOOLEAN ;
(* Postcondition: returns TRUE if n and m are
   adjacent and n precedes m *)

PROCEDURE IsSuccessor ( g : Graph ; n, m : Node ) :
                                             BOOLEAN ;
(* Postcondition: returns TRUE if n and m are
   adjacent and n succeeds m *)
```

The comment for the procedure AddEdge (g, n, m) must be changed to show that a directed edge is added from n to m, i.e. n is the source and m the destination.

```
PROCEDURE AddEdge ( g : Graph ; n, m : Node ) : Graph ;
(* Postcondition: returns a graph which consists of
   the same nodes and edges as the graph g and an edge
   from n to m if it did not previously exist in G *)
```

The semantics therefore acquire the following new axioms, in place of those for Is-Adjacent.

Semantics

IsPredecessor (Empty, n, m) = FALSE

IsPredecessor (AddNode (g, n), p, q) = *if* (n = p or n = q) *then* FALSE
                else IsPredecessor (g, p, q)
IsPredecessor (AddEdge (g, n, m), p, q) = *if* (n = p and m = q) *then* TRUE
                else IsPredecessor (g, p, q)
IsSuccessor (Empty, n, m) = FALSE
IsSuccessor (AddNode (g, n), p, q) = *if* (n = p or n = q) *then* FALSE
                else IsSuccessor (g, m, p)
IsSuccessor (AddEdge (g, n, m), p, q) = *if* (n = q and m = p) *then* TRUE
                else IsSuccessor (g, p, q)

Example

A project is made up of a number of separate activities, some of which must be completed before others may commence. If the time that each activity will take is known then the latest completion date for the entire project can be calculated. A *critical path* is a path from the start to the end of the project such that if any activity on it is delayed by an amount T, then the entire project is delayed by T. The interactions between activities may be expressed as a directed graph and for a computer application we might obtain the digraph in figure 10.3.

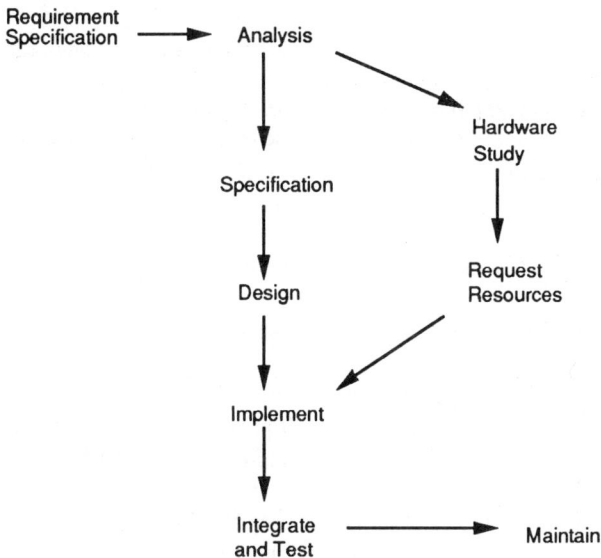

Figure 10. 3

Definition

A node W is *reachable* from a node V if and only if there exists a path from V to W. More formally, a node W is said to be reachable from a node V if:

(1) W and V are the same node; or

(2) W is reachable from some node that is a successor of V.

For each node of a graph there exists a set of nodes which can be reached from that node, called the *reachable set* (figure 10.4). The nodes which can be reached from node 1 in figure 10.4 are 1, 2, 3, 5 and 6 and the reachable sets for all the nodes are:

    reachable (1) = (1, 2, 3, 5, 6)
    reachable (2) = (2, 3, 5, 6)
    reachable (3) = (3, 5, 6)
    reachable (4) = (3, 4, 5, 6)
    reachable (5) = (5, 6)
    reachable (6) = (6)

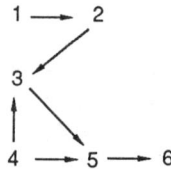

Figure 10.4

A node W is *directly* reachable from a node V if and only if the two nodes are adjacent and W is the successor of V. For example, in figure 10.4 the node 5 is directly reachable from both node 3 and node 4. Node 6 is only directly reachable from node 5.

GRAPH TRAVERSAL

Graph traversal is an extension of the traversal of trees which we have already discussed. The aim is to print the contents of each node in a graph exactly once. There are various ways to do this: the methods which we are going to look at are called *depth first* and *breadth first*.

The algorithms which we are going to discuss will print all the nodes which are reachable from one particular node. If a graph were disconnected then the algorithm would have to be called for each disjoint subgraph.

In depth-first traversal, first some node n1 is processed. Then an adjacent node, n2 (which has not previously been visited) is processed and a depth-first search is started from n2. When a node is reached whose adjacent nodes have all been processed the algorithm back-tracks to the last node visited which has a neighbour still to be processed, and a depth-first search is started from there. Finally, we reach a point where no more nodes can be reached from any of the processed nodes.

For example, possible depth first traversals for the graph in figure 10.5, starting at A, are:

A, B, C, D, F, E, G, H
A, B, E, F, D, C, G, H
A, G, H, B, C, D, F, E
A, G, H, B, E, F, D, C

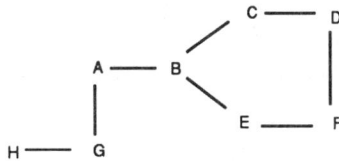

Figure 10. 5

PROCEDURE DepthFirst (g: graph ; n : node) ;
(* Postcondition: prints all the nodes which are reachable from n in depth first order *)

print n
while there is another node n1 adjacent to n *do*
   DepthFirst (g, n1)
end

In a breadth first traversal we first process some node, then *all* its neighbours, followed by all the neighbours of all these nodes, and so on. For example, possible breadth-first traversals of the graph in figure 10.5 are:

A, B, G, C, E, H, D, F
A, G, B, H, E, C, F, D

The pseudocode for this traversal is given below. We use a local variable of type *queue*.

PROCEDURE BreadthFirst (g: graph ; n : node)
(* Postcondition: prints all the nodes which are reachable from n in breadth first order
   *)

VAR q : Queue ;

add n to q
while q is not empty *do*
   remove the item at the front of the queue and print it
   add all of its neighbours which have not been inserted in q to q
end

IMPLEMENTATION

There are many possible implementations for the abstract data type graph. We will consider just two, *adjacency matrices* and *adjacency lists*. The former will be (essentially) a static implementation and the latter dynamic.

An *adjacency matrix* is a square matrix of boolean values, where TRUE is taken to mean that there is an edge from one node (indexing the row) to another (indexing the column) and FALSE to mean that there is not. For example, suppose that the contents of the graph are capital letters and suppose that we have the declarations:

```
TYPE
  Node = ['A'..'Z'] ;
  AdjacencyMatrix = ARRAY Node, Node OF BOOLEAN ;
  Graph = POINTER TO AdjacencyMatrix ;
```

then `AdjacencyMatrix [ i, j ]` = TRUE if (and only if) j is the successor of i (i.e. j is directly reachable from i).

In fact this implementation is not truly static because of the use of a pointer in the declaration of the type `Graph`. This is (as stated in previous chapters) so that variables of type `Graph` can be returned from functions and because we want to declare `Graph` as an opaque type.

As an example if this implementation, consider figure 10.6. In this example the contents of each node are used as indices into the array. If each node consists of a number of values it may be necessary to store the contents of the nodes in a table. A cardinal number could then be assigned to each node and used to index both the table and the adjacency matrix.

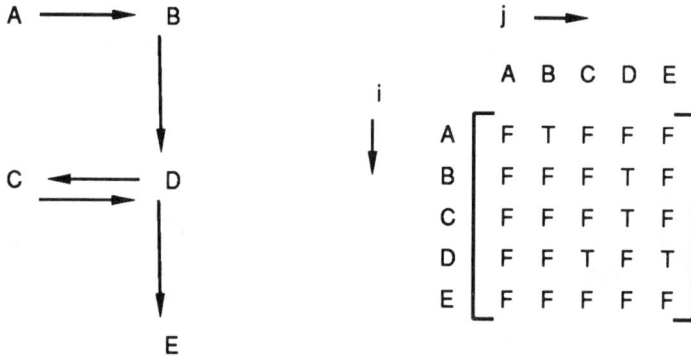

Figure 10.6

Note that we can implement unconnected graphs in this way, since if node i (say) were unconnected it would just mean that A[i, i] would be set to be TRUE. (This assumes that the graph does not have any degenerate cycles in it, i.e. paths from a node to itself which do not visit any other node.)

We therefore have the following implementation for the access procedures:

```
PROCEDURE Empty ( ) : Graph ;
(* Postcondition: returns an empty graph *)

VAR
  i, j : Node ;
  temp : Graph ;

BEGIN
  NEW ( temp ) ;
  FOR i := 'A' TO 'E' DO (* depending on maximum size and
                                    domain of the graph *)
    FOR j := 'A' TO 'E' DO
      temp^ [ i, j ] := FALSE
    END
```

```
      END
      RETURN temp
   END Empty ;


   PROCEDURE AddEdge ( g : Graph ; n1, n2 : Node ) : Graph ;
   (* Postcondition: returns a graph which has the
      same nodes and edges as the graph g and an edge
      from n1 to n2 if it did not previously exist in G *)


   VAR temp : Graph ;


   BEGIN
      NEW (temp) ;
      temp^   := g^ ;            (* copy the graph - see footnote¹ *)
      temp^[ n1, n2 ] := TRUE ;
      RETURN temp ;
   END AddEdge ;


   PROCEDURE IsPredecessor ( g : Graph ; n1, n2 : Node ) :
   BOOLEAN ;
   (* Postcondition: returns TRUE if n1 and n2 are
      adjacent and n1 precedes n2 *)


   BEGIN
      RETURN g^[ n1, n2 ]
   END IsPredecessor ;
```

The other access procedures are left as an exercise for the reader.

The dynamic or *adjacency list* implementation maintains lists of all the neighbours of every node in the graph. Consequently we can implement a graph as a list of lists, using access procedures which mimic the ones for the type list. For example, we could have a procedure HeadOfGraph, which returns a list of nodes which are all adjacent, and so on. Therefore the implementation should not present any difficulty for anyone who has implemented the type list.

A diagram of the implementation of the graph in figure 10.6 is shown in figure 10.7. One way to implement this data structure is as follows:

```
   TYPE
      List = POINTER TO Cell ;
      Cell = RECORD
                  Data : InfoType ;
                  Link : List
               END ;

      Graph = POINTER TO GraphNode ;
      GraphNode = RECORD
                     Info : List ;
                     Next : Graph;
                  END ;
```

---

1   If we know that there are no other copies of the graph being used and efficiency is important then we could alter the original graph g by using the statement temp : = g in place of temp^ : = g^.

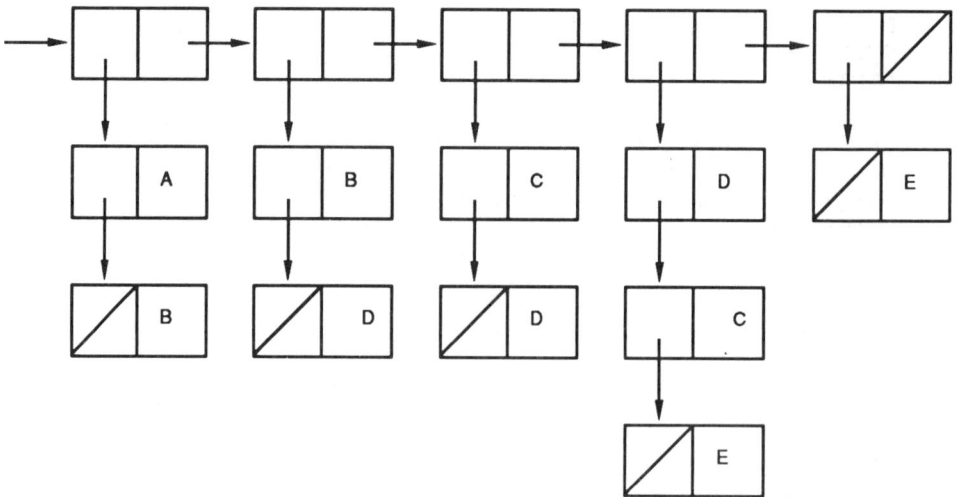

Figure 10.7

Implementation of the access procedures is left as an exercise for the reader.

Of course, there are other implementations for lists of lists. For example, we could use an array of records with two fields, one being the contents of the node and the other a pointer to a list of adjacent nodes. Alternatively. we could have a list of header nodes with three fields: data, a pointer to a list of adjacent nodes and a pointer to the next node in the graph (this is an optimization of our adjacency list method). We could also make use of a variant record, and follow the implementation of generalized lists which we discussed earlier. If there are very few nodes and edges in the graph then the graph is said to be *sparse* and could be implemented as discussed in Chapter 9.

How do the two techniques (adjacency matrices and adjacency lists) compare? Consider two operations:

(1) Given two nodes, determine whether one succeeds the other. For the adjacency matrix we simply inspect the boolean value at the location indexed by the two nodes, whereas for the adjacency list we need to find and then traverse the relevant list.
(2) Find all the neighbours succeeding one particular node. For the adjacency matrix we have to traverse the row indexed by the node, and for the adjacency list we have to find and then traverse the relevant list, which will (in general) be a shorter traversal.

When considering which implementation method to use we should take into account the operations which are most likely to be performed.

The techniques can also be compared from the point of memory requirements. The matrix implementation obviously limits at compile time the number of nodes we can have in the graph. A matrix which is not implemented as a sparse matrix will need $N*N$ booleans, where N is the number of nodes in the graph. For an adjacency list, on the other hand, the number of entries depends on the number of nodes and edges in the graph.

APPLICATION

The final section of this chapter considers an application of the abstract data type graph, called *graph reduction*, which is concerned with the evaluation of applicative expressions of the type written in functional languages.

The data type tree is often used in the analysis of programs written in imperative languages. With functional languages there are no side-effects, and so arguments may be shared between expressions: hence the type graph may be used to represent the application of a function.

Graph reduction

The term *graph reduction* (Wadsworth 1971) is used to describe the evaluation of expressions given by such graphs. In order to explain graph reduction we first need to consider the lambda calculus, which we view as a simple, low-level language into which functional languages may be translated before they are implemented.

In the lambda calculus functions can be defined without names by using *lambda abstraction*, which is denoted by the letter λ. An example of a lambda abstraction is:

$$\lambda x \, . + x \, 1$$

This is read as 'the function of x which adds x to 1' and may be thought of as the function f, where f is defined to be $f(x) = x+1$ in more conventional notation. To apply this function to an argument we simply juxtapose the two; for example:

$$(\lambda x \, . + x \, 1) \, 3$$

and this is read as 'apply the function (which adds its argument to 1) to the number 3'. Another way of writing this is $(\lambda x \, . \, \text{succ} \, x) \, 3$, where *succ* is the successor function on the integers. To apply the function to the argument we simply replace the formal parameter (x) in the body of the λ abstraction (everything which follows the '.') by the argument (3), giving us $+ \, 3 \, 1$, which is then evaluated as 4. This process is called *rewriting* (or *reduction*). We have used rewriting throughout this book to simplify expressions. This particular form of reduction is called β-reduction.

As another example, consider the expression $(\lambda x \, . + x \, y) \, 3$. This can be reduced to $+ \, 3 \, y$, but cannot be fully evaluated because the value of y is not known. The variable x is said to be *bound* by the λ, whereas y is said to be *free*.

Representing lambda expressions as graphs

The expression to be evaluated is held in the form of its syntax tree. Function application is represented by a tree which has the special symbol '@' at its root. The application of a function to several arguments is written in *curried* form. For example, to express $1 + 3$ we write $+ \, 1 \, 3$, where this is interpreted as 'the function which is applied to 3 is the result of applying the function $+$ to 1' (i.e. the successor function). The syntax tree for this function is shown in figure 10.8. Although this is in fact a tree, in general we need a graph because of the sharing of nodes which may occur in the evaluation of expressions.

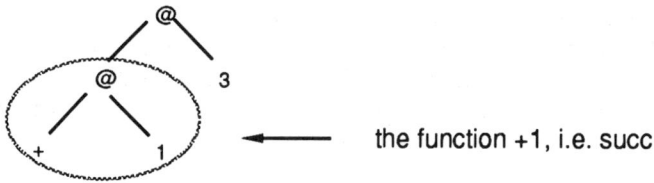

the function +1, i.e. succ

Figure 10. 8

Lambda abstractions of the form λ*x.B* are represented by a tree which has λ at its root, the bound variable *x* as its left subtree and the body of the abstraction, *B* as its right one. For example, the abstraction (λ*x* . succ *x*) is represented in figure 10.9.

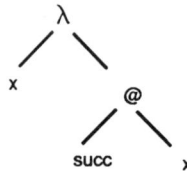

Figure 10. 9

The lambda expression (λ *x* . succ *x*) 3 can then be represented by the tree shown in figure 10.10.

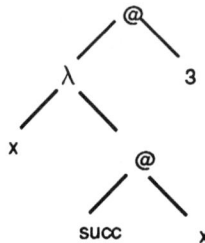

Figure 10.10

Reducing lambda expressions

A *reducible expression* (or *redex*), is one which can be reduced to a simpler form. There are two stages in the reduction of a graph representing a redex that is a lambda expression:

(1) Substitute for arguments.
(2) Overwrite the root of the graph representing the redex.

We will now explain each of these stages in detail.

(1) We substitute arguments for formal parameters by replacing the formal parameter by a link or pointer to the argument (i.e. the part of the graph which represents the argument). If an argument is shared then we have two pointers to it (hence the need for a graph rather than a tree). Because of possible sharing, we must make a copy of the body of the lambda abstraction before substituting for the bound variable: the graph representing the lambda abstraction might be shared itself. For example, the graph in figure 10.11 represents the expression ($\lambda x . + x x$) (* 2 4).

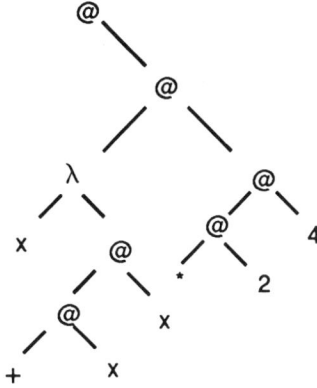

Figure 10.11

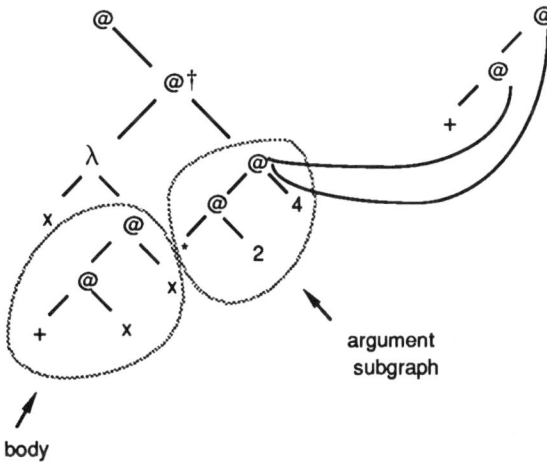

Figure 10.12

The graph in figure 10.12 is the result of copying the body of the lambda abstraction (the subgraph containing $(+ x x)$) and substituting pointers to the argument subgraph for the bound variable x.

The pseudocode for this part of the process is given below:

Copy the body of the λ abstraction
Traverse this graph
    if there is an edge between an @ and an x, *then*
      remove the edge
      add an edge from the @ to the right subgraph of the redex @ node in the whole graph

(2) We then overwrite the root of the reducible expression (marked by † in figure 10.12) with its value (shown here by redirecting the link from the @ node marked with a *).

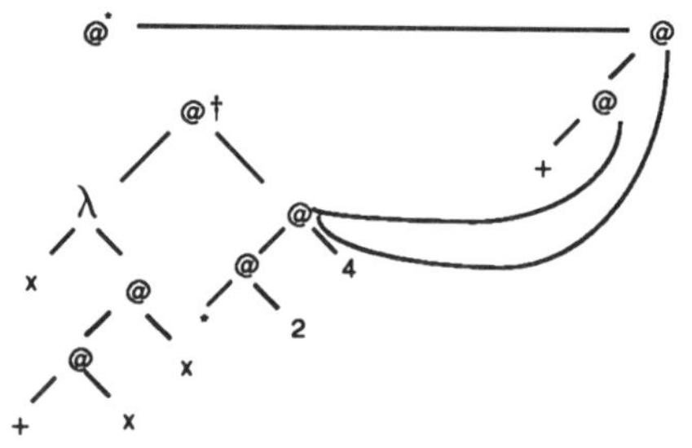

Figure 10.13

When the arguments are evaluated this root node will be reduced to the single node 16.

The explanation above shows how to reduce graphs containing lambda abstractions: there are other forms of expressions which can be reduced by extending this technique. We hope that this has given the reader a flavour of how graph reduction can be used to evaluate expressions which are written in functional languages.

EXERCISES

1. Implement the access procedures for the abstract data type graph either statically or dynamically.
2. Implement either the depth-first or the breadth-first procedure for graph traversal.
3. Implement a procedure to copy a graph.

SUMMARY

The abstract data type *graph* consists of a finite set of *nodes* and a set of *edges*, where an edge is a connection between two nodes, together with a number of access procedures.

Two nodes are said to be *adjacent*, or *neighbours*, if there is an edge connecting them.

A *path* is a sequence of nodes n, n_2, ..., n_m such that for all i from 1 to $(m-1)$, each pair of nodes (n_i, n_{i+1}) are adjacent.

A path is *simple* if each of its nodes occurs only once in the sequence. A *cycle* is a path that is simple except that the first and last nodes are the same.

If a path from a node to itself does not contain any other nodes then it is said to be a *degenerate cycle*.

An *acyclic* graph is a graph which does not have any cycles.

A *directed graph*, or *digraph*, is defined to be one in which the edges are *directed*.

In depth-first traversal, first some node n1 is processed. Then an adjacent node, n2 (which has not previously been visited) is processed and a depth first search is started from n2. When a node is reached whose adjacent nodes have all been processed the algorithm back-tracks to the last node visited which has a neighbour still to be processed, and a depth first search is started from there. Finally, we reach a point where no more nodes can be reached from any of the processed nodes.

In a breadth first traversal we first process some node, then *all* its neighbours, followed by all the neighbours of all these nodes, and so on.

There are many possible implementations for the abstract data type graph, two of which are *adjacency matrices* and *adjacency lists*.

The term *graph reduction* is used to describe a method which evaluates expressions written in functional languages.

APPENDIX 1

Review of Pointers in Modula-2

Readers who are unfamiliar with the use of pointer variables should read the following section carefully before any of the sections in the book concerned with implementing abstract data types.

The memory of a computer can be thought of as a large array. Each static variable declared in a program is allocated a storage location where its value will be stored. This is called *direct access*. A pointer is a variable that *references* or *points* to a particular memory (storage) location. The contents of the location can be changed through the pointer. This is called *indirect access*. The value of a pointer is called an *address*.

Variables which are identified by pointer values are called *dynamic variables* because they can be created dynamically during the execution of a block. They are useful because it is not always possible to predict a program's memory requirements at the time the program is written.

Many imperative languages (such as Modula-2 and Pascal) supply pointer types to model the concept of accessing memory locations. Thus a pointer type, like all language-defined types, is an abstract data type.

A pointer type is denoted by prefixing a type identifier with the reserved words POINTER TO:

```
TYPE IntegerPtr  = POINTER TO INTEGER ;
```

This declares that the type `IntegerPtr` is a pointer to an integer.

The declaration

```
VAR P : IntegerPtr ;
```

states that the value of P is a pointer to an integer. The integer which is associated with P is referred to by following P by an up-arrow, `P^`. This integer can be treated just like any other integer variable. For example:

```
P^ := 27
```

assigns 27 to the variable pointed to by P.

The relationship can be illustrated diagramatically:

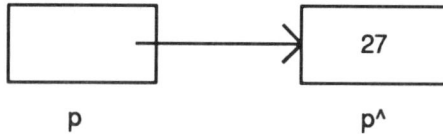

The arrow goes from the memory location holding the pointer value to the variable being pointed to.

Pointers to any other types, including user-defined types, are declared in a similar way. In the following example we use a type String which we assume has been declared previously:

```
TYPE
   EmployeeRecord = RECORD
                      Name : String ;
                      Age    : CARDINAL
                    END ;


EmployeePtr = POINTER TO EmployeeRecord ;
```

Sometimes a pointer is not associated with any object. For example, the last item in a list does not point to anything. This is indicated by the reserved word NIL. After the assignment

```
   P := NIL ;
```

the value of P does not point to any variable. The expression P^ is meaningless when the value of P is NIL. There are several ways of denoting P := NIL, three of which are shown below:

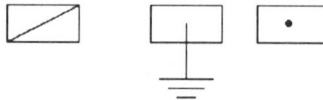

Pointer P becomes equal to NIL.

THE CREATION OF DYNAMIC VARIABLES

How can a pointer variable be made to point to a particular memory cell? The variables declared by standard variable declarations are allocated *static* memory; the memory is allocated before the block (i.e. the procedure or module) is executed.

However, pointer variables point to memory cells which are allocated *dynamically*. This is why pointers are so useful—they can be used to create data structures whose size varies during the execution of a block. Until a memory cell is created for a pointer to point to, it does not point to anything (its value is undefined). Dynamic variables are created by calling the standard procedure NEW. For example, after the declaration

```
VAR P : IntegerPtr ;
```

the statement:

```
NEW (P)
```

creates a new integer variable and makes P point to it. P is assigned the address of the allocated storage. If P is an integer pointer only integers can be placed in this new cell.

We will use diagrams of boxes as a way of clarifying pointer operations. For example, the declaration

```
VAR P : IntegerPtr ;
```

has the effect of creating P. However, P does not yet point to anything:

P

and the statement:

```
NEW (P)
```

is depicted by:

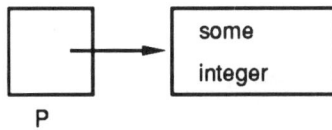

P

some integer

The procedure DISPOSE is the reverse of NEW. The statement

```
DISPOSE(P)
```

where P points to an unwanted dynamic variable, recovers the space for future use and leaves P undefined, so that once again we have:

P

Example

```
MODULE Example ;

FROM InOut IMPORT WriteInt ;
    (* used to output the value of an integer *)

TYPE IntegerPtr = POINTER TO INTEGER;

VAR  P : IntegerPtr ;

BEGIN
  NEW(P) ;                (* allocate a memory cell of type
                             integer *)
  P^ := 23 ;              (* give the new cell a value *)
  WriteInt(P^, 2) ;  (* writes out the value of the
                             integer in the cell P points to,
                             i.e. 23 *)
  P^ := 2 + P^ ;          (* The right hand side is evaluated
                             and the result is assigned to the
                             cell to which P points *)
  WriteInt(P^, 2) ;  (* writes out the new value, i.e. 25 *)

END Example.
```

USE OF POINTERS

A pointer value can be:

(1) Assigned to a pointer variable of the same type. NIL can be assigned to any pointer variable;
(2) Passed as a parameter;
(3) Compared with another pointer variable or with NIL;
(4) Used to access dynamic variables.

ASSIGNMENT STATEMENTS

Suppose p and q are pointer variables:

```
VAR  p,q : IntegerPtr;
```

It is important to realize the difference between the two assignment statements:

(i) q := p and (ii) q^ := p^

(i) q := p assigns the value of the pointer p to the pointer q. Pointer q now points to the same memory cell that p points to.

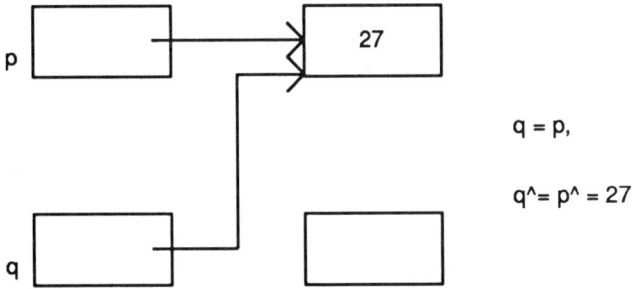

$$q = p,$$

$$q^\wedge = p^\wedge = 27$$

(ii) $q^\wedge := p^\wedge$ assigns the value of the variable pointed to by p to the variable pointed to by q.

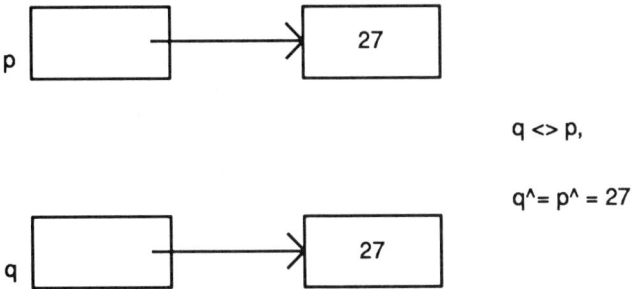

$$q <> p,$$

$$q^\wedge = p^\wedge = 27$$

$p^\wedge$ and $q^\wedge$ are called *referenced* variables.

Example

Suppose xptr and yptr are pointer variables :

```
VAR xptr, yptr : IntegerPtr;
```

The following extract of code shows pointer variables being manipulated.

```
BEGIN
  NEW (xptr);
  xptr^ := 10;
  NEW (yptr);
  yptr^ := 20;
  WriteInt ( xptr^, 2 );    (* xptr^ = 10 *)
  WriteInt ( yptr^, 2 );    (* yptr^ = 20 *)
  xptr^ := yptr^ + 7;
  WriteInt ( xptr^, 2 );    (* xptr^ = 27 *)
  WriteInt ( yptr^, 2 );    (* yptr^ = 20 *)
  xptr   :=   yptr;         (* both pointers now point
                              to the same physical location *)
  WriteInt ( xptr^, 2 );    (* xptr^ = 20 *)
  WriteInt ( yptr^, 2 );    (* yptr^ = 20 *)
  xptr^ := 17;
```

```
WriteInt ( xptr^, 2 );        (* xptr^ = 17 *)
WriteInt ( yptr^, 2 );        (* yptr^ = 17 *)
NEW ( xptr );
yptr := xptr;                 (* xptr, yptr undefined *)
```

EXERCISES

1. In the following fragment of code will the IF – THEN statement be executed?

```
FROM InOut IMPORT WriteInt ;
               (* used to output the value of an integer *)

TYPE IntegerPtr = POINTER TO INTEGER;

VAR  ptr1, ptr2 : IntegerPtr ;

BEGIN
  NEW(ptr1) ;
  ptr1^ := 23 ;
  WriteInt(ptr1^, 2) ;
  NEW(ptr2) ;
  ptr2^ := 23 ;
  IF ptr1 = ptr2 THEN ...
```

2. Predict the output of the following module:

```
MODULE Pointers;

FROM InOut IMPORT WriteInt ;

TYPE
  NumPointer = POINTER TO INTEGER;

VAR
  ptr1 : NumPointer;

PROCEDURE Change (P : Numpointer);

BEGIN
  p^ := 42
END Change;

BEGIN
  NEW(ptr1);
  ptr1^ := 23;
  WriteInt (ptr1^, 2 );
  Change (ptr1);
  WriteInt (ptr1^, 2 )
END Pointers.
```

APPENDIX 2

Modula-2 for Pascal Programmers

Modula-2 was developed in the late 1970s by Niklaus Wirth. It is a direct descendant of Pascal, and so any reader who is familiar with Pascal should have no difficulty with the syntax of Modula-2. The popularity of Pascal can be seen from the large number of machines for which compilers are available. However, there are certain aspects of Pascal which make it unsuitable for use as a language in a textbook on abstract data types, and certain features of Modula-2 which make it eminently suitable.

In Modula-2 there are two sorts of subprograms or *modules: definition* and *implementation.* Definition modules contain only the definitions (type declarations and procedure headings) of the procedures whose implementation is contained in the corresponding implementation module. The modules can be compiled separately, and so the user can be given the definition module which gives the procedure names and the compiled form of the implementation module. In this way the data type is truly abstract and its integrity is guaranteed. This facility is called *data hiding.*

The inability to separate the specification of an abstract data type from its implementation is perhaps the most serious shortcoming of Pascal and prevents it being a language which supports data abstraction. Data types in Pascal are bound to a particular implementation. Various dialects of Pascal do provide separate compilation of procedures and functions, but these are *extensions* to standard Pascal. For example, Pro Pascal[1] provides separate compilation by the use of SEGMENTS, UCSD Pascal[2] by the use of UNITs and LIGHTSPEED PASCAL[3] by means of a separate compilation module called a unit, which is divided into *interface* and *implementation* parts. However, none of these extensions allow the physical separation of specification from implementation, which are still tied together in the same compilation unit.

Modula-2 goes a step further in supporting the concept of abstract data types than the above implies: instead of giving the declaration of a type in the definition module we can declare it to be *opaque*, which means that its implementation is hidden from the user in the corresponding implementation module. For example, we might have the declaration:

```
TYPE List ;
```

in a definition module: this declares a type which is called List, but says nothing about its implementation (which is exactly what is wanted for an abstract data type).

---

1 Pro Pascal [TM] is a registered trademark of Prospero Software..
2 UCSD Pascal is a trademark of the Regents of the University of California.
3 LIGHTSPEED PASCAL [TM] is a registered trademark of LIGHTSPEED, Inc.

The rest of this appendix highlights some of the differences between Pascal and Modula-2. It is not a comprehensive account, but it does cover the points which are relevant to this text.

INPUT AND OUTPUT

The philosophy behind input and output in Modula-2 is entirely different to that of Pascal. Only the lowest-level routines are provided in Modula-2: all other routines (such as `ReadInt`, `WriteInt` etc.) are supplied in separate libraries, and have to be imported into any module which wishes to use them. The library used for input and output throughout this book is called `InOut`, which is the library for input and output provided by Wirth's group. Other frequently used libraries include `RealInOut`, `MathLib`, `System`, and so on.

Example

The following program in Pascal:

```
PROGRAM SquareRoot (INPUT, OUTPUT) ;
(* Postcondition: returns the square root of the number
    provided by the user *)

VAR
  x: real ;

BEGIN
  writeln('What square root do you want ?') ;
  read(x) ;
  IF x >= 0 THEN
    write(SQRT(x))
  ELSE write (x, 'does not have a real square root !')
END .
```

translates to the Modula-2 code below:

```
MODULE SquareRoot;
(* Postcondition: returns the square root of the number
    provided by the user *)

FROM InOut IMPORT WriteLn, WriteString ; (*see Appendix 4*)
FROM RealInOut IMPORT ReadReal, WriteReal ; (*see Appendix
                                                     4 *)

VAR
  x: real ;

BEGIN
  WriteString ('What square root do you want ?') ;
  WriteLn ( ) ;
  ReadReal (x) ;
  IF x >= 0 THEN
    WriteReal (sqrt(x), 2)
  ELSE
    WriteReal (x) ;
```

```
      WriteString ('does not have a real square root!')
    END (* needed in Modula-2 *)
END SquareRoot.
```

MINOR DIFFERENCES

1. In Modula-2 declarations of constants, types, variables and procedures can occur in any order.
2. The word FUNCTION is not used: instead, procedures in Modula-2 are allowed to return a value by means of the RETURN statement. For example, the factorial function is given below, first in Pascal and then in Modula-2.

```
FUNCTION Factorial (n : INTEGER ) : INTEGER ;
(* Pascal *)
(* Precondition: n ≥ 0
   Postcondition: returns factorial n *)

BEGIN
  IF n = 0 THEN
    factorial := 1
  ELSE factorial := n * factorial(n - 1)
END ;

PROCEDURE Factorial (n : INTEGER ) : INTEGER ;
(* Modula-2 *)
(* Precondition: n ≥ 0
   Postcondition: returns factorial n *)

BEGIN
  IF n = 0 THEN
    RETURN 1
    ELSE
    RETURN n * factorial(n - 1)
END Factorial ;
```

According to the language definition, functions can return structured types. However, this facility is rarely supported by compilers.
3. The syntax of control structures is slightly different in that the word BEGIN is no longer needed to mark the start of the block. For example:

```
PROGRAM Average ;
(* Pascal *)
(* Postcondition: returns the average of n numbers*)

VAR
  count,n : INTEGER ;
  average, sum, value : REAL ;

BEGIN
  writeln('how many numbers are there ?') ;
  read (n) ;
  sum := 0 ;
```

```
    writeln('please type in', n:4 , 'numbers') ;
    FOR count := 1 TO n DO

    BEGIN
      read (value) ;
      sum := sum + value ;
    END ;
    average := sum/n ;
    writeln ('the average is', average:5:2 )
  END.
```

translates to the following Modula-2 code:

```
  MODULE Average ;
  (* Modula-2 *)
  (* Postcondition: returns the average of n numbers*)

  FROM InOut IMPORT WriteLn, WriteString ;
  FROM RealInOut IMPORT ReadReal, WriteReal ;

  VAR
    count, n : INTEGER ;
    average, sum, value : REAL ;

  BEGIN
    WriteString ('how many numbers are there ?') ;
    WriteLn ( ) ;
    ReadInt (n) ;
    sum := 0 ;
    WriteString ('please type in') ;
    WriteInt ( n, 4 ) ;
    WriteString (' numbers') ;
    WriteLn ( ) ;
    FOR count := 1 TO n DO
      ReadReal (value) ;
      sum := sum + value ;
    END ; (* for *)
    average := sum/n ;
    WriteString ('the average is') ;
    WriteReal ( average, 2 ) ;
    WriteLn ( ) ;
  END Average.
```

4. The IF..THEN..ELSE construct has an accompanying END and there is a reserved word ELSIF which is used for nested if tests. For example:

```
  IF n = 0 THEN
    RETURN 0
  ELSIF ( n = 1 ) THEN
    RETURN 1
  ELSE
    RETURN Fib ( n - 1) + Fib ( n - 2 )
  END ; (* if *)
```

5. The CASE statement of Modula-2 has an ELSE part. The selections are separated by a vertical bar ('l'), and the use of subranges in case constant lists is allowed.

Example

```
VAR day : (sun,mon,tues,wed,thu,fri,sat) ;

CASE day OF
   sun : ; |
   mon .. fri : BEGIN
                     (* go to college ,
                        work,
                        go home *)
              END ;
   ELSE (* go shopping *)
END; (* case *)
```

6. The boolean functions EOLN and EOF are not provided by the Modula-2 language: their equivalent must be obtained from library routines.

7. The syntax for set operations is different to that of Pascal. Braces are used and also the type of the set must precede the braces to ensure that the type is known to the compiler. For example:

```
TYPE
   Charset = SET OF CHAR ;
VAR
   Current : CHAR ;
   IncludedLetters : Charset ;

BEGIN
   IncludedLetters := Charset { } ;
   Read (Current ) ;
   IncludedLetters := IncludedLetters + Charset {Current }
```

There is a type BITSET in Modula-2, which can be used to model a machine word. (See Chapter 5 for more details of sets in Modula-2.)

8. There is a HALT statement which causes a program to terminate execution.

9. Conformant arrays are allowed. This means that an array can be passed as a parameter to a procedure without its size being declared. For example:

```
PROCEDURE Hash ( AKey : ARRAY OF CHAR ) : Index ;
```

This procedure takes an array of characters whose size has not been specified. The upper bound of the array is returned by the intrinsic function HIGH.

10. Modula-2 is case sensitive.

Example

This example prints the first seven factorials.

```
PROGRAM PrintFact (output) ;
(* Pascal *)
(* Postcondition: prints the first 7 factorials *)

VAR num: INTEGER ;

FUNCTION factorial (n :INTEGER ) : INTEGER ;

VAR i,f : INTEGER ;

BEGIN
  f := 1 ;
  FOR i := 1 TO n DO
    f := f * i ;
  factorial := f
END ; (* factorial *)

BEGIN
  writeln ('number':10, 'factorial':10 ) ;
  writeln ;
  FOR num := 0 TO 6 DO
    writeln ( num:10, factorial(num):10 )
END.

MODULE PrintFact ;
(* Modula-2 *)
(* Postcondition: prints the first 7 factorials *)

FROM InOut IMPORT WriteString, WriteInt ;

VAR num: INTEGER ;

PROCEDURE factorial (n :INTEGER ) : INTEGER ;

VAR i,f : INTEGER ;

BEGIN
  f := 1 ;
  FOR i := 1 TO n DO
    f := f * i ;
  END ;
  RETURN f
END factorial;

BEGIN
  WriteString ('number') ;
  WriteString ('          ') ;
  WriteString ('factorial' ) ;
  WriteLn ( ) ;
  FOR num := 0 TO 6 DO
   WriteInt ( num, 10 ) ;
    WriteInt ( factorial(num), 10 ) ;
  END ;
END PrintFact.
```

APPENDIX 3

Modula-2 Syntax Diagrams[1]

ident

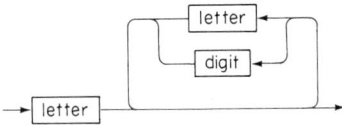

number

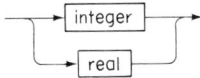

integer

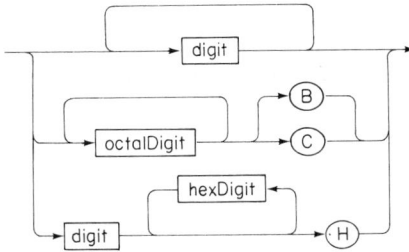

real

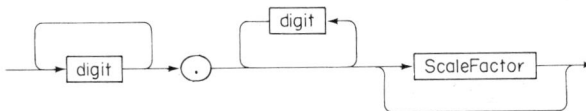

1   Reproduced by permission from Wirth, N. (1988). *Programming in Modula-2*. 4th edn. © 1988 Springer-Verlag.

ScaleFactor

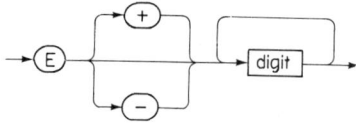

hexDigit

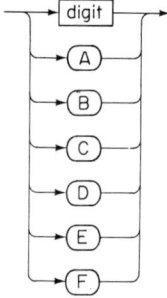

digit

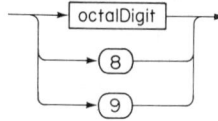

octalDigit

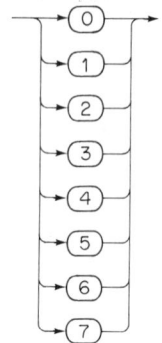

qualident

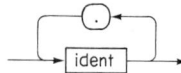

relation

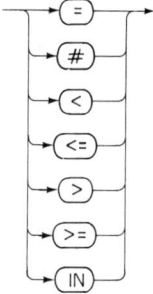

AddOperator

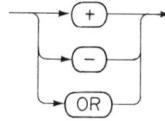

MulOperator

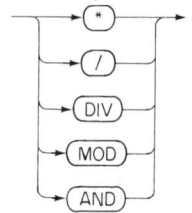

string

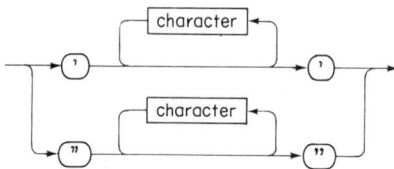

ConstExpression

TypeDeclaration

enumeration

type

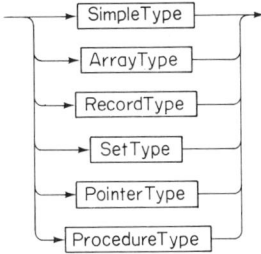

SimpleType

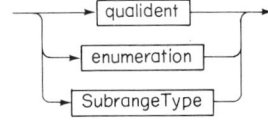

IdentList

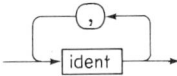

SubrangeType

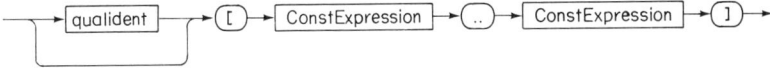

ArrayType

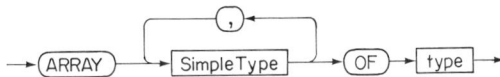

RecordType

FieldListSequence

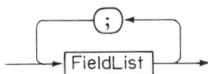

FieldList

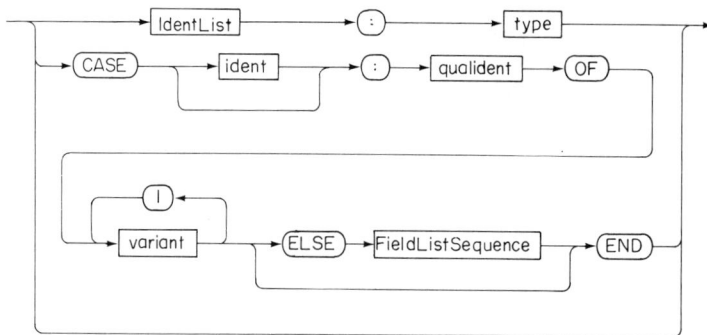

variant

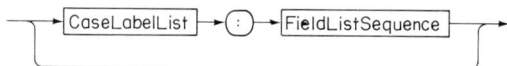

CaseLabelList

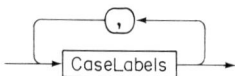

CaseLabels

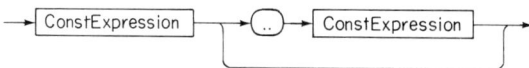

SetType

PointerType

ProcedureType

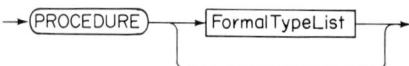

FormalParameters

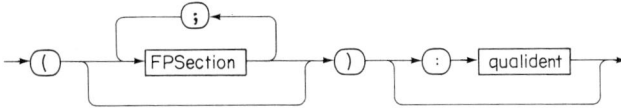

FPSection

FormalType

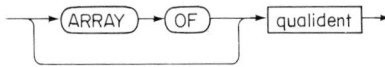

priority

ModuleDeclaration

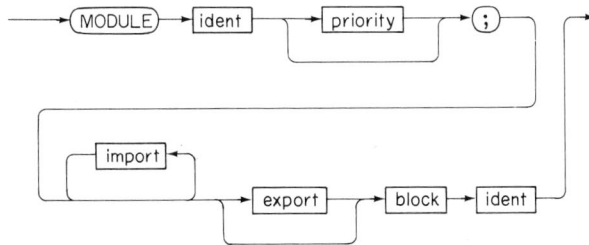

export

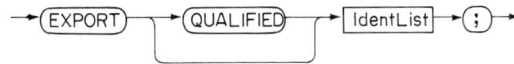

import

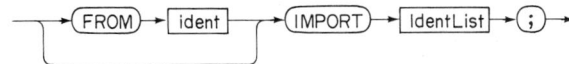

factor

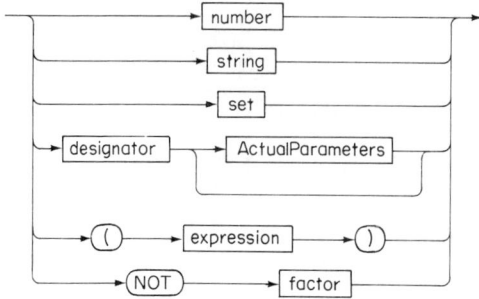

set

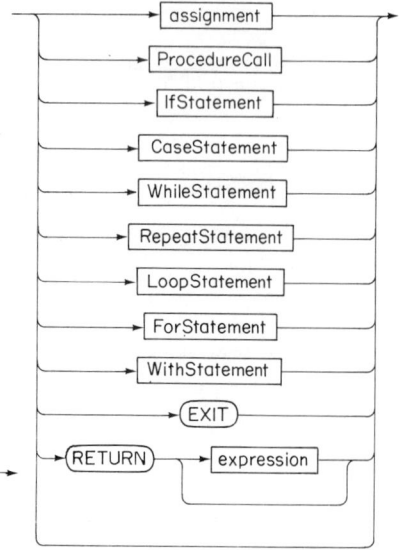

statement

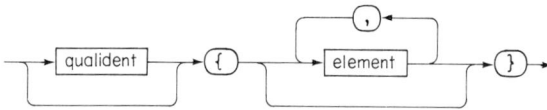

element

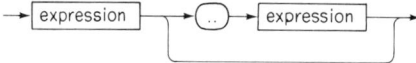

ActualParameters

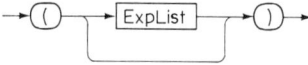

assignment

ProcedureCall

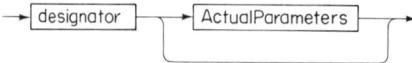

StatementSequence

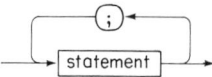

IfStatement

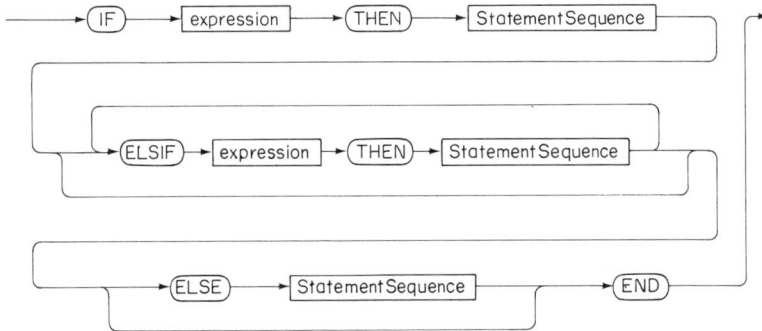

CaseStatement

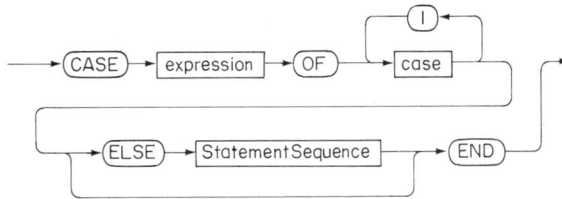

case

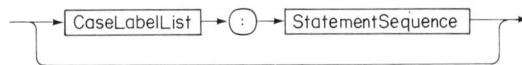

WhileStatement

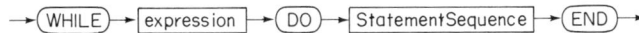

RepeatStatement

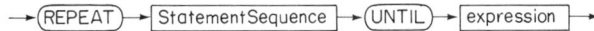

ForStatement

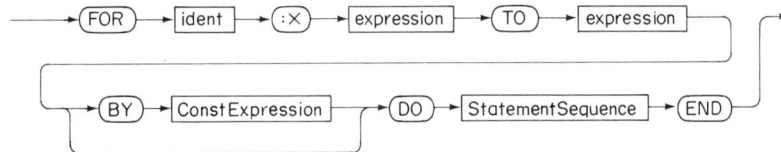

LoopStatement

WithStatement

ProcedureDeclaration

ProcedureHeading

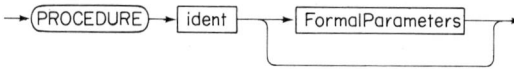

block

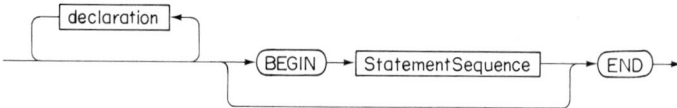

declaration

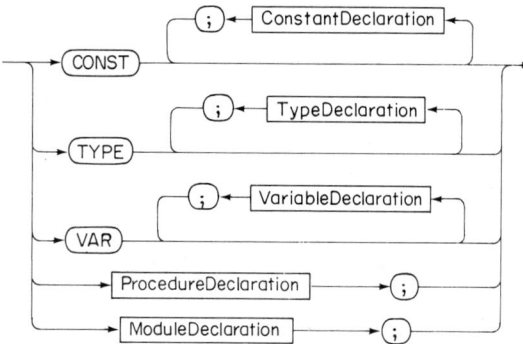

FormalTypeList

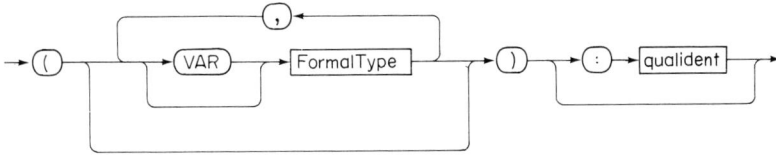

VariableDeclaration

designator

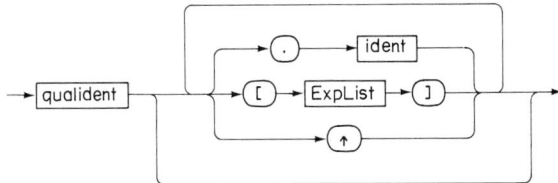

ExpList

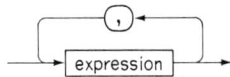

expression

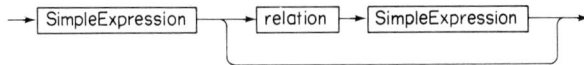

SimpleExpression

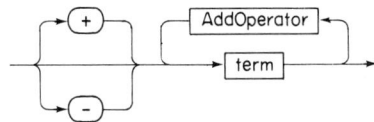

term

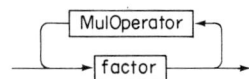

DefinitionModule

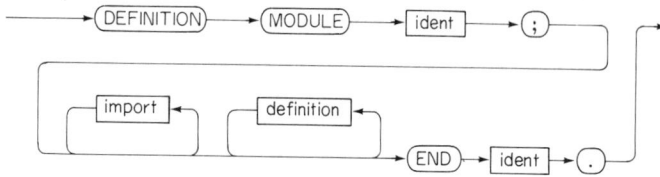

definition

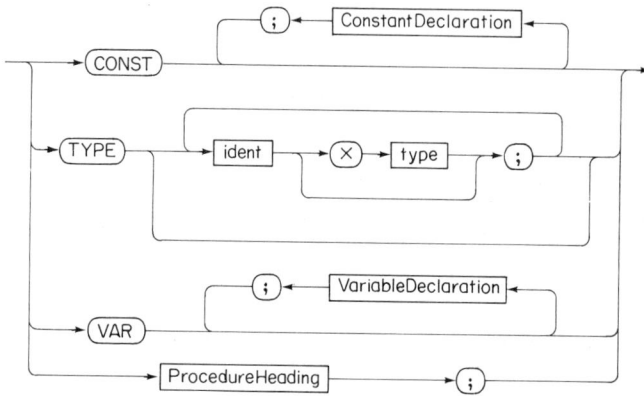

ProgramModule

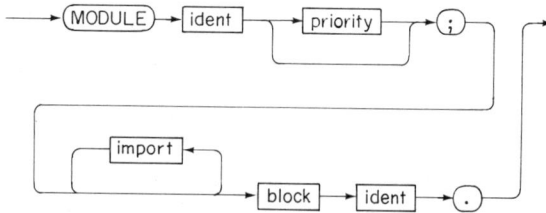

CompilationUnit

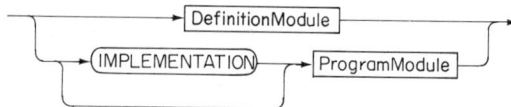

APPENDIX 4

Modula-2 Standard Utility Modules[1]

```
DEFINITION MODULE Terminal; (*S.E. Knudsen*)
 PROCEDURE Read (VAR ch: CHAR);
 PROCEDURE BusyRead(VAR ch: CHAR);
 PROCEDURE ReadAgain;
 PROCEDURE Write(ch: CHAR);
 PROCEDURE WriteString(string: ARRAY OF CHAR);
 PROCEDURE WriteLn;
END Terminal.

DEFINITION MODULE FileSystem; (*S.E. Knudsen*)
 FROM SYSTEM IMPORT ADDRESS, WORD;

 TYPE
  Flag =     (er, ef, rd, wr, ag, bm);
  FlagSet =   SET OF Flag;

  Response =  (done, notedone, lockerror, permissionerror,
                notsupported, callerror,
                unknownmedium, unknownfile, filenameerror,
                toomanyfiles, mediumfull,
                deviceoff, parityerror, harderror);

  Command =   (create, open, opendir, close, rename,
                setread, setwrite, setmodify, setopen, doio,
                setpos, getpos, length
                setpermission, getpermission,
                setpermanent, getpermanent);

  Lock =      (nolock, sharedlock, exclusivelock);
  Permission = (noperm, ownerperm, groupperm, allperm);
  MediumType = ARRAY [0 .. 1] OF CHAR;

  File =      RECORD
                bufa: ADDRESS;
                ela: ADDRESS;
                elodd: BOOLEAN;
                ina: ADDRESS;
```

---

1 Reproduced by permission from Wirth, N. (1988) *Programming in Modula-2* 4th edn. © Springer-Verlag.

```
            inodd: BOOLEAN;
            topa: ADDRESS;
            flags: FlagSet;
            eof: BOOLEAN;
            res: Response;
            CASE com: Command OF
            create, open: new: BOOLEAN; lock: Lock
            | opendir: selections: BITSET;
            | setpos, getpos, length: highpos, lowpos:
              CARDINAL
            | setpermission, getpermission
              readpermission, modifypermission:
              Permission
            | setpermanent, getpermanent, on: BOOLEAN
            END;
            mt: MediumType;
            mediumno: CARDINAL;
            fileno: CARDINAL;
            versionno: CARDINAL;
            openedfile: ADDRESS;
          END;

PROCEDURE Create(VAR f: File; filename: ARRAY OF CHAR);
PROCEDURE Lookup(VAR f: File; filename: ARRAY OF CHAR;
                                   new: BOOLEAN);
PROCEDURE Close(VAR f: File);
PROCEDURE Delete(VAR f: File);
PROCEDURE Rename(VAR f: File; filename: ARRAY OF CHAR);

PROCEDURE SetRead(VAR f: File);
PROCEDURE SetWrite(VAR f: File);
PROCEDURE SetModify(VAR f: File);
PROCEDURE SetOpen(VAR f: File);
PROCEDURE Doio(VAR f: File);

PROCEDURE SetPos(VAR f: File; highpos, lowpos: CARDINAL);
PROCEDURE GetPos(VAR f: File; VAR highpos, lowpos:
                                       CARDINAL);
PROCEDURE Length(VAR f: File; VAR highpos, lowpos:
                                       CARDINAL);

PROCEDURE Reset(VAR f: File);
PROCEDURE Again(VAR f: File);

PROCEDURE ReadWord(VAR f: File; VAR w: WORD);
PROCEDURE WriteWord(VAR f: File; w: WORD);
PROCEDURE ReadChar(VAR f: File; VAR ch: CHAR);
PROCEDURE WriteChar(VAR f: File; ch: CHAR);

(*The following declarations are only useful when
programming or importing drivers.*)

PROCEDURE FileCommand(VAR f: File);
PROCEDURE DirectoryCommand(VAR f: File; filename: ARRAY OF
                                            CHAR);
```

```
TYPE
 FileProc =          PROCEDURE (VAR File);
 DirectoryProc = PROCEDURE (VAR File, ARRAY OF CHAR);

PROCEDURE CreateMedium(mt: MediumType; mediumno: CARDINAL;
           fp: FileProc; dp: DirectoryProc; VAR done:
                                               BOOLEAN);

PROCEDURE DeleteMedium(mt: MediumType; mediumno: CARDINAL;
              VAR done: BOOLEAN);

PROCEDURE  AssignName(mt: MediumType; mediumno: CARDINAL;
              mediumname: ARRAY OF CHAR;
              VAR done: BOOLEAN);

PROCEDURE DeassignName
              (mediumname: ARRAY OF CHAR;
              VAR done: BOOLEAN);

PROCEDURE ReadMedium(index: CARDINAL;
              VAR mt: MediumType; VAR mediumno: CARDINAL;
              VAR mediumname: ARRAY OF CHAR;
              VAR original: BOOLEAN;
              VAR done: BOOLEAN);

PROCEDURE LookupMedium(VAR mt: MediumType; VAR mediumno:
                                               CARDINAL;
              Mediumname: ARRAY OF CHAR;
              VAR done: BOOLEAN);

END FileSystem.

DEFINITION MODULE InOut; (*N. Wirth*)
 FROM SYSTEM IMPORT WORD;
 FROM  FileSystem IMPORT File;

CONST EOL = 36C;
 VAR Done: BOOLEAN;
 termCH; CHAR; (*terminating character in Readint,
                                      ReadCard*)
 in, out: File; (*for exceptional cases only*)

PROCEDURE OpenInput(defext: ARRAY OF CHAR);
  (*request a file name and open input file *in*.
   Done := "file was successfully opened".
   If open, subsequent input is read from this file.
   If name ends with ".", append extension defext*)

PROCEDURE OpenOutput(defext: ARRAY OF CHAR);
  (*request a file name and open output file "out"
   Done := "file was successfully opened.
   If open, subsequent output is written on this file*)

PROCEDURE CloseInput;
  (*closes input file; returns input to terminal*)

PROCEDURE CloseOutput;
  (*closes output file; returns output to terminal*)
```

```
  PROCEDURE Read(VAR ch: CHAR);
   (*Done := NOT in.eof*)

  PROCEDURE ReadString(VAR s: ARRAY OF CHAR);
   (*read string, i.e. sequence of characters not containing
    blanks nor control characters; leading blanks are ignored.
    Input is terminated by any character <="";
    this character is assigned to termCH.
    DEL is used for backspacing when input from terminal*)

  PROCEDURE ReadInt(VAR x; INTEGER);
   (*read string and convert to integer. Syntax:
    integer = ["+"|"-"] digit {digit}.
   Leading blanks are ignored.
   Done := "integer was read"*)

  PROCEDURE ReadCard(VAR x: CARDINAL);
   (*read string and convert to cardinal. Syntax:
    cardinal = digit {digit}.
   Leading blanks are ignored.
    Done := "cardinal was read"*)

  PROCEDURE ReadWrite(VAR w: WORD);
   (*Done := NOT in.eof*)

  PROCEDURE Write(ch: CHAR);
  PROCEDURE WriteLn;   (*terminate line*)
  PROCEDURE WriteString(s: ARRAY OF CHAR);

  PROCEDURE WriteInt(x: INTEGER:n: CARDINAL);

 . (*write integer x with (at least) n characters on file
                                              "out".
   If n is greater than the number of digits needed,
   blanks are added preceding the number*)

  PROCEDURE WriteCard(x, n: CARDINAL);
  PROCEDURE WriteOct(x, n: CARDINAL);
  PROCEDURE WriteHex(x, n: CARDINAL);
  PROCEDURE WriteWrd(w: WORD);
  END InOut.

  DEFINITION MODULE RealInOut; (*N.Wirth*)
   VAR Done: BOOLEAN;

   PROCEDURE ReadReal(VAR x: REAL);
   (*Read REAL number x from keyboard according to syntax:

     ["+"|"-"] digit {digit} ["."digit {digit}] ["E"["+"|"-"]
             digit [digit]]

   Done := "a number was read".
   At most 7 digits are significant, leading zeros not
   counting. Maximum exponent is 38. Input terminates
```

with a blank or any control character. DEL is used
for backspacing*)

PROCEDURE WriteReal(x: REAL; n: INTEGER);
 (*Write x using n characters. If fewer than n characters
 are needed, leading blanks are inserted*)

PROCEDURE WriteFixPt(x: REAL; n, k: INTEGER);
(*Write x using n characters with k digits after decimal
 point.
If fewer than n characters are needed, leading blanks are
inserted*)

PROCEDURE WriteRealOct(x: REAL);
(*Write x in octal form with exponent and mantissa*)
END RealInOut.

DEFINITION MODULE Windows; (*J. Gutknecht*)
 CONST Background = 0; FirstWindow = 1; LastWindow = 8;
 TYPE Window = [Background .. LastWindow];
  RestoreProc = PROCEDURE(Window);

 PROCEDURE OpenWindow(VAR u: Window; x,y,w,h: CARDINAL;
  Repaint: RestoreProc; VAR done: BOOLEAN);
 (*Open new window. Repaint will be invoked to restore*)

 PROCEDURE DrawTitle (u: Window, title: ARRAY OF CHAR);
 PROCEDURE RedefineWindow(u: Window: x,y,w,h: CARDINAL; VAR
 done: BOOLEAN);

 PROCEDURE CloseWindow(u: Window);
 PROCEDURE PlaceOnTop(u: Window);
 PROCEDURE PlaceOnBottom(u: Window);
 PROCEDURE OnTop(u: Window); BOOLEAN;
 PROCEDURE UpWindow (x,y: CARDINAL): Window;
 (*Return window or Background corresponding to screen
 coordinates (x,y)*)
END Windows.

 DEFINITION MODULE TextWindows; (*J. Gutknecht*)
 IMPORT Windows;

 TYPE Window = Windows.Window;
  RestoreProc = Windows.RestoreProc;

 VAR Done: BOOLEAN; (*Done = "previous operation was
 successfully executed"*)
   termCH: CHAR; (*termination characters*)

 PROCEDURE OpenTextWindow(VAR u: Window; x,y,w,h: CARDINAL;
             name: ARRAY OF CHAR);

 PROCEDURE RedefTextWindow(u: Window; x,y,w,h: CARDINAL);
 PROCEDURE CloseTextWindow(u: Window);

```
    PROCEDURE AssignFont(u: Window; frame, charW, lineH:
                                              CARDINAL);
    (*Assign non proportional font to window u*)
    PROCEDURE AssignRestoreProc(u: Window; r: RestoreProc);
    PROCEDURE AssignEOWAction(u: Window; r: RestoreProc);
     (*Assign reaction on "end of window" condition for window
                                                          u*)


    PROCEDURE  ScrollUp(u: Window);
     (*Scroll one line up in window u (standard EOW-action(*)
    PROCEDURE DrawTitle(u: Window, name: ARRAY OF CHAR);
    PROCEDURE DrawLine(u: Window; line, col: CARDINAL);
             (*col = 0: draw horizontal line at line;
             line = 0: draw vertical line at col*)
    PROCEDURE SetCaret(u: Window; on: BOOLEAN);
    PROCEDURE Invert(u: Window; on: BOOLEAN);


    PROCEDURE IdentifyPos(u:Window;x,y: CARDINAL; VAR line,
                                    col: CARDINAL:);
    PROCEDURE GetPos(u: Window; VAR line, col: CARDINAL);
    PROCEDURE SetPos(u: Window; line, col: CARDINAL);


    PROCEDURE ReadString (u: Window; VAR a: ARRAY OF CHAR);
    PROCEDURE ReadCard (u: Window; VAR x: CARDINAL);
    PROCEDURE ReadInt(u: Window; VAR x: INTEGER);


    PROCEDURE Write(u: Window; ch: CHAR);
     (*Write character ch at current position.
       Interpret BS, LF, FF, CR, CAN, EOL and DEL*)
    PROCEDURE WriteLn(u: Window);
    PROCEDURE WriteString(u: Window; a: ARRAY OF CHAR);
    PROCEDURE WriteCard(u: Window; x, n: CARDINAL);
     (*Write Integer x with (at least) n characters.
     If n is  greater than the numbers of digits needed.
     blanks are added preceding the number*)
    PROCEDURE WriteInt(u: Window; x: INTEGER; n: CARDINAL);
    PROCEDURE WriteOct(u: Window; x, n: CARDINAL);
END TextWindows.

DEFINITION MODULE GraphicWindows; (*E. Kohen*)
 IMPORT Windows;
 TYPE Window = Windows. Window
 RestoreProc = Windows. RestoreProc;
 Mode = (replace, paint, invert, erase);

VAR Done: BOOLEAN; (*Done = "operation was successfully
                            executed"*)

   PROCEDURE OpenGraphWindow(VAR u: Window; x,y,w,h: CARDINAL;
    VAR name: ARRAY OF CHAR; Reprint: RestoreProc);
   (*Open new graphic window. Draw title bar if"name" not
     empty*)


   PROCEDURE Redefine(u: Window; x,y,w,h: CARDINAL);
   PROCEDURE Clear(u: Window);
```

```
PROCEDURE CloseGraphWindow(u: Window);
PROCEDURE SetMode(u: Window; m: Mode);
PROCEDURE Dot(u: Window; x,y: CARDINAL);

PROCEDURE SetPen(u: Window; x,y: CARDINAL);
PROCEDURE TurnTo(u: Window; angle: INTEGER);
PROCEDURE Turn(u: Window; d: INTEGER);
PROCEDURE Move(u: Window; n: CARDINAL);
PROCEDURE MoveTo(u: Window; x,y: CARDINAL);
PROCEDURE Circle(u: Window; x,y,r: CARDINAL);
  (*draw circle with center at (x,y) and radius r*)
PROCEDURE Area(u: Window; c: CARDINAL; x,y,w,h: CARDINAL);
    (*paint rectangular area of width w and height h at
      coordinate x,y) in colour c: 0: white, 1: light grey,
    21: dark grey, 3: black*)
PROCEDURE CopyArea (u: Window; sx,sy,dx,dy,dw,dh:
                                          CARDINAL);
  (*copy rectangular area at (sx, sy) into rectangle at
  (dx, dy) of width dw and height dh*)

PROCEDURE Write(u: Window; ch; CHAR);
PROCEDURE WriteString(u: Window; s: ARRAY OF CHAR);
PROCEDURE GetPos(VAR u: Window; VAR x,y: CARDINAL);
  (*return uppermost opened window and the window oriented
  coordinates (x,y) for given screen coordinates (x,y)*)
END GraphicWindows.

DEFINITION MODULE CursorMouse; (*J. Gutknecht*)
 CONST ML = 15; MM = 14; MR = 13;

 TYPE Pattern = RECORD
                   height: CARDINAL;
                   raster: ARRAY [0 .. 15] OF BITSET
                END;

   ReadProc =      PROCEDURE(VAR BITSET, VAR CARDINAL, VAR
                                          CARDINAL);

 PROCEDURE SetMouse(x,y: CARDINAL);
 PROCEDURE GetMouse(VAR s: BITSET; VAR x,y: CARDINAL);
 *(          ML IN s = "Left mouseKey pressed";
             MM IN s = "Middle mouseKey pressed";
             MR IN s = "Right mouseKey pressed"*)

 PROCEDURE ReadMouse(VAR s: BITSET; VAR x,y: CARDINAL);
 PROCEDURE Assign(p: ReadProc);
 PROCEDURE MoveCursor(x,y: CARDINAL);
 PROCEDURE EraseCursor;
 PROCEDURE SetPattern(VAR p: Pattern); (*of cursor*)
 PROCEDURE ResetPattern; (*to standard arrow patterns*)
END CursorMouse.

DEFINITION MODULE Menu; (*J. Gutknecht*)
 PROCEDURE ShowMenu(X,Y: CARDINAL;
 VAR menu: ARRAY OF CHAR;  VAR cmd; CARDINAL);
```

```
(*menu = title {"|" item}.
 item = name ["(" menu ")"]
 name = {char}.
 char = 'any character except OC, "|". "(". ")"'.
 title = name.
```

Nonprintable characters and characters exceeding maximum
namelength are ignored.
The input value of "cmd" specifies the command initially to
be selected.
The sequence of selected items is returned via the digits
of "cmd" (from right to left).
interpreted as an octal number*)
END Menu.

```
DEFINITION MODULE MathLib0; (*N. Wirth*)
  PROCEDURE sqrt(x: REAL): REAL,
  PROCEDURE exp(x: REAL): REAL;
  PROCEDURE ln(x: REAL): REAL;
  PROCEDURE sin(x: REAL): REAL;
  PROCEDURE cos(x: REAL): REAL;
  PROCEDURE arctan(x: REAL): REAL;
  PROCEDURE entier(X: REAL): INTEGER;
END MathLib0.
```

APPENDIX 5

Modula-2 Reserved Words and Standard Procedures[1]

RESERVED WORDS

Operators and *delimiters* are the special characters, character pairs or reserved words listed below. These reserved words consist exclusively of capital letters and *must not* be used in the role of identifiers. The symbols # and <> are synonyms, and so are &, AND and ~, NOT.

+	=	AND	FOR	QUALIFIED
-	#	ARRAY	FROM	RECORD
*	<	BEGIN	IF	REPEAT
/	>	BY	IMPLEMENTATION	RETURN
:=	<>	CASE	IMPORT	SET
&	<=	CONST	IN	THEN
.	>=	DEFINITION	LOOP	TO
,	..	DIV	MOD	TYPE
;	:	DO	MODULE	UNTIL
(	)	ELSE	NOT	VAR
[	]	ELSIF	OF	WHILE
{	}	END	OR	WITH
↑	|	EXIT	POINTER	
~		EXPORT	PROCEDURE	

Comments may be inserted between any two symbols in a program. They are arbitrary character sequences opened by the parenthesis (* and closed by *). Comments may be nested, and they do not affect the meaning of a program.

STANDARD PROCEDURES

Standard procedures are predefined. Some are *generic* procedures that cannot be explicitly declared, i.e. they apply to classes of operand types or have several possible parameter list forms. Standard procedures are:

---

1 Reproduced by permission from Wirth, N. (1988). *Programming in Modula-2*, 4th edn. © 1988 Springer-Verlag.

ABS(x)	absolute value: result type = argument type.
CAP(ch)	if ch is a lower-case letter, the corresponding capital letter; if ch is a capital letter, the same letter.
CHR(x)	the character with ordinal number x, CHR(x) = VAL(CHAR,x)
FLOAT(x)	x of type INTEGER represented as a value of type REAL.
HIGH(a)	high index bound of array a.
MAX(T)	the maximum value of type T.
MIN(T)	the minimum value of type T.
ODD(x)	x MOD 2 # 0.
ORD(x)	ordinal number (of type CARDINAL) of x in the set of values defined by type T of x. T is an enumeration type, CHAR, INTEGER or CARDINAL.
SIZE(T)	the number of storage units required by a variable of type T.
TRUNC(x)	real number x truncated to its integral part (of type INTEGER).
VAL(T,x)	the value with ordinal number x and with type T. T is any enumeration type, or CHAR, INTEGER or CARDINAL. VAL(T, ORD(x) = x, if x of type T.
DEC(x)	x := x−1
DEC(x,n)	x := x−n
EXCL(s,i)	s := s − {i}
HALT	terminate program execution
INC(x)	x := x+1
INCL(x,n)	x := x+n
INCL(s,i)	s:= s + {i}

The procedures INC and DEC also apply to operands x of enumeration types and of type CHAR. In these cases they replace x by its (nth) successor or predecessor.

APPENDIX 6

Solutions to Selected Exercises

CHAPTER 2

2.1

1.

```
PROCEDURE Last (L: List) : InfoType ;
(* Precondition: L is not empty
   Postcondition: return the last item of the list L *)

BEGIN
    IF IsEmpty ( Tail (L) )
       THEN RETURN Head (L)
    ELSE
       RETURN Last(Tail (L))
    END (* if *)
  END Last ;
```

2.

```
PROCEDURE IsIn ( I : Infotype; L : List) : BOOLEAN ;
(* Postcondition: return TRUE if item I is in list L,
   otherwise FALSE *)

BEGIN
  IF IsEmpty (L) THEN
    RETURN FALSE
  ELSIF IsEqual (I, Head (L)) THEN
    RETURN TRUE
  ELSE
    RETURN IsIn (I, Tail (L))
  END (* if *)
END IsIn ;
```

3.

```
PROCEDURE Duplicate ( L : List ) : List ;
(* Postcondition: returns a list in which each item is
   duplicated.
```

For example, Duplicate ('A', 'C', 'M') should return
('A', 'A', 'C', 'C', 'M', 'M') *)

```
  BEGIN
    IF IsEmpty L THEN
      RETURN L
    ELSE
      RETURN Cons ( Head ( L ), Cons ( Head ( L ),
                                  Duplicate (Tail (L ))))
    END (* if *)
  END Duplicate;
```

4.
```
  PROCEDURE AllOut ( I : Infotype; L : List ) : List ;
  (* Postcondition:  returns a  list in  which all
     occurrences of the item I have been removed *)

    BEGIN
      IF IsEmpty (L) THEN
        RETURN L
      ELSIF
      IsEqual (I, Head (L)) THEN RETURN AllOut ( I, Tail ( L )
      ELSE
        RETURN Cons ( Head ( L ), AllOut (I, Tail (L)) )
      END (* if *)
    END AllOut;
```

5.
```
  PROCEDURE FirstOut ( I : Infotype; L : List ) : List ;
  (* Postcondition: returns a list in which the first
     occurrence of the item I has been removed *)

    BEGIN
      IF IsEmpty (L) THEN
        RETURN L
      ELSIF IsEqual (I, Head (L)) THEN
        RETURN Tail ( L )
      ELSE
        RETURN Cons ( Head ( L ), FirstOut (I, Tail (L)))
      END (* if *)
    END FirstOut ;
```

6.
```
  PROCEDURE Take ( n : CARDINAL ; L : List ) : List ;
  (* Postcondition: returns a list which consists of the
     first n items of the list L*)

    BEGIN
      IF n = 0 THEN
        RETURN Empty ( )
      ELSIF Length (L) <= n THEN
        RETURN  L
      ELSE
        RETURN Cons ( Head ( L ), Take ( n - 1, Tail (L)))
      END (* if *)
    END Take;
```

7.
```
PROCEDURE Drop ( n : CARDINAL ; L : List ) : List ;
(* Postcondition: returns a list without the first n
    items of the list L*)

  BEGIN
    IF n = 0 THEN
      RETURN L
    ELSEIF Length (L) <= n THEN
      RETURN Empty ( )
    ELSE
      Drop ( n - 1, Tail (L))
    END (* if *)
  END Drop;
```

8.
```
PROCEDURE PrettyPrintlist ( L : List);
(* Postcondition: prints the contents of the list to the
    screen in such a way that the list is enclosed by
    brackets and consecutive items are separated by commas*)

  PROCEDURE Printlist ( L : List);

  BEGIN
    IF NOT IsEmpty (L) THEN
      Write (Head(L) ) ;
      IF NOT IsEmpty ( Tail (L)) THEN Write(",") ; END ;
      Printlist(Tail(L)) ;
    END; (*IF *)
  END Printlist ;

BEGIN
  Write ( '(' ) ;
  Printlist(L) ;
  Write (')') ;
END PrettyPrintlist;
```

9.
```
PROCEDURE Replace ( new, old: Infotype; L : List ) : List ;
(* Postcondition : return a list in which the first
    ccurrence of old has been replaced by new *)

  BEGIN
    IF IsEmpty (L) THEN
      RETURN L
    ELSIF HEAD ( L ) = old THEN
      RETURN Cons ( new, Tail ( L ) )
    ELSE
      RETURN Cons ( Head ( L ) , Replace ( new, old, Tail
                                                ( L ) ) )
    END
  END Replace ;
```

10.
```
PROCEDURE ReplaceAll ( new, old : Infotype ; L : List ) :
                                                List ;
(* Postcondition : return a list in  which all
   occurrences of old have been replaced by new *)


  BEGIN
     IF IsEmpty (L) THEN
        RETURN L
     ELSIF HEAD ( L ) = old THEN
        RETURN Cons ( new, ReplaceAll (new, old, Tail ( L)) )
     ELSE
        RETURN Cons ( Head ( L ) , ReplaceAll ( new, old, Tail
                                                ( L ) ) )
     END
  END ReplaceAll ;
```

11.
```
PROCEDURE InBefore ( new, old : Infotype ; L : List ) :
                                                List ;
(* Postcondition : return a list in which new has been
   inserted before every occurrence of old *)


  BEGIN
     IF IsEmpty (L) THEN
        RETURN L
     ELSIF HEAD ( L ) = old THEN
        RETURN Cons ( new, Cons ( Head ( L ),
                          InBefore (new, old, Tail ( L ))) )
     ELSE
      RETURN Cons ( Head ( L ) , InBefore ( new, old, Tail
                                                ( L ) ) )
     END
  END InBefore ;
```

12.
```
PROCEDURE InAround ( new, old : Infotype ; L : List ) :
                                                List ;
(* Postcondition : return a list in which new has been
   inserted before and after every occurrence of old *)


  BEGIN
     IF IsEmpty (L) THEN
        RETURN L
     ELSIF HEAD ( L ) = old THEN
        RETURN Cons ( new, Cons ( Head ( L ),
          Cons ( new, InAround (new, old, Tail ( L )))) )
     ELSE
      RETURN Cons ( Head ( L ) , InAround ( new, old, Tail
                                                ( L ) ) )
     END
  END InAround ;
```

2.2

We could use an expression such as

```
Reduce ( Sum, ( Map ( Ones, L )), 0 )
```

where Ones is a monadic function which takes a list and returns a list of the same length with every item equal to one.

2.3

1.
```
PROCEDURE Length ( l: List) : CARDINAL ;
(* Postcondition : returns the length of l *)

BEGIN
    IF IsEmpty (l) THEN
      RETURN 0
    ELSE
      RETURN (1 + Length(Tail(l)))
    END
  END Length ;
```

2.
```
PROCEDURE Reverse (l: List) : List ;
(* Precondition: l is a generalized list
    Postcondition: returns a list consisting of the
    items in l (including sublists) reversed *)

  BEGIN
    IF IsEmpty (l) THEN
      RETURN l
    ELSE
      IF ContainsData ( l ) THEN
        RETURN Append ( Reverse(Tail(l)), Cons(Head
                                      (l),Empty()))
      ELSE
        RETURN Append ( Reverse ( Tail ( l )),
      ConsList ( Reverse (ListHead ( l )), Empty ()))
      END
    END
  END Reverse ;
```

3.
```
PROCEDURE PrettyPrintlist ( L : List);
(* Postcondition: prints the contents of a generalized
    list to the screen in such a way that the list is
    enclosed by brackets and consecutive items are separated
    by commas *)

  PROCEDURE Printlist ( L : List);
```

```
BEGIN
    IF NOT IsEmpty (L) THEN
      IF ContainsData ( L ) THEN
        Write (Head(L) )
      ELSE
        PrettyPrintlist ( ListHead ( L)) ;
      END ;
      IF NOT IsEmpty ( Tail (L)) THEN
        Write(",") ;
      END ;
      Printlist(Tail(L)) ;
    END;
  END Printlist ;


  BEGIN
    Write ( '(' ) ;
    Printlist (L) ;
    Write (')') ;
  END PrettyPrintlist;
```

CHAPTER 3

3.1

3. The specification is the same as that of a list, except that Cons should no longer be visible to the user, but a procedure which will insert an item in order into a priority queue should be provided instead.

CHAPTER 4

4.1

1.

(a)
```
PROCEDURE Last (L: List) : InfoType ;
(* Precondition: L is not empty
   Postcondition: return the last item of the list L *)

  BEGIN
    WHILE NOT IsEmpty ( Tail (L)) DO
      L := Tail ( L )
    END
    RETURN Head (L)
  END Last ;
```

(b)
```
PROCEDURE IsIn ( I : Infotype; L : List) : BOOLEAN ;
(* Postcondition: return TRUE if item I is in list L,
   otherwise FALSE *)
```

```
  BEGIN
    WHILE NOT IsEmpty (L) DO
      IF IsEqual (I, Head (L)) THEN
        RETURN TRUE
      END ;
      L := Tail ( L ) ;
    END ;
    RETURN FALSE
  END IsIn ;
```

CHAPTER 5

5.1

1.

(a)
```
  PROCEDURE PrimeFactors ( n : CARDINAL) : Bag ;
  (* Postcondition: returns a bag containing the prime
     factors of n *)

    VAR b : Bag ;

    BEGIN
      b := Insert ( 1, Empty ( )) ;
      test := 2 ;
      WHILE n <> 1 DO
       IF n MOD test = 0 THEN
          Insert ( test, b ) ;
          n := n DIV test
       ELSE
          test := test + 1
       END
      END
      RETURN b
    END PrimeFactors ;
```

(b)
```
  PROCEDURE CommonFactors ( n1, n2, n3 : CARDINAL ) : Bag ;
  (* Postcondition: returns a bag containing the prime
     factors of n1, n2, and n3 *)

  BEGIN
   RETURN Intersection (Intersection ( PrimeFactors (n1),
                                 PrimeFactors ( n2 )),
                             PrimeFactors ( n3 ))
  END CommonFactors ;

  PROCEDURE Multiply ( b : Bag ; acc : CARDINAL ) :
  CARDINAL ;
  (* Postcondition : returns the result of multiplying
     the items in b together *)
```

```
BEGIN
    IF NOT IsEmpty ( b ) THEN
        Multiply ( Tail ( b ), acc * Head ( b ) )
    END ;
    RETURN acc
  END Multiply ;

PROCEDURE HCF ( n1, n2, n3 : CARDINAL ) : CARDINAL ;
(* Postcondition : returns the highest common factor of
    3 numbers *)

  BEGIN
    RETURN Multiply ( CommonFactors ( n1, n2, n3 ), 1 )
  END HCF ;
```

5.2

```
PROCEDURE BinarySearch ( key, low, high : CARDINAL;
                    A : ARRAY OF InfoType ) : CARDINAL ;
(* Precondition: 'key' is in the array 'A' of items
    stored in increasing order. The bounds of A are 'low'
    and 'high'.
    Postcondition: returns the index  of the position
    which holds 'key' *)

  VAR mid : CARDINAL ;

  BEGIN
    Mid := (low + high ) DIV 2 ;
    IF key = A [mid] THEN
      RETURN mid
    ELSIF key < A [mid] THEN
      RETURN BinarySearch ( key, low, mid - 1 )
    ELSE
      RETURN BinarySearch ( key, mid + 1, high )
    END (* if *)
  END BinarySearch ;
```

CHAPTER 6

6.1

```
PROCEDURE Shortest ( t : Tree ) : Tree ;
(* Postcondition: returns the shortest path of the binary
    tree t *)

  BEGIN
    IF IsEmptyTree ( t ) THEN
      RETURN 0
    ELSE
      RETURN ( 1 + Min ( Height ( LeftTree ( t )) ,
                            Shortest ( RightTree ( t ))))
    END
  END Shortest ;
```

6.2

1.
```
PROCEDURE Preorder ( t : Tree ) ;
(* Postcondition: prints the items of tree t in preorder *)


   BEGIN
     IF NOT IsEmptyTree(t) THEN
       WriteItem( Root(t));
       Preorder (LeftTree(t));
       Preorder (RightTree(t)) ;
     END
   END PreOrder;


PROCEDURE Postorder ( t : Tree ) ;
(* Postcondition: prints the items of tree t in postorder *)


   BEGIN
     IF NOT IsEmptyTree(t) THEN
       PostOrder(LeftTree(t));
       PostOrder(RightTree(t));
       WriteItem(Root(t));
     END
   END PostOrder;
```

2.

Inorder :	$a * b - c + d / e$
Preorder :	$+ * a - b c / d e$
Postorder:	$a b c - * d e / +$

6.3

2.
```
PROCEDURE Reduce ( F: Dyadic; T : Tree ; b: CARDINAL ) :
CARDINAL ;
(* Precondition: takes a tree T, a dyadic function F
   and a base case b
   Postcondition: returns a tree in which the function
   has been applied to the base case and every item *)


   BEGIN
     IF IsEmptyTree ( T ) THEN
       RETURN b
     ELSE
       RETURN F( Root ( T ), Reduce ( F, LeftTree ( T ),
                   b ), Reduce ( F, RightTree( T ), b) ))
     END
   END Reduce;
```

CHAPTER 7

7.1

1.

```
PROCEDURE Insert (c : InfoType ; t : Tree ) : Tree ;
(* Precondition: i is an item and t is a binary search tree
   Postcondition: returns a binary search tree with i
   inserted in the correct position *)

   BEGIN
     IF IsEmptyTree(t) THEN
       RETURN ConsTree(c, EmptyTree(), EmptyTree())
     ELSIF (c < Root(t)) THEN
       RETURN ConsTree(Root(t), Insert(c, LeftTree(t)),
                                      RightTree(t))
     ELSE
       RETURN ConsTree(Root(t), LeftTree(t), Insert(c,
                                      RightTree(t)))
     END
   END Insert;
```

2.

```
PROCEDURE BuildTree ( l : List ; t : Tree ) : Tree ;
(* Precondition: receives a list of items and a binary
   search tree
   Postcondition: returns a binary search tree *)

   BEGIN
     IF IsEmpty ( l ) THEN
       RETURN t
     ELSE
       RETURN BuildTree (Tail ( l ), Insert(Head ( l ), t))
     END
   END BuildTree;
```

4.

```
PROCEDURE Contains( t : Tree ; key : InfoType ) : BOOLEAN ;
(* Precondition: takes a binary search tree (t) and an
   item (key).
   Postcondition: returns TRUE if key is in t, otherwise
   FALSE *)

   BEGIN
     IF IsEmptyTree ( t ) THEN
       RETURN FALSE
     ELSIF Root ( t ) = key THEN
       RETURN TRUE
     ELSIF Root ( t ) > key THEN
       RETURN Contains( LeftTree ( t ), key )
     ELSE
       RETURN Contains( RightTree ( t ), key )
     END
   END Contains;
```

5.
```
PROCEDURE FindTree ( t : Tree ; key : InfoType ) : Tree ;
(* Precondition: takes a binary search tree (t) and an
   item (key).
   Postcondition: returns the subtree which has the item at
   its root, or the empty tree if the item is not in the
   tree *)


   BEGIN
     IF IsEmptyTree ( t ) THEN
       RETURN EmptyTree ()
     ELSIF Root ( t ) = key THEN
       RETURN t
     ELSIF Root ( t ) > key THEN
       RETURN FindTree ( LeftTree ( t ), key )
     ELSE
       RETURN FindTree ( RightTree ( t ), key )
     END
   END FindTree ;
```

7.3

1.
```
PROCEDURE FindLast ( t : Tree ) : InfoType ;
(* Precondition: takes a complete tree
   Postcondition: returns the rightmost item in the lowest
   level of the tree *)


   BEGIN
     IF IsEmptyTree ( LeftTree ( t )) THEN
       RETURN Root (t)
     ELSIF IsEmptyTree ( RightTree ( t )) THEN
       RETURN FindLast ( LeftTree (t))
     ELSIF (Height(LeftTree(t)) > Height (RightTree(t))) THEN
       RETURN FindLast ( LeftTree (t))
     ELSE
       RETURN FindLast ( RightTree(t))
     END
   END FindLast ;
```

CHAPTER 8

8.1

1.
```
PROCEDURE PrintTree (t : Tree);
(* Precondition: t is a 2-3 search tree
   Postcondition: prints the items in t in increasing
   order *)
```

```
      BEGIN
        IF IsEmptyTree ( t ) THEN
        ELSE
          PrintTree (LeftTree ( t ));
          IF ( NumberOfValues ( t ) = one ) THEN
            WriteItem (Root ( t ));
          ELSE
            WriteItem (MinVal ( t ));
            PrintTree (MiddleTree ( t ));
            WriteItem (MaxVal ( t )) ;
          END ;
          PrintTree (RightTree ( t ))
        END ;
      END PrintTree;
```

2.

(i)   (g, m, (a, c), (j), (n))
(ii) (g, m, (a, c), (j), (n, p))
(iii) (g, m, (a, c), (j, h), (n, p))
(iv) (j, (g, (a, c), (h)), (m, (k), (n, p)))
(v)   (j, (b, g, (a), (c), (h)), (m, (k), (n, p)))

4.

```
  PROCEDURE OrderFlatten ( t : Tree ) : List ;
  (* Precondition: takes a 2-3 search tree
     Postcondition: returns a list (in ascending order) of
     the items which are in the tree *)

    BEGIN
      IF IsEmptyTree ( t ) THEN
        RETURN Empty()
      ELSIF (NumberOfValues(t) = one ) THEN
        RETURN Append (OrderFlatten (LeftTree (t)), Cons
                                          (Root(t),
                            OrderFlatten (RightTree (t))))
      ELSE
        RETURN Append (Append (OrderFlatten (LeftTree (t)),
                    Cons (MinVal(t), OrderFlatten ( MiddleTree
                                                  (t)))),
                    Cons (MaxVal(t), OrderFlatten (RightTree
                                                  (t))))
      END
    END OrderFlatten ;
```

5.

(i)   (j, (a), (m, n))
(ii)   (g, (a), (j, n))
(iii) (g, (a), (j, n))
(iv)   (j, (g), (m, n))
(v)   (g, (a), (m, n))
(vi)   (k, (e, (c, (a), (d)), (g, (f), (h))), (p, (n, (l), (o)), (r, (q), (u))))

CHAPTER 9

9.1

6.

```
BASIC 34              COBOL 7
FORTRAN 20            COMAL 4
PASCAL 36             MODULA 10
APL 21                ALGOL60 29
ALGOL68 37            MODULA2 20
HOPE 20 ML 33         MIRANDA 28
ADA 38                PL1 5
FORTH 27              PROLOG 27
SIMULA 19             CORAL 9
LISP 32
```

7.

0	10 MODULA	20 FORTRAN	30 PROLOG (rehash)
1	11	21 APL	31
2	12	22 MODULA2 (rehash)	32 LISP
3	13	23 HOPE (rehash)	33 ML
4 COMAL	14	24	34 BASIC
5 PL1	15	25	35
6	16	26	36 PASCAL
7 COBOL	17	27 FORTH	37 ALGOL68
8	18	28 MIRANDA	38 ADA
9 CORAL	19 SIMULA	29 ALGOL60	39

8. Seventeen programming language names can be reached by hashing their names, one (MODULA2) requires three probes and two (HOPE and PROLOG) requires four probes. Therefore it takes

$$(17*1 + 1*3 + 2*4) / 20 = 1.4$$

probes on average to locate a valid programming language name.

9. It takes 2.1 probes on average to find that a language name is invalid:

$$(20*1 + 7*2 + 6*3 + 4*4 + 2*5 + 1*6) / 40 = 2.1$$

Bibliography

Bayer, R., and McCreight, C., (1972). Organization and maintenance of large ordered indexes. *Acta Informatica*, **1**, No. 3, 173–89

Burstall, R. M. MacQueen D. B., and Sanella D. T., (1980). Hope: An experimental applicative language. *Proceedings 1st International LISP Conference*, Stanford, California, pp. 136–43.

Downs, E., Clare, P., and Coe, I., (1988). *Structured Systems Analysis and Design Method*, Englewood Cliffs, NJ: Prentice Hall.

Feller, W., (1950). *An Introduction to Probability Theory and Its Applications*, Vol. 1, New York: John Wiley.

Field, A. J., and Harrison, P. G., (1988). *Functional Programming*, Reading, Mass.: Addison-Wesley.

Glaser, H., Hankin, C., and Till, D., (1984). *Principles of Functional Programming*, Englewood Cliffs, NJ: Prentice-Hall.

Goldberg, A., and Robson, D., (1983). *Smalltalk-80—The Language and its Implementation*, Reading, Mass.: Addison-Wesley.

Guttag, J. V., (1977). Abstract data types and the development of data structures, *Communications of the ACM*, **20**, 397–404.

Guttag, J. V., (1978). The algebraic specification of abstract data types. *Acta Informatica*, **10**, No. 1, 27–52.

Guttag, J. V., (1980). Notes on type abstraction. *IEEE Transactions on Software Engineering*, **SE-6**, No.1, 13–23.

Guttag, J. V., (1982). Some notes on putting formal specifications to productive use. *Science of Computer Programming*, **2**(1), 53–68.

Guttag, J. V., Horowitz, E., and Musser, D. R., (1978). Abstract data types and software validation, *Communications of the ACM*, **21**, 1048–64.

Harper, R., MacQueen, D., and Milner, R., (1986). *Standard ML*, Edinburgh University Internal Report LFCS–86–2.

Hoare, C.A.R., (1969). The axiomatic basis of computer programming, *Communications of the ACM*, **12**, 576–83.

Hoare, C.A.R., (1972). Proofs of Correctness of Data Representations, *Acta Informatica*, **1**, No. 1, 271–81.

Horowitz, E., and Sahni, S., (1976) *Fundamentals of Data Structures*, Rockville, Maryland: Computer Science Press.

Jones, C. B., (1986). *Systematic Software Development Using VDM*, Englewood Cliffs, NJ: Prentice-Hall.

Knuth, D. E. (1973). *The Art of Computer Programming: Sorting and Searching*, Vol. 3, Reading, Mass.: Addison-Wesley.

Liskov, B. H., and Zillies, S. N. (1975). Specification techniques for data abstractions, *IEEE Transactions on Software Engineering* 1, No. 1, 7–19.

Lum,V. Y., Yuen, P. S. T., and Dodd, M., (1971). Key-to-address transform techniques: a fundamental performance study on large existing formatted files. *Communications of the ACM* **14**, No. 4, 228–39

MacQueen, D., (May 1985). *Modules for Standard ML*, AT&T Bell Laboratories.

Radke, C. E., (February 1970). The use of quadratic residue search. *Communications of the ACM*, **13**, No. 12, 103–05.

Turner, D. A., (1985). Miranda: A non-strict functional language with polymorphic types, Functional Programming Languages and Computer Architectures, New York: Springer-Verlag, 1–16.

Stevens, W. P., Myers, G. J., and Constantine, L. L., (1974). Structured design. *IBM Systems Journal*, No. 2.

Stroupstrup, B., (1985). *The C++ Programming Language*, Reading, Mass.: Addison Wesley.

Stoy. J. E., (1981). *Denotational Semantics: The Scott-Strachey Approach to Programming Language Theory*, Cambridge, Mass.: The MIT Press.

Tenenbaum, A. M., and Augenstein, M. J., (1986). *Data Structures Using Pascal*, Englewood Cliffs, NJ: Prentice-Hall.

US Department of Defense, (1983). *Reference Manual for the Ada Programming Language*, ANSI/MIL-STD-1815A.

Wadsworth, C. P., (1971). *Semantics and Pragmatics of the Lambda Calculus*. D.Phil Thesis, University of Oxford.

Williams, J. W. J., (1964). Heapsort. *Communications of the ACM* 7, No. 6, 347–48.

Wirth, N, (1971). Program development by stepwise refinement. *Communications of the ACM*, **14** No. 4, 221–7.

Wirth, N., (1986) *Algorithms and Data Structures*, Englewood Cliffs, NJ: Prentice-Hall.

Wirth, N., (1988). *Programming in Modula-2*, 4th edn, New York: Springer-Verlag.

Index